T0246227

"Failing is such an important part of living and leading. Finally, we have the book that will help us learn how to fail well. In it, Amy shares with us very practical tools and advice illustrated by many inspiring, jaw-dropping stories. A breakthrough book that every leader needs to study and begin applying. It will make the world a better place."

—Hubert Joly, senior lecturer at Harvard Business School, former Best Buy chairman and CEO, and author of *The Heart of Business*

"Edmondson continues to help us get to the essential simplicity on the far side of complexity. Contrary to the often prevailing belief that 'failing is not an option,' she makes it abundantly clear that, both personally and organizationally, we must embrace the notion that 'failing well is the only option,' for advancing healthier thinking, breakthrough learning, and the potential for radical growth. It really is that simple. Bravo, Amy!"

—Douglas R. Conant, founder of ConantLeadership, retired president and CEO of the Campbell Soup Company, and retired chair of Avon Products

RIGHT KIND OF WRONG

RIGHT HAND OF WAR

RIGHT KIND OF WRONG

THE SCIENCE OF FAILING WELL

AMY EDMONDSON

ATRIA BOOKS

New York   London   Toronto   Sydney   New Delhi

ATRIA
BOOKS

An Imprint of Simon & Schuster, Inc.
1230 Avenue of the Americas
New York, NY 10020

First Atria Books hardcover edition September 2023

ATRIA BOOKS and colophon are trademarks of Simon & Schuster, Inc.

For information about special discounts for bulk purchases, please contact Simon & Schuster Special Sales at 1-866-506-1949 or business@simonandschuster.com.

The Simon & Schuster Speakers Bureau can bring authors to your live event. For more information or to book an event, contact the Simon & Schuster Speakers Bureau at 1-866-248-3049 or visit our website at www.simonspeakers.com.

Interior design by Kyoko Watanabe

Manufactured in the United States of America

9 10

Library of Congress Cataloging-in-Publication Data

Names: Edmondson, Amy C., author.
Title: The right kind of wrong / Amy Edmondson.
Description: First Atria books hardcover edition. | New York : Atria Books, [2023] | Includes bibliographical references and index.
Identifiers: LCCN 2022061950 (print) | LCCN 2022061951 (ebook) | ISBN 9781982195069 (hardcover) | ISBN 9781982195076 (paperback) | ISBN 9781982195083 (ebook)
Subjects: LCSH: Failure (Psychology) | Psychology, Industrial. | Organizational learning—Psychological aspects.
Classification: LCC BF575.F14 E46 2023 (print) | LCC BF575.F14 (ebook) | DDC 158.1—dc23/eng/20230501
LC record available at https://lccn.loc.gov/2022061950
LC ebook record available at https://lccn.loc.gov/2022061951

ISBN 978-1-9821-9506-9
ISBN 978-1-9821-9508-3 (ebook)

For Jack & Nick

With abiding love and growing admiration

I am not afraid of storms, for I'm learning how to sail my ship.

—Louisa May Alcott

Contents

Prologue   1

Introduction   5

PART ONE:

The Failure Landscape

CHAPTER 1: Chasing the Right Kind of Wrong   23

CHAPTER 2: Eureka!   49

CHAPTER 3: To Err Is Human   87

CHAPTER 4: The Perfect Storm   125

PART TWO:

Practicing the Science of Failing Well

CHAPTER 5: We Have Met the Enemy   167

CHAPTER 6: Contexts and Consequences   199

CHAPTER 7: Appreciating Systems   227

CHAPTER 8: Thriving as a Fallible Human Being   259

Acknowledgments   295

Notes   299

Index   337

RIGHT KIND OF WRONG

Prologue

June 1993. I'm sitting at the old wooden desk in my fifteenth-floor office in William James Hall, where I'm a student in the new Harvard PhD program in organizational behavior. I lean in to look more closely at the small black-and-white screen on my bulky Apple computer.* A stack of paper surveys I'd used to measure teamwork in two nearby hospitals sits pushed up against the wall at the edge of the desk. Six months ago, hundreds of nurses and doctors had filled out those surveys, giving me a glimpse into how their teams were working. I've analyzed the data enough to learn that some of the teams were working together a whole lot better than others. Now it's time for me to discover how many mistakes they've been making. In my hand, a small computer disk holds the long-awaited data on medication errors in each team, painstakingly collected by nurses over the past six months. All I need to do is run the statistical analysis to see if the team survey data correlate with the hospitals' error data.

This is the moment right before my first major research failure.

---

*The same model (Macintosh Classic Desktop Computer, 1989) that's today in the permanent collection of New York's Museum of Modern Art, https://www.moma.org /collection/works/142222.

Soon I would find myself thinking, not for the first time, that maybe I wasn't cut out for a PhD program. I had been ambivalent about graduate school. I admired people who made meaningful contributions in the world without the leg up of an advanced degree. If you were smart and resourceful, it seemed to me, you should be able to carve out a unique path forward, doing work that made a difference in the world. But a decade after graduating from college, I'd had to admit defeat.

True, much of that decade had been creative and, from certain vantages, enviable. I'd worked as chief engineer for Buckminster Fuller—the visionary inventor of the geodesic dome. After that, I made the shift from engineering to organizational development after a chance meeting with the founder of a consulting company and was soon fascinated by organizations (and their failures!). I worked with some of the oldest and largest companies in America. I met managers in the U.S. car industry in the late 1980s who saw that customers wanted fuel-efficient, high-quality cars, such as the new imports from Japan, but couldn't get their giant organizations to retool to make them. Everywhere I looked, thoughtful managers bemoaned their organization's inability to adapt to clear changes in what the world needed. I enjoyed the work immensely. My sense of defeat came from concluding that I'd gone as far as I could on my own steam. To be more effective in my new field of organizational behavior and management, I would have to go back to school. Then perhaps I could contribute in a meaningful way to the goal slowly taking shape in my mind: *helping people and organizations learn so they can thrive in a world that keeps changing.*

I had no idea how to study this, nor how to contribute to changing how organizations worked. But it seemed like a problem worth solving, and I believed that I could learn from the professors in psychology and organizational behavior and somehow find a way to make a difference in understanding—and altering—the dynamics that make it hard for people and organizations to learn and thrive.

Because of my interest in how organizations learn, as a brand-new PhD student I had been glad to accept the invitation to join a team of researchers studying medication errors at nearby Harvard Medical School. This ready-made project would help me learn how to conduct original research. Your first-grade teacher probably told you that errors are a crucial source of learning. And medication errors, as anyone who has ever spent time in a hospital knows, are numerous and consequential.

But suddenly, this did not seem an auspicious beginning to a research career. I had unequivocally failed to support my hypothesis. I had predicted that better teamwork would lead to fewer medication errors, measured by nurse investigators stopping in several times a week to review patient charts and talk to the nurses and doctors who worked there. Instead, the results were suggesting that better teams had *higher*—not lower—error rates. I was not just wrong. I was completely wrong.

My hope of publishing a paper on my findings evaporated as I started to question again whether I could make it as a researcher. Most of us feel ashamed of our failures. We're more likely to hide them than to learn from them. Just because mistakes happen in organizations doesn't mean learning and improvement follow. Ashamed of being wrong, I felt afraid to tell my adviser.

Within a few days, this surprise finding—this failure—would lead me gently to new insights, new data, and follow-up research projects that saved and changed the course of my academic career. I would publish a research paper from this first study called "Learning from Mistakes Is Easier Said Than Done," a precursor to so much of my later work—and a theme that runs throughout my life's work and this book.

I would also begin to understand how success as a researcher *necessitates* failure along the way. If you're not failing, you're not journeying into new territory. Since those early days, in the back of my mind, a more nuanced understanding of terms such as *error* and *failure* and *mishap* has taken shape. Now I can share it with you.

Introduction

Success is stumbling from failure to failure
with no loss of enthusiasm.

—Winston Churchill

The idea that people and organizations should learn from failure is popular and even seems obvious. But most of us fail to learn the valuable lessons failures can offer. We put off the hard work of reflecting on what we did wrong. Sometimes, we're reluctant to admit that we failed in the first place. We're embarrassed by our failures and quick to spot those of others. We deny, gloss over, and quickly move on from—or blame circumstances and other people for—things that go wrong. Every child learns, sooner or later, to dodge blame by pointing the finger elsewhere. Over time, this becomes habitual. Worse, these habits make us avoid stretch goals or challenges where we might fail. As a result, we lose out on countless opportunities to learn and develop new skills. This pernicious combination of human psychology, socialization, and institutional rewards makes mastering the science of failing well far more challenging than it needs to be.

It's impossible to calculate the wasted time and resources created by our failure to learn from failure. It's just as hard to measure its emotional toll. Most of us go out of our way to avoid experiencing failure, robbing ourselves of adventure, accomplishment, and even love.

This book is about what makes learning from failure so difficult to put into practice in our day-to-day lives and in the institutions we build. It's also about how we can do better. As you've already read, I've not only studied mistakes and failures, I've experienced plenty of them myself and had to learn firsthand how to feel better about being so fallible. I've had more papers than I can count get rejected from top journals. I've had my car break down by the side of the road and spent a precarious night contemplating preventive maintenance. Freshman year in college many years ago, I failed a first-semester multivariable-calculus exam. I've missed important Little League games and disappointed both of my sons. The list goes on. *And on*. To come to terms with my shortcomings, and to help others do the same, I decided to get scientific about it.

I believe that part of successfully navigating failure to reap its rewards—and, importantly, to avoid the wrong kinds of failure as often as possible—starts with understanding that not all failures are created equal. As you will see, some failures can rightly be called bad. Fortunately, most of these are also preventable. Other failures are genuinely good. They bring important discoveries that improve our lives and our world. Lest you get the wrong idea, I've had my share of failures that were bad, along with some that were good.

This book offers a typology of failure that helps you sort the "right kind of wrong" from the failures that you should work hard to prevent. You will also learn how to think differently about yourself and failure, recognize contexts in which failures are likely, and understand the role of systems—all crucial competencies for mastering the science of failing well. You will meet a handful of *elite failure practitioners* from different fields, countries, and even centuries. As their examples make clear, learning from failure takes emotional fortitude and skill. It requires learning how to conduct thoughtful experiments, how to categorize failure, and how to glean valuable lessons from failures of all types.

The frameworks and lessons in this book are the direct result of my quarter century as an academic researcher in social psychology and organizational behavior. In this role, I've interviewed people and collected data from surveys and other sources in corporations, government agencies, start-ups, schools, and hospitals. Talking with hundreds of people in these varied organizations—managers, engineers, nurses, physicians, CEOs, and frontline employees alike—I began to see patterns that yielded a new typology of failure, as well as a host of best practices for managing and learning from failure.

Let's return to the beginning of this long journey, which started with my participation in a pioneering study of hospital medication errors.

Learning from Mistakes Is Easier Said Than Done

I sat, dumbfounded, staring at the computer screen starkly displaying my failure to find support for my study hypothesis. My first thought was, How could I admit how wrong I had been to my supervisor and to the doctors leading the study? I had spent hundreds of hours developing the survey, attending biweekly research meetings with the doctors and nurses who tracked drug errors in two nearby hospitals, and periodically jumping on my bicycle to get to the hospital soon after a caregiver had reported a major error, to interview people to identify the error's underlying causes. I had been entrusted with the medical-error data and permitted to ask hundreds of busy doctors and nurses to fill out my survey. I felt guilty for taking up their valuable time and ashamed of my failure.

One of the people I'd have to talk to about the failure was Dr. Lucian Leape, a pediatric surgeon who had shifted his professional attention later in his career to the study of medical errors. Well over six feet tall, with thick white hair and eyebrows, Lucian was both avuncular and intimidating. He was also determined. One research goal for the larger study was simple: to measure the rate of medication errors in hospitals.

Back then, little was known about how frequently errors happened, and Lucian and his colleagues had a National Institutes of Health (NIH) grant to find out. Adding to that goal, inspired by some research in aviation that showed that better teamwork in the cockpit meant safer flights, Lucian had asked whether the same might be true in hospitals.

The aviation research that inspired Lucian hadn't intended to look at teamwork, but rather at fatigue in the cockpit. It was another failed hypothesis. A team of researchers at NASA, led by human-factors expert H. Clayton Foushee, ran an experiment to test the effects of fatigue on error rates. They had twenty two-person teams; ten were assigned to the "postduty" or "fatigue" condition. These teams "flew" in the simulator as if it were the last segment of a three-day stint in the short-haul airline operations where they worked. The fatigued teams had already flown three eight- to ten-hour daily shifts. Those shifts included at least five takeoffs and landings, sometimes up to eight. The other ten teams (the "pre-duty," well-rested condition) flew in the simulator after at least two days off duty. For them, the simulator was like their first segment in a three-day shift.

Simulators provide a safe context for learning. Pilots I've spoken to say the simulator looks and feels like a real cockpit, and they feel fear when something goes wrong. But errors in a simulator don't bring down a plane. This makes it a great environment to reflect on what went wrong, so as to perfect the skills needed to safely transport hundreds of passengers in real flights. These same features also make the simulator a great research tool. While it would never be ethical to randomly assign tired pilots to fly real flights with real passengers, experimenting is fine in a simulator.

To his surprise, Foushee discovered that the teams who'd just logged several days flying together (the fatigued teams) performed *better* than the well-rested teams. As expected, the fatigued *individuals* made more errors than their well-rested counterparts, but because they had spent time working together through multiple flights, they'd made fewer errors *as teams*. Apparently, they were able to work well together, catching and correcting one another's errors throughout the flight, avoiding serious mishaps. The fatigued pilots had essentially turned themselves into good teams after working together for a couple of days. In contrast, the well-rested pilots, unfamiliar with one another, didn't work as well as teams.

This surprise finding about the importance of teamwork in the cockpit helped fuel a revolution in passenger air travel called crew resource management (CRM), which is partly responsible for the extraordinary safety of passenger air travel today. This impressive work is one of many examples of what I call the science of failing well.

Research on cockpit crews blossomed in the 1980s and included the work of J. Richard Hackman, a Harvard psychology professor, who studied the interplay of pilots, copilots, and navigators on both civilian and military planes to understand what effective teams had in common. His cockpit-crew research had attracted the attention of Lucian Leape. Seeing a parallel between the high-stakes work of cockpit crews and that of hospital clinicians, Lucian picked up the phone to see if Richard might be willing to help with Lucian's medication-error study. Lacking the time to commit to the project, Richard suggested that I, his doctoral student, might be put to work instead. Which is how I found myself hunched over my findings, gripped by anxiety.

I'd hoped to build on the aviation research to add another small finding to the team-effectiveness literature. The research question was simple: Does better teamwork in the hospital lead to fewer errors? The idea was to replicate the aviation findings in this new context. So what if it would not be a major discovery? As a new graduate student, I wasn't trying to set the world on fire, but just to satisfy a program requirement. Simple, unsurprising, would be just fine.

A small team of nurses would do the hard work of tracking error rates for six months in the hospital wards, talking with doctors and nurses and reviewing patients' charts several times a week. All I had to do was distribute a survey to measure teamwork in these same wards in the first month of the six-month study. Then I had to wait patiently for the error data to be collected so I could compare the two data sets—

connecting my team measures with the error data collected over the full six months. I had Hackman's ready-made "team diagnostic survey" to get me started for measuring team effectiveness. Working with the doctors and nurses in the research team, I modified the wording to include numerous items to assess different aspects of teamwork, such as "Members of this unit care a lot about it and work together to make it one of the best in the hospital" and "Members of this unit share their special knowledge and expertise with one another," or the negatively worded item "Some people in this unit do not carry their fair share of the overall workload." The response options ranged from strongly agree to strongly disagree. I computed averages of individual responses to these types of items to assess the quality of teamwork, which I then averaged again to compute scores for each team. A healthy 55 percent of the surveys I distributed were returned, and the data showed plenty of variance across teams. Some teams appeared to be more effective than others. So far so good.

Would those differences predict the teams' propensity to make mistakes?

At first glance, everything looked fine. I immediately saw a correlation between the error rates and team effectiveness, and better yet, it was statistically significant. For those who haven't taken a stats course, this was reassuring.

But then I looked more closely! Leaning toward my computer screen, I saw that the correlation was in the *wrong* direction. The data were saying the opposite of what I'd predicted. Better teams appeared to have higher, not lower, error rates. My anxiety intensified, bringing a sinking feeling in my stomach.

Although I didn't yet know it, my no longer straightforward research project was producing an intelligent failure that would lead to an unexpected discovery.

Surprises, often in the form of bad news for a researcher's hypothesis, are common in research. None last long as scientists if they can't stand to fail, as I would soon learn. Discovery stories don't *end* with failure; failures are stepping stones on the way to success. There is no shortage of popular quotes on that point—many of them are sprinkled throughout this book—and for good reason. These kinds of informative, but still *undesired*, failures are the *right kind of wrong*.

Being Wrong in New Territory

These failures are "intelligent," as my colleague Duke professor Sim Sitkin first suggested back in 1992, because they involve careful thinking, don't cause unnecessary harm, and generate useful learning that advances our knowledge. Despite happy talk about celebrating failures in Silicon Valley and around the world, intelligent failures are the only type genuinely worth celebrating. Also referred to as smart failures or good failures, they occur most characteristically in science, where failure rates in a successful laboratory might be 70 percent or higher. Intelligent failures are also frequent and essential in company innovation projects, say, as part of building a popular new kitchen tool. Successful innovation is only possible as a result of insights from incremental losses along the way.

In science, as in life, intelligent failures can't be predicted. A blind date set up by a mutual friend may conclude in a tedious evening (a failure) even if the friend had good reasons to believe you'd like each other. Whether an intelligent failure is small (a boring date) or large (a failed clinical trial), we must welcome this type of failure as part of the messy journey into new terrain, whether it leads to a lifesaving vaccine or a life partner.

Intelligent failures provide valuable new knowledge. They bring discovery. They occur when experimentation is necessary simply because answers are not knowable in advance. Perhaps a particular situation hasn't been encountered before, or perhaps one is truly standing on the front lines of discovery in a field of research. Discovering new drugs, launching a radical new business model, designing an innovative product, or testing customer reactions in a brand-new market are all tasks that require intelligent failures to make progress and succeed. *Trial and error* is a common term for the kind of experimentation needed in these settings, but it's a misnomer. *Error* implies that there was a "right" way to do it in the first place. Intelligent failures are not errors. This book will elaborate on this and other vital distinctions that we must make if we wish to learn to put failure to good use.

Solving the puzzle

That day in William James Hall, staring at the failure displayed on my old Mac screen, I tried to think clearly, pushing aside the anxiety that only intensified as I envisioned the moment when I, a lowly graduate student, would have to tell the esteemed Richard Hackman that I had been wrong, that the aviation results didn't hold in health care. Perhaps that anxiety forced me to think deeply. To rethink what my results might mean.

Did better teams *really* make more mistakes? I thought about the need for communication between doctors and nurses to produce error-free care in this perpetually complex and customized work. These clinicians needed to ask for help, to double-check doses, to raise concerns about one another's actions. They had to coordinate on the fly. It didn't make sense that good teamwork (and I didn't doubt the veracity of my survey data) would lead to more errors.

Why else might better teams have higher error rates?

What if those teams had created a better work environment? What if they had built a climate of openness where people felt able to speak up? What if that environment made it easier to be open and honest about error? To err is human. Mistakes happen—the only real question is whether we catch, admit, and correct them. Maybe the good teams, I suddenly thought, don't *make* more mistakes, maybe they *report* more. They swim upstream against the widely held view of error as indicative of incompetence, which leads people everywhere to suppress acknowl-edging (or to deny responsibility for) mistakes. This discourages the systematic analysis of mistakes that allows us to learn from them. This insight eventually led me to the discovery of psychological safety, and why it matters in today's world.

Having this insight was a far cry from proving it. When I brought the idea to Lucian Leape, he was at first extremely skeptical. I was the novice on the team. Everyone else had a degree in medicine or nursing and deeply understood patient care in a way that I never would. My sense of failure deepened in the face of his dismissal. That in those fraught moments Lucian reminded me of my ignorance was under-standable. I was suggesting a reporting bias across teams, effectively calling into question a primary aim of the overall study—to provide a good estimate of the *actual* error rates in hospital care. But his skepti-cism turned out to be a gift. It forced me to double down on my efforts to think about what additional data might be available to support my (new and still-shaky) interpretation of the failed results.

Two ideas occurred to me. First, because of the overall study's focus on error, when I had edited the team survey to make its wording ap-propriate for hospital work, I had added a new item: "If you make a mistake in this unit, it won't be held against you." Fortunately, the item correlated with the detected error rates; the more people believed that making a mistake would not be held against them, the higher the de-tected errors in their unit! Could that be a coincidence? I didn't think so. This item, later research would show, is remarkably predictive of whether people will speak up in a team. This, along with several other secondary statistical analyses, was entirely consistent with my new hypothesis. *When people believe mistakes will be held against them, they are loath to report them.* Of course, I had felt this myself!

Second, I wanted to get an objective read on whether palpable differences in the work environment might exist across these work groups, despite all being in the same health-care system. But I couldn't do it myself: I was biased in favor of finding such differences.

Unlike Lucian Leape, with his initial skepticism, Richard Hackman immediately recognized the plausibility of my new argument. With Richard's support, I hired a research assistant, Andy Molinsky, to study each of the work groups carefully with no preconceptions. Andy didn't know which units had more mistakes, nor which ones had scored better on the team survey. He also didn't know about my new hypothesis. In research terminology, he was *double-blind*. I simply asked him to try to understand what it was like to work in each of the units. So, Andy observed each unit for several days, quietly watching how people interacted and interviewing nurses and physicians during their breaks to learn more about the work environment and how it differed across units. He took notes on what he observed, including jotting down things people said about working in their unit.

With no prompting from me, Andy reported that the hospital units in the study appeared wildly different as places to work. In some, people talked about mistakes openly. Andy quoted the nurses as saying such things as a "certain level of error will occur" so a "non-punitive environment" is essential to good patient care. In other units, it seemed nearly impossible to speak openly about error. Nurses explained that making a mistake meant "you get in trouble" or you get put "on trial." They reported feeling belittled, "like I was a two-year-old," for things that went wrong. His report was music to my ears. It was exactly the kind of variance in work environment that I had suspected might exist.

But were these differences in climate correlated with the error rates so painstakingly collected by the medical researchers? In a word, yes. I asked Andy to rank the teams he'd studied from most to least *open*, the word he had used to explain his observations. Astonishingly, his list was nearly perfectly correlated with the detected error rates. This meant that the study's error-rate measure was flawed: when people felt unable to reveal errors, many errors remained hidden. Combined, these secondary analyses suggested that my interpretation of the surprise finding was likely correct. My eureka moment was this: better teams probably don't *make* more mistakes, but they are more able to discuss mistakes.*

Discovering psychological safety

Much later I used the term *psychological safety* to capture this difference in work environment, and I developed a set of survey items to measure it, thereby spawning a subfield of research in organizational behavior. Today, over a thousand research papers in fields ranging from education to business to medicine have shown that teams and organizations with higher psychological safety have better performance, lower burnout, and, in medicine, even lower patient mortality. Why might this be the case? Because psychological safety helps people take the interpersonal risks that are necessary for achieving excellence in a fast-changing, interdependent world. When people work in psychologically safe contexts, they know that questions are appreciated, ideas are welcome, and errors and failure are discussable. In these environments, people can focus on the work without being tied up in knots about what others might think of them. They know that being wrong won't be a fatal blow to their reputation.

Psychological safety plays a powerful role in the science of failing well. It allows people to ask for help when they're in over their heads, which helps eliminate preventable failures. It helps them report—and hence catch and correct—errors to avoid worse outcomes, and it makes it possible to experiment in thoughtful ways to generate new discoveries. Think about the teams that you've been a part of at work, or at school, in sports, or in your community. These groups probably varied in psychological safety. Maybe in some you felt completely comfortable speaking

---

* Note that in this study it was not possible to assess *actual*-error rates; detected-error rates were discovered to be a necessarily biased measure because of the discovered differences across units in psychological safety.

up with a new idea, or disagreeing with a team leader, or asking for help when you were out of your depth. In other teams you might have felt it was better to hold back—to wait and see what happened or what other people did and said before sticking your neck out. That difference is now called psychological safety—and I have found in my research that it's an emergent property of a group, not a personality difference. This means your perception of whether it's safe to speak up at work is unrelated to whether you're an extrovert or an introvert. Instead, it's shaped by how people around you react to things that you and others say and do.

When a group is higher in psychological safety, it's likely to be more innovative, do higher-quality work, and enjoy better performance, compared to a group that is low in psychological safety. One of the most important reasons for these different outcomes is that people in psychologically safe teams can admit their mistakes. These are teams where candor is expected. It's not always fun, and certainly it's not always comfortable, to work in such a team because of the difficult conversations you will sometimes experience. Psychological safety in a team is virtually synonymous with a learning environment in a team. Everyone makes mistakes (we are all fallible), but not everyone is in a group where people feel comfortable speaking up about them. And it's hard for teams to learn and perform well without psychological safety.

What Is the Right Kind of Wrong?

You might think that the right kind of wrong is simply the smallest possible failure. Big failures are bad, and small failures are good. But size is actually not how you will learn to distinguish failures, or how you will assess their value. Good failures are those that bring us valuable new information that simply *could not have been gained any other way.*

Every kind of failure brings opportunities for learning and improvement. To avoid squandering these opportunities, we need a mix of emotional, cognitive, and interpersonal skills. These will be spelled out in this book in a way that I hope makes it easy to start applying them immediately.

But before we go any further, a few definitions are in order. I define *failure* as an outcome that deviates from desired results, whether that be failing to win a hoped-for gold medal, an oil tanker spilling thousands of tons of raw oil into the ocean instead of arriving safely in a harbor, a start-up that dives downward, or overcooking the fish meant for dinner. In short, failure is a lack of success.

Next, I define *errors* (synonymous with *mistakes*) as unintended deviations from prespecified standards, such as procedures, rules, or policies. Putting the cereal in the refrigerator and the milk in the cupboard is an error. A surgeon who operates on a patient's left knee when the right knee was injured has made an error. The important thing about errors and mistakes is that they are unintended. Errors may have relatively minor consequences—cereal stored in the refrigerator is inconvenient and milk left in the cupboard may spoil—while other mistakes, such as the patient who received the wrong-site surgery, have serious repercussions.

Finally, *violations* occur when an individual intentionally deviates from the rules. If you deliberately pour flammable oil on a rag, light a match to it, and throw it into an open doorway, you are an arsonist and have violated the law. If you forget to properly store an oil-soaked rag and it spontaneously combusts, you have made a mistake.

All of these terms can be so emotionally loaded that we may be tempted to simply turn and flee. But in so doing, we miss out on the intellectually (and emotionally) satisfying journey of learning to dance with failure.

Bad Failure, Good Failure

Maybe you are one of the many people who deep down believe that failure is bad. You've heard the new rhetoric about embracing failure but find it hard to take it seriously in your day-to-day life. Maybe you also believe that learning from failure is pretty straightforward: reflect on what you did wrong (not trying hard enough in math class, steering the boat too close to the rocks) and just do better next time, whether by studying more or ensuring that you have the latest maps for accurate navigation. This approach sees failure as shameful and largely the fault of the one who fails.

This belief is as widely held as it is misguided.

First, failure is not always bad. Today, I don't doubt that my failure to find support for the simple research hypothesis that guided my first study was the best thing that ever happened to my research career. Of course, it didn't feel that way in the moment. I felt embarrassed and afraid that my colleagues wouldn't keep me on the research team. My thoughts spiraled out to what I would do next, after dropping out of graduate school. This unhelpful reaction points to why each of us must learn how to take a deep breath, think again, and hypothesize anew. That simple self-management task is part of the science of failing well.

Second, learning from failure is not nearly as easy as it sounds. Nonetheless, we can learn how to do it well. If we want to go beyond superficial lessons, we need to jettison a few outdated cultural beliefs and stereotypical notions of success. We need to accept ourselves as fallible human beings and take it from there.

Road Map for the Journey Ahead

This book offers frameworks that I hope will help you think about, talk about, and practice failure in a way that allows you to work and live more joyfully.

Part one introduces a framework of failure types. The first chapter offers key concepts in failure science, followed by three chapters to describe the three failure archetypes: intelligent, basic, and complex. Understanding this taxonomy will give you a deeper understanding of failure's mechanisms and of what it means to fail well. This will help you design your own experiments to stretch beyond limits, self-imposed or otherwise. I will share best practices related to each type of failure—for learning from them, as well as for preventing some of them. This survey of the failure landscape will help you truly welcome the good kinds of failure, while getting better at learning from all kinds.

Intelligent failures, the subject of chapter 2, are the "good failures" that are necessary for progress—the small and large discoveries that advance science, technology, and our lives. Pioneers doing something new will always face unexpected problems. The key is to learn from them, rather than to deny or feel bad about them, give up, or pretend it should have been otherwise.

Chapter 3 digs into *basic failures*, the most easily understood and the most preventable. Caused by mistakes and slips, basic failures can be avoided with care and access to relevant knowledge. Mistakenly sending an email meant for your sister to a boss is a basic failure. Yes, some might call it catastrophic, but it's basic nonetheless. Checklists are just one of the tools you'll learn about for reducing basic failures.

As pernicious as basic failures can be, *complex failures*, described in chapter 4, are the real monsters that loom large in our work, lives, organizations, and societies. Complex failures *have not one but multiple causes* and often include a pinch of bad luck, too. These unfortunate breakdowns will always be with us due to the inherent uncertainty and interdependence we face in our day-to-day lives. This is why catching small problems before they spiral out of control to cause a more substantial complex failure becomes a crucial capability in the modern world.

Part two presents my latest thinking on *self-awareness, situation awareness*, and *system awareness*—and how these capabilities intersect with the three types of failure. This will be a chance to dig more deeply into tactics and habits that allow people to practice the science of failing well at work and in their lives. Chapter 5 explores *self-awareness* and its crucial role in the science of failure. Our human capacity for sustained self-reflection, humility, honesty, and curiosity propels us to seek out patterns that provide insight into our behavior. Chapter 6 digs into *situation awareness*—and learning how to read a given situation for its failure potential. You'll have a sense of what situations present an accident waiting to happen so as to help prevent unnecessary failure. Chapter 7 looks at *system awareness*. We live in a world of complex systems where our actions trigger unintended consequences. But learning to see and appreciate systems—say, family, organization, nature, or politics—helps us prevent a lot of failures.

These ideas and frameworks come together to help us answer the question, in chapter 8, of *how to thrive as a fallible human being*. All of us are fallible. The question is whether, and how, we use this fact to craft a fulfilling life full of never-ending learning.

PART ONE

THE FAILURE LANDSCAPE

CHAPTER 1

Chasing the Right Kind of Wrong

Only those who dare to fail greatly
can ever achieve greatly.

—Robert F. Kennedy

On April 6, 1951, forty-one-year-old cardiac surgeon Dr. Clarence Dennis was operating on five-year-old Patty Anderson in a state-of-the-art operating room. It wasn't going well. Dennis's desire to save the child, who had been diagnosed with a rare congenital heart defect, was intense and urgent. On the observation deck, several of his colleagues at University Hospital in Minnesota watched as Dennis connected his new heart-lung bypass machine to the little girl. Designed to function as the patient's lungs and heart during surgery, the machine had thus far only been tested on dogs in a laboratory. Extremely complicated, the machine required the assistance of sixteen people during the procedure; its rotating disks served as lungs; a pump performed the heart functions; and its many tubes acted as vessels moving blood throughout the body.

Dennis was among a handful of pioneering surgeons in the 1950s determined to discover a way to successfully operate on the heart of a living patient. Back then, one of the seemingly insurmountable hurdles had been containing the blood that spurted furiously out after cutting into a patient's heart. The heart's function, after all, is to pump blood, and it does it well. Another challenge lay in conducting the delicate surgical repairs on a beating heart. Stitching an organ that lay perfectly still was challenging enough. Yet, stopping the heart to facilitate the procedure would arrest the flow of blood through the body, without which the patient could not survive. Dennis's complicated machine was trying to solve these seemingly intractable problems.

At 1:22 p.m., Dennis ordered his team to tie off Patty's heart and start the pump. It's easy to imagine the entire team holding its collective breath as the first incision was made.

Then the unexpected. As the surgeon cut into the small heart's upper right-hand chamber, blood—way too much blood—flooded into the area surrounding the heart, and the team could not suction fast enough. Something was very wrong. The incision had revealed that the original diagnosis was incorrect. Patty did not have a single hole, as the doctors had thought, but rather several at the center of her heart. None of the surgeons had seen this condition before. Dennis and his team sutured as fast as they could, making eleven stitches in the biggest hole, but the bleeding continued, overwhelming their efforts, obscuring their field of vision, and rendering a complete repair impossible. After forty minutes, they disconnected the little girl from the machine, but it took another forty-three minutes until Dennis admitted defeat. Patty died a day before her sixth birthday.

A month later, Dennis tried again, operating with a colleague on two-year-old Sheryl Judge, as thirty-two-year-old Clarence Walton "Walt" Lillehei, who would later be dubbed the Father of Open Heart Surgery, observed. Sheryl had been diagnosed with an atrial septal defect—a single hole in the wall between the two upper chambers of the heart. Once again, this congenital condition, if left untreated, would soon prove fatal for the child.

This time, when the surgeon opened the heart, a different problem occurred: air began to leak out of the coronary vessels, blocking the flow of blood. One of the technicians (who, it later turned out, was suffering from a mild cold) had let the machine's reservoir of clean blood run dry, pumping the patient full of air, poisoning her brain, heart, and liver. The consequences were devastating. After eight hours, Sheryl Judge died. Here, a tragic instance of human error—in what was still terribly unfamiliar territory—muddied the results of the surgeons' efforts to push the limits of medical possibility.

These devastating failures are difficult for most of us to contemplate. We might even find ourselves feeling outraged by the idea of experiments that have life-and-death implications. Yet for these patients, their only hope was a surgical repair. Stepping back, we can appreciate that most of today's taken-for-granted medical miracles—including open heart surgery on diseased vessels and valves—were once the impossible dream of medical pioneers. As cardiologist Dr. James Forrester wrote, "In medicine, we learn more from our mistakes than from our successes. Error exposes truth." But the truth of Forrester's statement does little on its own to make it easy for the rest of us to navigate failure's painful side effects. We need a little more help to overcome the emotional, cognitive, and social barriers to failing well.

Why Is It So Hard to Fail Well?

Failing well is hard for three reasons: *aversion*, *confusion*, and *fear*. Aversion refers to an instinctive emotional response to failure. Confusion arises when we lack access to a simple, practical framework for distinguishing failure types. Fear comes from the social stigma of failure.

In our day-to-day lives, most of us will never face the kinds of high-stakes failures Clarence Dennis experienced, but, still, learning from elite failure practitioners such as Dennis can be illuminating—just as watching professional sports teams can help and inspire the weekend athlete. Even if you're not a medical pioneer or a professional athlete, it's helpful to understand what they confront and overcome to advance their craft. If Robert F. Kennedy, whose quote opened this chapter, was right in claiming that great achievement requires great failure, most of us have work to do.

Although the first successful open-heart surgery did not occur that April day in Minneapolis, today ten thousand surgeons in six thousand centers around the globe perform more than 2 million of these life-saving medical procedures each year—typically using a sophisticated, streamlined descendant of Dennis's heart-lung bypass machine. It would take another four years for Dennis and his team to perform their first successful operation with the machine, and it would take place at SUNY Downstate Medical Center in New York. During those four years not only did Dennis and other surgeons continue to experience failures in these early machines, but their attempts at other innovative ways to solve the vexing problems of cardiac surgery also met with varying degrees of failure (along with some small successes).

Aversion: a spontaneous emotional response to failure

Failure is never fun, and nowhere is that more starkly true than in hospitals, where life and death are at stake. But even our ordinary failures—our mistakes, the unimportant things we do wrong, the small defeats when we hoped for victory—can be surprisingly painful and difficult to come to terms with. You trip on the sidewalk; a comment in a meeting falls flat; you're the last kid selected for the team in an impromptu soccer game. Small failures, to be sure, but for many of us the sting is real.

Rationally, we know that failure is an unavoidable part of life, certainly a source of learning, and even a requirement for progress. But, as research in psychology and neuroscience has shown, our emotions don't always keep up with our clear-eyed, rational understanding. Numerous studies show that we process negative and positive information differently. You might say we're saddled with a "negativity bias." We take in "bad" information, including small mistakes and failures, more readily than "good" information. We have more trouble letting go of bad compared to good thoughts. We remember the negative things that happen to us more vividly and for longer than we do the positive ones. We pay more attention to negative than positive feedback. People interpret negative facial expressions more quickly than positive ones. Bad, simply put, is stronger than good. This is not to say we agree with or value it more but rather that we notice it more.

Why are we so sensitive to negative information and criticism? Well, it seems to have offered a survival advantage for early humans, when the threat of rejection from the tribe could mean death. This left us disproportionately sensitive to threats, even the merely interpersonal threat of looking bad in the eyes of others. Today, many of the interpersonal threats we detect in our day-to-day lives are not truly harmful, but we're hardwired to react, even overreact, to them. We also suffer from what celebrated psychologist Daniel Kahneman called "loss aversion"—a tendency to overweigh losses (of money, possessions, or even social status) compared to equivalent wins. In one study, participants were given a coffee mug and later offered the chance to sell it. To part with their mug, participants had to be given twice as much in compensation as the amount they were willing to pay to acquire the mug. Irrational, yes. And profoundly human. We don't want to lose; we don't want to fail. The pain of failing, even in simple activities, is more emotionally salient than the pleasure of succeeding.

Aversion to failure is real. Rationally, we know that everyone makes mistakes; we know we live in a complex world where things will go wrong even when we do our best; we know we should forgive ourselves (and others) when we fall short. But failure and fault are inextricably linked in most households, organizations, and cultures.

A friend in the Netherlands told me a story recently that highlights the universality of dodging blame—and how early it takes hold.

Sander's small car was in for repairs, and the garage had loaned him a large BMW. On the drive back to the garage to return the borrowed car, Sander took his children to school. Dropping off the older child first, he continued on to take his three-year-old to day care. In a hurry, Sander navigated the car through a narrow street made narrower by the parked cars lining the sidewalk. And suddenly, bang! The BMW's outside mirror on the passenger side, where the child was sitting in the back seat, collided with a parked car. Not a second had passed before the startled child looked up and shouted, "I didn't do anything, Papa!"

We can laugh at the impossibility of a three-year-old child in the back seat being culpable for a damaged exterior car mirror. Clearly, his instinct to dodge blame superseded any possibility of his being at fault. Yet the story illustrates how deep-rooted is our instinct to dodge blame. Even when the stakes are low, the blame-dodging reflex thwarts learning. And it doesn't stop in childhood. Sydney Finkelstein, a Dartmouth professor who studied major failures at over fifty companies, found that those higher in the management hierarchy were more likely to blame factors other than themselves compared to those with less power. Oddly, those with the most power seem to feel they have the least control. So much for the "buck stops here" thinking popularized by U.S. president Harry Truman.

Ironically, our aversion to failures makes experiencing them more likely. When we don't admit or point out small failures, we allow them to turn into larger ones. When you put off telling your boss about a problem that could derail a critical project—and perhaps miss an important deadline for the customer—you convert a potentially solvable small issue into a larger, more consequential failure. Similarly, in our lives, when we won't admit that we're struggling, we don't get the help we need. Our aversion to our failures also leaves us vulnerable to feelings of relief when someone else fails. We're instantly glad it's not us. We may experience an automatic, if fleeting, feeling of superiority. Worse, we can be quick to judge others' failures. When I teach extended case studies of significant failures in the Harvard Business

School classroom—for example, one of NASA's two failed shuttle missions—a third of the students express anger, sometimes even outrage, that NASA could have allowed these failures to occur.

It's human to feel anger and blame, but it's not a strategy for helping us avoid and learn from failure. The complex failures in NASA's Space Shuttle program are fascinating to me and my students. I try to put them to good use to help those of us who are not rocket scientists—or managers of large, complex, high-stakes operations—to learn vicariously (with an open mind and immense humility about the challenges NASA faced) about how to avoid certain kinds of failures in our own lives.

One of the most important strategies for avoiding complex failures is emphasizing a preference for speaking up openly and quickly in your family, team, or organization. In other words, make it psychologically safe to be honest about a small thing before it snowballs into a larger failure. Too many of the large organizational failures I've studied could have been prevented if people had felt able to speak up earlier with their tentative concerns.

Oddly, our aversion holds for both little failures and big ones. We want to feel good about ourselves (not incidentally an important element of mental health), and we want to accomplish things. It's not only surgeons pursuing ambitious dreams of saving lives who hold such hopes. We want our children to go to college and for holidays to always be joyous. Yet in reality we say things we regret, companies and products fail, children struggle, and holidays include conflict and disappointment. Examining our failures carefully is emotionally unpleasant and chips away at our self-esteem. Left to our own devices, we will speed through or avoid failure analysis altogether.

I still remember the humiliation I felt when I failed to make my high school basketball team. A day after the tryouts the coach posted a sheet of paper with two lists. To the left were the names of all who'd been accepted to the team—many of my friends and classmates. To the right was the list of those who'd tried and failed. That list had only one name: mine. Which is what made it so embarrassing. I didn't want to analyze why I'd failed to make the team, and certainly I didn't want to dwell on the unpleasant feelings it evoked. It's not that I thought I was particularly skilled, but being the only player rejected hurt. No surprise—I didn't die from this rejection. I didn't devote much time to learning from it, either.

Athletes in general possess a relatively enlightened understanding of failure's relationship to success. As Canadian ice hockey superstar Wayne Gretzky famously said, "You miss one hundred percent of the shots you don't take." Sports training and competition naturally entail accepting and learning from multiple failures as part of gaining mastery. Soccer star and Olympic gold medalist Abby Wambach points out that failure means you are "in the game." In her 2018 commencement speech at Barnard College in New York, Wambach exhorted graduates to make failure their "fuel." Failure, she explained, "is not something to be ashamed of, it's something to be powered by. Failure is the highest-octane fuel your life can run on."

Surprising—and revelatory—however, is the study that found athletes who placed third in an Olympic event, earning a bronze medal, appeared happier and *less* likely to feel the sting of failure than the athletes who finished second and received a silver medal.

Why did silver-medaling Olympic competitors in the study feel as if they'd failed, while their bronze-medaling counterparts felt a measure of success? Psychologists say it's caused by "counterfactual thinking"—the human tendency to frame events in terms of "what if" or "if only." The silver medalists, disappointed at not having won gold, framed their performance as a failure relative to winning gold. Those who came in third place framed the result as a success—they earned a medal at the Olympics! They were acutely aware of how easily they might have missed the chance to stand on the Olympic podium in glory and not come home with a medal at all.

The bronze medalists had *reframed* their result—from a loss to a gain. That simple—and scientifically valid—reframe gave them joy instead of regret. As you will learn in this book, how we frame or *reframe* failure has a great deal to do with our capacity to fail well. Reframing failure is the life-enhancing skill that helps us overcome our spontaneous aversion to failure.

It starts with the willingness to look at yourself—not to engage in extensive self-criticism or to enumerate your personal flaws, but to become more aware of universal tendencies that stem from how we're wired and are compounded by how we're socialized. This is not about rumination—a repetitive negative thought process that isn't productive—or self-flagellation. But it may mean taking a look at some of your idiosyncratic habits. Without this, it's hard to experiment with practices that help us think and act differently.

Clinical psychology research shows that failures in our lives can trigger emotional distress, anxiety, and even depression. Yet, some people are more resilient than others. What makes them different? First, they are less prone to perfectionism, less likely to hold themselves to unrealistic standards. If you expect to do everything perfectly or to win every contest, you will be disappointed or even distressed when it doesn't happen. In contrast, if you expect to try your best, accepting that you might not achieve everything you want, you're likely to have a more balanced and healthy relationship with failure.

Second, resilient people make more positive attributions about events than those who become anxious or depressed. How they explain failures to themselves is balanced and realistic, rather than exaggerated and colored by shame. If you attribute not getting a job offer you wanted to a highly competitive applicant pool or to the company's idiosyncratic preferences, you're more likely to recover from the disappointment than if you think, "I'm just not good enough." Attributional style has been studied at length by Martin Seligman, the University of Pennsylvania psychologist who launched a revolution in "positive psychology" in the 1990s. Seligman shifted from his field's focus on pathology to instead study human strengths that enable individuals and communities to thrive. In particular, he studied how people develop positive or negative explanations of the events in their lives. Fortunately, forming positive attributions is a learnable skill. For instance, when you weren't selected for that job you wanted, maybe a good friend helped you reframe the situation to think constructively about it. If you bring that learning forward to your next experiences, you are on your way to a healthier relationship with failure.

Note that healthy attributions about failure not only stay balanced and rational, they also take account of the ways—small or large—that you may have contributed to what happened. Maybe you didn't prepare sufficiently for the interview. This is not to beat yourself up or wallow in shame. Quite the contrary; it's about developing the self-awareness and confidence to keep learning, making whatever changes you need so as to do better next time.

Each of us is a fallible human being, living and working with other fallible human beings. Even if we work to overcome our emotional aversion to failure, failing effectively isn't automatic. We also need help to reduce the confusion created by the glib talk about failure that is especially rampant in conversations on entrepreneurship.

Confusion: not all failure is alike!

Although "fail fast, fail often" has become a Silicon Valley mantra meant to celebrate failure, and corporate failure parties and failure résumés have become popular, much of the discussion in books, articles, and podcasts is simple and superficial—more rhetoric than reality. For instance, it's clear that no company should celebrate a plant manager whose automobile assembly line fails fast and often. Ditto for today's heart surgeons. No wonder we are confused!

Fortunately, this confusion can be reduced by understanding the three types of failure, and how differences in context matter. For instance, in some situations well-developed knowledge about how to achieve desired results makes routines and plans generally unfold as expected; for example, following a recipe to bake a cake or drawing patients' blood in a phlebotomy lab. I call these *consistent contexts*. Other times you're in brand-new territory—forced to try things to see what works. The pioneering cardiac surgeons we met at the start of this chapter were clearly in new terrain, and most of their failures were intelligent. Other examples of *novel contexts* include designing a new product or figuring out how to get protective masks to millions of people during a worldwide pandemic.

Failures are more likely in novel than consistent contexts, so we don't get upset about them, right? Wrong. Your amygdala—that small part of your brain responsible for activating a fight-or-flight response—detects a threat no matter the context. Relatedly, you might be surprised to discover that your negative emotional reaction to failures, regardless of the level of *real* danger, can be surprisingly similar. But, a simple typology for distinguishing failures can help us make healthy attributions about them, counteracting the amygdala hijack.

In addition to novel and consistent contexts, all of us frequently find ourselves in *variable contexts*—those moments in life when knowledge exists to handle that particular type of situation, but life throws you a curveball. For example, doctors and nurses working in a hospital emergency room, no matter how seasoned or experienced, may encounter patients presenting a cluster of previously unseen symptoms, as in the early days of the COVID virus. Pilots must be prepared to fly through unexpected weather patterns. In our daily lives, we face situations where we have extensive prior knowledge but still face meaningful uncertainty. The most experienced teachers never know in advance what challenges a new class of students will bring. If you move to a new place or take a new job, you can never be sure how you might or might not fit in—even if you've talked to people there and tried to learn what you could about its culture. Until you arrive, you have an informed prediction, not a guarantee, about what it will be like.

Over the years I've studied people working in manufacturing assembly lines (consistent context), corporate research and development labs (novel context), and cardiac surgery operating rooms (variable context). I've noticed that different organizational contexts set the stage for different expectations about failing, as depicted in Table 1.1. Yet even though common sense dictates that people should be less allergic to failure in a lab than in a production line, it's not always true. Nobody likes to fail. Period.

Most of us don't stop to challenge our spontaneous emotional responses to the events in our lives. But you can learn how to do this—and it's a crucial skill to bring more learning and joy into your life. Imagine you join a community tennis team—hoping to have fun and improve your skills. Early on you'll make many mistakes and fail to return many of your opponents' shots. How should you feel? Despondent? Of course not. You force yourself to remember that you're simply trying to get better at a new activity. When you teach your teenager to drive, preferably in a large empty parking lot at first, you don't yell at him for mistakenly putting the car in reverse or stalling the engine. Instead, with an encouraging voice, you talk through what happened and what to do next time. In your family or in a social group you care about, having more honest and logical conversations about expectations and disappointments is liberating. And the cognitive skills you need to process failures productively, rather than painfully, can be learned, as you will see in chapter 5.

The correlation between context type and failure type is substantial (clearly, for instance, scientific laboratories and intelligent failures go hand in hand)—but context and failure type are not 100 percent aligned. A basic failure can happen in a laboratory when a scientist mistakenly uses the wrong chemical—wasting both materials and time. Similarly, an intelligent failure occurs on an assembly line when a thoughtful process improvement suggestion turns out not to work as hoped. Nonetheless, an appreciation for the role of context helps you anticipate the kinds of failures likely to happen, as you will explore in chapter 6.

Our confusion about failure gives rise to illogical policies and prac-

TABLE 1.1: **Implications of Context for Failure**

Context	Consistent	Variable	Novel
Example	Vehicle assembly line	Surgical operating room	Scientific laboratory
The state of knowledge	Well-developed	Well-developed knowledge, vulnerable to unexpected events	Limited
Uncertainty	Low	Medium	High
Most common failure type	Basic failure	Complex failure	Intelligent failure

tices. For example, meeting with senior executives in a large financial services firm in April 2020, I listened as they explained that the current business environment made failure temporarily "off-limits." Understandably concerned about an economic climate increasingly challenged by a global pandemic, these business leaders wanted everything to go as well as possible. Generally speaking, they were sincere in their desire to learn from failure. But enthusiasm about failing was acceptable when times were good, they told me; now that the future looked uncertain, pursuing unerring success was more imperative than ever.

These smart, well-intentioned people needed to rethink failure. First, they needed to appreciate the context. The need for fast learning from failure is most critical in times of uncertainty and upheaval, in part because failures are more likely! Second, while encouraging people to minimize basic and complex failures may help them focus, welcoming intelligent failures remains essential to progress in any industry. Third, they needed to recognize that the most likely outcome of their prohibition on failure wasn't perfection but rather not hearing about the failures that do occur. When people don't speak up about small failures—say, an accounting error—these can spiral into larger failures, such as massive banking losses.

In my work with companies, I've encountered this issue often enough to see it as a common error. The instinct to exhort people to do their best work in challenging times is understandable. It's tempting to believe that if we just hunker down, we can avoid failure altogether. It's also wrong. The relationship between effort and success is imperfect. The world around us changes constantly and keeps presenting us with new situations. The best-laid plans encounter problems in an uncertain context. Even when people work hard and are committed to doing the right thing, failure is always possible in a new situation. Sure, sometimes failures are caused by people who are careless or don't work hard, but even hard work can end in failure when a situation is new and different or some unexpected event happens. Finally, and most perversely, sometimes sheer luck allows you to mail it in and succeed anyway.

An upheaval such as a global pandemic causes an extreme degree of uncertainty and change. But even before COVID-19 dominated the news cycle, the interdependence of the world in which we live and work had long made uncertainty and change part of our lives. Our interdependence—being dependent on others to achieve some goal (including the goal of continuing to exist)—makes us vulnerable. We cannot ever know for sure what others will do, and what other systems we depend on might break down. Nineteenth-century German military strategist Helmuth von Moltke's advice has been interpreted as "No plan survives contact with the enemy." When we take into consideration our interdependence, we are forced to become more thoughtful and vigilant in expecting the unexpected.

Now consider what happens when senior executives, or parents, for that matter, state unequivocally that failure is off-limits, that only *good* results are acceptable. Failures don't stop. They simply go underground. Unwittingly, the financial services executives I spoke with were at risk of inhibiting the transmission of bad news. That wasn't their goal. Their goal was to encourage excellence. But it's human nature to hide the truth when it's clear that sharing it will bring punishment—or even just disapproval. Our fear of rejection presents the third barrier to practicing the science of failing well.

Interpersonal fear: stigma and social rejection

Adding to our emotional aversion and cognitive confusion is a deep-rooted fear of looking bad in the eyes of others. This is more than just a preference. The fear induced by the risk of social rejection can be traced back to our evolutionary heritage when rejection could literally mean the difference between staying alive and dying of starvation or exposure. Our modern brains fail to distinguish between the fear of rejection that is irrational in most settings and more rational fears, such as that of an oncoming bus barreling toward you on a city street. Research by Matthew Lieberman and Naomi Eisenberger at UCLA shows that many of the brain circuits for social pain and physical pain overlap.

Fear activates the amygdala, as previously noted, inducing the fight-or-flight response, where "flight" does not necessarily mean running away but instead doing what you can to avoid looking bad. When your heart pounds or your palms sweat before you speak up in an important meeting, especially one in which you are feeling judged or criticized, that's due to the automatic responses of your amygdala. This survival mechanism in our brains helped us elude saber-toothed tigers in prehistoric times, but today often leads us to overreact to harmless stimuli and to shy away from constructive risk-taking. The fear response, designed to be protective, can be counterproductive in the modern world when it keeps us from taking the small interpersonal risks that are essential to speaking up or trying new things.

First, fear inhibits learning. Research shows that fear consumes physiologic resources, diverting them from parts of the brain that manage working memory and process new information. In a word, learning. And that includes learning from failure. It is hard for people to do their best work when they're afraid. It's especially hard to learn from failure because doing so is a cognitively demanding task.

Second, fear impedes talking about our failures. Today's never-ending chore of self-presentation has exacerbated this ancient human tendency. The pressure to look successful has never been greater than in this age of social media. Studies find today's teens, in particular, are obsessed with putting forward a sanitized version of their lives, endlessly checking for "likes" and suffering emotionally from comparisons and slights, real or perceived. Our emotional reaction to a perceived rejection is the same as to an actual one, because it's how we interpret a situation that shapes our emotional response. And it's not just the kids who worry. Whether in professional accomplishment, attractiveness, or social inclusion, keeping up appearances can feel as necessary as breathing to full-grown adults. The real failure, I've found, is believing that others will like us more if we are failure-free. In reality, we appreciate and like people who are genuine and interested in us, not those who present a flawless exterior.

In my research, I've amassed a fair amount of evidence that psychological safety is especially helpful in settings where teamwork, problem-solving, or innovation are needed to get the job done. Psychological safety—an environment where you don't fear rejection for being wrong—is the antidote to the interpersonal fear that prevents us from failing well. Failure lurks in the background in most studies of psychological safety. This is because psychological safety helps us do and say the things that allow us to learn and make progress in our changing, uncertain world. This interpersonal climate factor—such a "soft" thing—turned out to be crucial in predicting team performance in challenging environments, ranging from those in leading academic medical centers to Fortune 500 companies to your family.

Have you ever worked in a team where you were genuinely not worried that others would think less of you if you asked for help or admitted that you were wrong about something? Maybe you felt confident that people supported and respected one another—and all were trying to do their best. If so, you probably weren't afraid to ask questions, to admit mistakes, and to experiment with unproven ideas. My research has shown that psychologically safe environments help teams avoid preventable failures. They also help them pursue intelligent ones. Psychological safety reduces the interpersonal barriers to failing well, so people can take on new challenges with less fear, such that we can try to succeed and walk away wiser when we don't. That, I believe, is the right kind of wrong.

Yet few organizations have enough psychological safety for the benefits of learning from failure to be fully realized. Managers I've interviewed in places as different as hospitals and investment banks admit to being torn: How can they respond constructively to failures without encouraging lax performance? If people aren't held accountable for failures, what would make them do their best work? Parents ask the same question.

These concerns stem from a false dichotomy. A culture that makes it safe to talk about failure can coexist with high standards, as depicted in Figure 1.1. This is as true in families as it is at work. Psychological

FIGURE 1.1: The Relationship between Psychological Safety and Standards in Failure Science

safety isn't synonymous with "anything goes." A workplace can be psychologically safe and still expect people to do excellent work or meet deadlines. A family can be psychologically safe and still expect everyone to wash dishes and take out the trash. It's possible to create an environment where candor and openness seem feasible: an honest, challenging, collaborative environment.

I'd go so far as to say that insisting on high standards without psychological safety is a recipe for failure—and not the good kind. People are more likely to mess up (even for things they know how to do well) when they're stressed. Similarly, when you have a question about how to do something but don't feel able to ask someone, you're at risk of running headlong into a basic failure. Also, when people encounter intelligent failures, they need to feel safe enough to tell other people about them. These useful failures are no longer "intelligent" when they happen a second time.

Maybe it's occurred to you that in contexts where certainty is high—such as an assembly line—it's possible to succeed without psychological safety. There will be fewer failures in the first place. But because certainty is not the norm today, reducing interpersonal fear by destigmatizing failure is important. Learning happens best when we're challenged *and* psychologically safe enough to experiment and to talk openly about it when things don't work out as we'd hoped. It's not just your own learning from failure that matters; it's also your willingness to share those lessons with others.

In sum, our aversion to failure, confusion about failure types, and fear of rejection combine to make practicing the science of failing well more difficult than it needs to be. Fear makes it hard to speak up when we need help to avoid a mistake or to engage in honest conversation so we can learn from a failed experiment. Lacking the vocabulary and rationale to distinguish basic, complex, and intelligent failures, we're more likely to maintain our aversion to all failures. Fortunately, reframing, discerning, and psychological safety can help us get unstuck, as summarized in Table 1.2.

TABLE 1.2: **Overcoming the Barriers to Failing Well**

Why We Fail at Failure	What Helps
Aversion	Reframing to build healthy attributions
Confusion	A framework to discern failure types
Fear	Psychological safety

Failure's Range of Causes

At first glance, commitment to excellence and tolerance of failure seem to be in tension. But let's consider a hypothetical spectrum of reasons for failure such as I've depicted in Figure 1.2. At one end we find misconduct or sabotage (say, breaking a law or violating a safety procedure); at the other, we find a thoughtful experiment that fails (as scientists endure daily). It becomes clear that not all failures are caused by blameworthy acts. Some are downright praiseworthy.

When someone deliberately sabotages a process or violates a safety practice, blame is appropriate. But after that, you face a judgment call that cannot be made without more information about the context. For example, carelessly not paying attention might be blameworthy. But what if that person was overcome by fatigue after being required to work two straight shifts? Here, we might wish to blame the manager

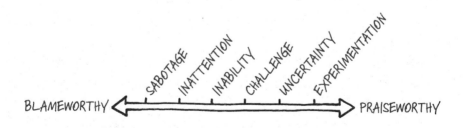

FIGURE 1.2: A Spectrum of Causes of Failure

who assigned the shifts, rather than the employee who fell asleep, but we'd need to know more before we could be certain who or what was at fault. As we go across the spectrum, it gets more illogical to blame anyone! Lack of ability? All of us have been novices in various activities. No one takes off on a bicycle the first time without a fall. Unless someone deliberately undertook a dangerous procedure before receiving training, it's hard to call *inability* blameworthy.

Next, some tasks persist in being too challenging for reliably failure-free performance. Consider the Olympic gymnast who fails to execute a flawless back-full on the balance beam. Blameworthy? Of course not. It's one of the most challenging moves in gymnastics. The gymnast starts it from a standing position, executes a backward somersault with a straight body throughout and a full twist in the middle, then lands back on her feet on the beam. Top competitors who can execute the move perfectly in practice may still fail to do so in an important competition.

As we continue across the spectrum, uncertainty gives rise to unavoidable failures. When a friend sets you up on a blind date, there's no way to know for sure if it will work out. If you agree to go and the date proves a failure, neither you nor your friend deserves blame. Lastly, a failure that results from thoughtful experimentation yields new knowledge. It's praiseworthy. The pioneering surgeons' failures in the early days of open heart surgery are clearly praiseworthy. These failures were unavoidable stepping stones on the path to today's taken-for-granted miracle.

I've conducted the following thought experiment with audiences around the world: "Take a look at the Blameworthy–Praiseworthy spectrum: Which of the potential causes of failure do you consider blameworthy?"

Answers to this question vary. Some will say only sabotage can be considered blameworthy. Others will chime in that inattention should be as well. Pushing back on that, others immediately recognize that people might have been put in difficult situations where becoming distracted was not their fault. It doesn't matter to me *where* you draw the line. What matters is that you draw it and then contemplate your answer to the next question: "What percent of the failures in your organization or family can be considered blameworthy?" I've found that most people, when they think about it carefully, arrive at a small number: perhaps, 1 to 2 percent.

I then ask the most important question: "How many of these failures are *treated* as blameworthy by those who matter in your organization or life?"

Here, people will say (after a rueful pause or a laugh) 70 percent to 90 percent. Or, sometimes, "All of them!" The unfortunate consequence of this gap between a rational assessment of fault and the spontaneous response of those in charge is that failures—in our lives, households, and workplaces—are too often hidden. This is one of the ways we lose access to failure's lessons.

Succeeding through Failing

It should be clear by now that not everyone fails at failure. The pioneering cardiac surgeons such as Walt Lillehei and Clarence Dennis were stunningly successful at putting failure to work—to advance the lifesaving craft to which they devoted their lives. Seeking to alter the surgical landscape forever, Lillehei and Dennis were both contestants in a race that had thus far, as Lillehei's biographer G. Wayne Miller writes, "produced only corpses." Nearly all of these deaths were the result of what we might call "new" failures—failures occurring as part of a journey to accomplish a goal never before achieved. Innovations such as the room-size heart-lung machine, designed to remove carbon dioxide from the patient's blood and pump freshly oxygenated blood back into an artery, were necessary parts of that journey.

Watching Dennis operate in 1951, Dr. Lillehei had been determined to push ahead toward success. Over the next several years, he doggedly sought out opportunities to advance the science. He, too, would confront painful failures along the way.

On September 2, 1952, at the University Hospital, Dr. F. John Lewis, with Lillehei assisting, tried hypothermia as a means of facilitating patient stability. Miraculously, five-year-old Jacqueline Jones survived. Success? Although Lillehei and others would continue to operate successfully with hypothermia, the severely limited time a patient could be kept at such a low temperature—ten or twelve minutes—made longer and more complex surgical procedures impossible. A short-lived success.

On March 26, 1954, Lillehei, again in the University Hospital operating room, physically connected an infant, Gregory Glidden, born with a hole between the lower chambers of his heart, to his father's circulatory system. This was to keep the child alive while Lillehei operated on the infant's tiny heart. Several times since the autumn of 1953, and most recently in January of 1954, Lillehei had connected the circulatory systems of two dogs, allowing the donor dog to serve as life support for the patient dog during open heart surgery. Called cross-circulation, this new technique was Lillehei's inspired idea. If a pregnant woman could keep her infant's heart going via connections between their veins and arteries, could a similar but artificially induced connection function outside the womb? So far, the approach had worked, keeping the canine patients alive during delicate surgical procedures. But now the stakes were higher.

At 8:45 a.m., Gregory's father, Lyman, was brought into the operating room. Blood from Lyman's femoral artery, carrying freshly oxygenated blood from his heart, was pumped into Gregory through a cannula inserted into the baby's superior and inferior venae cavae to bring blood into his heart. Lillehei opened the baby's heart and located the ventricular septal defect (VSD), a dime-size hole, and repaired it. Gregory survived the operation but died on April 6, 1954, a little under two weeks later, of pneumonia.

None of the experiments that ultimately transformed cardiac surgery occurred without extensive thought about benefits and risks. Each was scientifically rigorous. Failures nonetheless occurred. Sometimes a presurgical diagnosis proved faulty. Sometimes an accident occurred during surgery because the doctors were not yet skilled enough. Most failures occurred because a hypothesis was wrong. In every case, the innovators were traveling into new terrain without a map—determined to reach their destination. Along the way, they needed to explain to so many parents, spouses, and children why a beloved family member had died in a sea of blood. You might say that everyone—surgeons, patients, and their families—were practicing the right kind of wrong. They understood that failures with serious consequences were possible. Each failed operation and each failed surgical innovation provided a chance to learn something that could lead to eventual success.

Lillehei's first triumph, which followed soon after Gregory's surgery, was a cross-circulation surgery on four-year-old Annie Brown, who was connected to her father, Joseph. Two weeks later, Lillehei held a press conference with the adorable, healthy girl, who would live well into adulthood. Yet, as so often happens, the path from failure to success was not a straight line. Immediately after Annie Brown, six out of seven of Lillehei's child patients died from similar surgeries. Equally troubling, a mistake in the cross-circulation rendered one of the parents permanently brain-dead. Operating on a child whose only hope for life was a risky surgery was one thing. But putting a healthy adult volunteer at such risk was much more difficult to tolerate.

Eventually, the heart-lung machine proved to be the most viable solution to the problems posed by open heart surgery. Originally invented by Dr. John Gibbon, improved upon by Clarence Dennis, and then further engineered in a collaboration with Thomas Watson at IBM, it gradually reduced the mortality rate for cardiac surgery to 10 percent by 1957. Today, the risk of dying from the surgery is estimated to be approximately 2 to 3 percent.

Innovation Never Ends

In 1998, a half century after these early surgical failures and successes, I got the chance to study a modern innovation in cardiac surgery. One of my Harvard colleagues had learned about a new surgical technology for conducting the lifesaving surgery less invasively. In most heart operations, including those performed back in the 1950s, the surgeons had to first cut longitudinally through the patient's chest, splitting the breastbone apart. This technique, called a median sternotomy, provides access to the heart, and it still dominates the practice today. It's effective but can involve a painful and lengthy recovery.

The new technology my colleague told me about had been designed to allow the surgeon to perform a repair through a small incision between the ribs, leaving the breastbone intact, with the promise of a shorter, less painful recovery. The downside? A substantial learning curve for the entire operating-room team. For surgeons, operating in a smaller, more restricted space in the body was not as big a shift as you might think. Their field of vision was narrowed, but the delicate stitching for repairing the heart remained relatively unchanged. But for the rest of the team, this new way was not easy to learn.

Of the sixteen cardiac surgery departments my colleagues and I studied, only seven stuck with the new technology. The other nine departments tried it out for a handful of operations, then abandoned it. The most important difference in the groups that succeeded was surgeon leadership—not surgeon skill, experience level, or seniority. When we started the study, we expected that the more elite academic medical centers would be more likely to succeed than the less well-known community hospitals. But we were wrong. Hospital type and status made no difference at all.

The challenge all these teams faced was more interpersonal than technical. The innovation challenged the traditionally hierarchical structure of operating rooms, where the surgeon typically issued orders that others carried out. Surgeons practicing the new technique were newly dependent on the rest of the operating-room team to coordinate aspects of the procedure and keep a "balloon clamp" in place inside the patient's artery as a way of restricting blood flow to the heart. The balloon's tendency to shift meant that the team had to monitor its location through ultrasound imagery to make adjustments. But unless people felt psychologically safe enough to speak up, these activities were hard to carry out. For instance, asking the surgeon to pause while the balloon was repositioned was both new and difficult for most nurses. Surgeons had to listen to other members of the team more often, and more intensely, than in traditional surgeries, where they had done most of the talking.

The successful innovators in our study recognized that they needed to *lead* differently. They had to make sure that everyone in the operating room could talk openly and immediately about what was needed from one another to make the procedure work. When my colleagues and I analyzed the teams that persisted in mastering the new approach, we found that all of them engaged in a few special activities that reflect core practices in the science of failing well.

First, these teams eliminated unnecessary risks to patients by conducting dry runs of the new procedure in the laboratory with animals, then by speaking openly and proactively about what they were doing and thinking as they worked together, and also by immediately reverting to the traditional procedure (the median sternotomy) if they had any concerns about the operation as it unfolded.

Second, these teams drove fear out of the operating room. How? The surgeons were explicit about the learning journey that lay ahead. They emphasized the life-enhancing purpose of the innovation—a chance to help patients recover more quickly. The surgeons let all on the team know their input was critical to making the new procedure work. In this way, the surgeons built psychological safety for speaking up. That some surgeons did this and others didn't allowed me to *prospectively* test the relationship between psychological safety and successful innovation; as the study began, I did not know which sites would succeed at innovating and which would fail. Later, I would be able to conclude that teams that worked to build psychological safety outperformed those that did not.

Third, in their explicit, reflective conversations about how things were going *during* the procedures, the successful teams ensured that there was no confusion about what was happening. In this more mature phase of cardiac surgery, the failures they encountered were more likely quick conversions to the traditional procedure from the minimally invasive one. Or, simply giving up on the new technology altogether—a failure, but not a life-threatening one. Although nine of the sixteen teams we studied failed to innovate, no team experienced a patient death in the many hundreds of minimally invasive operations in our data. By avoiding preventable harm, every team we studied was thus a thoughtful practitioner of the science of failing well.

Practicing the Science of Failing Well

Failures may never be fun, but with practice using new tools and insights they can become less painful and easier to learn from. Our instinctive aversion to failure, our confusion about its different forms, and our fear of rejection keep us stuck. The way out starts with reframing failure—as did so many Olympic bronze medalists—and setting realistic expectations about it. From the small setbacks we experience in our day-to-day lives to the tragic deaths that occurred in the early days of open heart surgery, failures are an unavoidable part of progress. This is as true for our personal lives as for the vital institutions that shape society. This is why it's so important—and ultimately so rewarding—to master the science of failure. Each of the chapters ahead brings foundational ideas and practices to help you do just that.

CHAPTER 2

Eureka!

I have not failed. I've just found ten
thousand ways that won't work.

—Attributed to Thomas A. Edison

Although most of us are familiar with the concept of DNA—the nucleic acids that determine so much of who we are—few of us have tried to manipulate these tiny naturally occurring chemicals to enhance their application in lifesaving therapeutics or game-changing nanotechnologies. That is what Dr. Jennifer Heemstra, working with the other members of her thriving research laboratory at Emory University, does for a living.

On the frontier in any scientific field, a thoughtful hypothesis not supported by data is the right kind of wrong. Scientists, along with inventors such as James West, whom you'll meet later in this chapter, don't last long in their fields if they can't stand to fail. They intuit the value intelligent failure brings. It would be a lie to claim these failures aren't disappointing. They are. Like Olympic bronze medalists, however, scientists and inventors learn healthy ways to think about failure.

And Dr. Heemstra is a scientist who not only practices this healthy thinking, she also preaches it—to the students in her lab and in tweets, articles, and videos.

I met with Jen on Zoom on a summer day in 2021. Scientists are among the most resilient and thoughtful practitioners of intelligent failure, and I wanted to learn more from Jen about how an intelligent failure might play out. When I ask her for a favorite failure story, Jen's hands fly up, palms open, facing me. "Failure is a part of science rather than a judgment," she says. Her warm, open smile threatens to burst from the confines of the small screen. She likes to tell her lab students, "We're going to fail all day." Heads of scientific labs need to normalize failure, she explains. Estimating that experiments fail 95 percent of the time, Jen adds, "Nine out of ten times people beat themselves up unnecessarily."

That's a lot of pain.

Unless, like Jen, you appreciate the difference between blameworthy and praiseworthy failures. Intelligent failures are praiseworthy because they are the necessary building blocks of discovery.

Dr. Heemstra came to this appreciation honestly. She says that she became a scientist because her eighth-grade science teacher told her that she was not good at science. Growing up in Orange County, California, when friends invited her to join a Science Olympiad in the 1990s, she went along—not with any hope of succeeding but because she needed an after-school activity. There, Jen discovered that she not only enjoyed but excelled at geology; eventually, the club coach made sure that she was accepted into the high school's advanced-placement science courses. Her initial failure as a science student led her to develop intrinsic motivation. Rather than studying for the grades (an extrinsic motivator if there ever was one), she memorized the names of rocks and sorted them into egg cartons because, she says, it was "a blast." When she saw the dystopian science fiction movie *Gattaca* shortly after its release, the movie influenced her to major in chemistry. Today, as the first woman to make full professor in the chemistry department at Emory, she still conveys an intrinsic delight in doing the work for its own sake—as she cheers on her students.

Dressed this afternoon in a blue blazer, she could be ready to address an auditorium full of students after our meeting or, just as easily, shed the blazer and head out for a run. Behind her, on the shelves behind her desk, are various models and action figures she's collected. She points to one and says it's named Steve, after a PhD student, Steve Knutson, who used a chemical reagent called glyoxal* to react with nucleotides in single-stranded RNA. When I ask why this might be important (revealing my relative ignorance about chemistry), Jen says, "Aha!" and explains that the lab had been ecstatic because of how many avenues of research and development glyoxal opened up. In addition to applications for controlled or time-release therapeutic drugs, they'd invented a kind of scientific tool for other chemists working in synthetic biology or research to control different gene circuits.

What about failure? Apparently, even someone as comfortable with failure as Jennifer Heemstra naturally begins a failure story with the ending—the successful outcome. Which only reinforces how difficult it is to talk about failure.

Jen takes a step back. Speaking rapidly, she explains that in trying to develop a method for isolating certain RNAs, they realized that it wouldn't happen when the RNA was folded, or double stranded. So the first problem was to unravel the RNA, a necessary step in getting a protein to bind. Steve began to experiment. Would adding a new reagent (an ingredient used to cause a chemical reaction) already in the lab work?

It didn't work.

Salt helps RNA fold. What if he experimented with depriving the RNA of salt? This didn't work either. Steve was disappointed. But not devastated, as he might have been had Jen not worked so hard to create

---

*Glyoxal is an organic compound often used to link other chemicals in scientific experiments.

an environment in the lab where the focus is on learning and discovery. As she explains, "High-performing individuals aren't used to making mistakes. It's important to learn to laugh at ourselves or we'll err on the side of being too afraid to try."

Her passion for the central role embracing failure plays in science research has led Heemstra to write about how students, and especially women, can easily be discouraged from pursuing careers in science, stating in a tweet, "The only people who never make mistakes and never experience failure are those who never try." But really, Steve's failures were not mistakes.

Mistakes are deviations from known practices. Mistakes happen when knowledge about how to achieve a certain result already exists but isn't used. Such as the time when Jen was a graduate student and collected weird data simply because she was using the pipette incorrectly. Proper pipette usage promptly produced data that made sense. She laughs at this story, too, explaining that she tries to create a lab culture where people can "laugh at and normalize silly mistakes."

That the protein failed to bind on double-stranded DNA when it had succeeded in binding on single-stranded RNA was not, however, a "silly mistake." It was the undesired result of a hypothesis-driven experiment. A failure, yes, but an intelligent failure—and an inevitable part of the fascinating work of science. Most important, that failure would inform the next experiment.

Clearly, there was more to learn about how to unfold RNA. Steve went back to the literature and found a paper written by Japanese biochemists in the 1960s, published in a German scientific journal, detailing the use of glyoxal in other, not unrelated, applications. He started to wonder about using glyoxal and set up an experiment with it.

Eureka! With some tweaking, the glyoxal allowed him to cage and re-cage the nucleic acids and restore total function. While not an announcement to flash electronically in twenty-foot letters on a Times Square billboard, for Jen and Steve as research scientists it was cause for celebration, and better yet, it led to new research questions. Their story shows how success in new territory depends on a willingness to endure the right kind of wrong—the intelligent kind.

When Failure Is Intelligent

What makes a failure qualify as intelligent? Here are four key attributes: it takes place in new territory; the context presents a credible opportunity to advance toward a desired goal (whether that be scientific discovery or a new friendship); it is informed by available knowledge (one might say "hypothesis driven"); and finally the failure is as small as it can be to still provide valuable insights. Size is a judgment call, and context matters. What a large company can afford to risk on a pilot project may be greater than what you can afford to risk on a new endeavor in your personal life. The point is to use time and resources wisely. A bonus attribute is that the failure's lessons are learned and used to guide next steps.

With these criteria in mind, anyone can try something out and feel good about the results even when they fall short of a hoped-for success. The failure is intelligent because it's the result of a thoughtful experiment—not a haphazard or sloppy one.

Thomas Edison has been called one of the greatest inventors in history. With 1,093 patents and an outsize impact on the modern world through his tangible inventions (electric light, sound recording, mass communication, motion pictures, to name a few), Edison also created the first research laboratory, Menlo Park, in New Jersey. There the incandescent light bulb was invented, and the lab was the model for R & D departments in today's companies—a place and a process for designers, scientists, engineers, and others to collaborate on new inventions. Much ink has already been spilled about Edison, but what I admire most is how he celebrated the necessity of getting things wrong along the way if you aspire to make progress in any field.

Variously told, my favorite Edison story depicts a former lab assistant expressing sympathetic dismay about the seemingly endless stretch of failure to get results in the inventor's quest to develop a new type of storage battery. Edison's famous retort—or a version of it—was used to open this chapter. In one telling, Edison, a grin on his face, turned to his former assistant and explained that, no, in fact he had thousands of "results"—each a valuable discovery of a way that would not work. That Edison operated in new territory and pursued opportunity is indisputable. That his experiments were informed, and appropriately sized, can be inferred. That he never gave up, such that his intelligent failures ultimately led to success, is itself a "light bulb moment" for all of us.

You don't need to hold these four criteria as a rigid litmus test. Think of them as a helpful guide for distinguishing intelligent failures from other types. Admittedly, these are not crisp yes-no distinctions but rather judgment calls. For instance, it's up to you, not to me or anyone else, whether you see an opportunity worth pursuing. What I hope is that you can use the framework to think about when and why a failure brings discovery—and thus value—in your personal life or in your job. Let's look at a handful of intelligent failures (and fail-ers)—across a range of settings—to get a better feel for each criterion.

New territory

From an early age, Jocelyn Bell Burnell found herself in places—literal and figurative—where no one had ever before been.

In 1940s Northern Ireland, for a girl to express a desire to learn science rather than prepare for a future solely as a wife and mother was unusual. Yet young Jocelyn Bell was utterly dismayed at school when the boys were sent to the lab to learn about chemicals and experiments while the girls were sent to the kitchen to learn domestic sciences. She went home and complained to her parents, who, fortunately, took their daughter's interest in science seriously and convinced the school to change its policy. Jocelyn then became one of three girls allowed to attend science class. She fell in love with astronomy by reading one of her father's books (an architect, he helped design Northern Ireland's Armagh Planetarium). In college, she was the only woman in her class; the lecture hall itself was new and, sadly, capricious territory—other students often greeted her entrance with hisses and catcalls. Perhaps her experiences as an outsider, a female pioneer in science, primed her to notice what no one else had seen.

As a postgraduate student in astronomy at Cambridge University in 1967, she was assigned to a research project to help build and then operate an enormous radio telescope and analyze the collected data— nearly a hundred feet a day of up-and-down lines on graph paper. Antony Hewish, the professor in charge of the project, was looking for quasars, those luminous centers of galaxies that generate enormous amounts of radio waves. One day, staring at the data charts, Jocelyn Bell saw a signal that she couldn't explain. As she recollected, "I shouldn't be seeing something like that. I wanted to understand what it was."

She took the problem to her professor, who at first dismissed her concerns: the aberrant lines, he maintained, were "interference" or perhaps she had set up the telescope wrong. But Jocelyn Bell believed that she had spotted something worthy of continued investigation. So, she dug into the puzzle to figure it out, enlarging the portion of the chart in question to scrutinize the radio signals more clearly. When she presented the enlarged visual data to Hewish, he, too, recognized that the signals signified something new. As Jocelyn Bell later explained, "That started a whole new research project. . . . What is it? How are we getting this curious signal?"

Jocelyn Bell's curiosity in new, uncertain territory—and the work that propelled her experiments with Hewish at the Mullard Radio Astronomy Observatory—eventually led to the Nobel Prize–winning discovery of the first pulsars. The Nobel, incidentally, did not include Jocelyn Bell among its winners.

Life and work place us in new territory all the time. New may mean new to an entire professional field, or simply new to you as in a new sport, a career move, or a first date. If you are picking up golf, it's all but guaranteed that the first encounter between your club and the ball will qualify as a failure. More meaningfully, most major life events, such as leaving home or moving to a new location, lead to new ground. This is true for happy life events, such as getting married. And sad ones, such as losing a parent.

Inventors or scientists such as Edison, Heemstra, and Jocelyn Bell navigate territory that's new to everyone. The challenge of new territory is that, whatever the domain, there is no way to look up the answer on the internet and use it to avoid failure. If you're interested in doing original thinking, moving away from the familiar is required. Scientists certainly study the work of their predecessors and colleagues to make sure a research question hasn't been answered before, but that doesn't circumvent failure in new areas. When you start a new job, you may receive information from friends or hiring managers or online employer reviews, but as you settle in, get introduced to new colleagues, and attend meetings where work is discussed, you may discover aspects of the situation that you didn't expect. If the job doesn't work out, it won't necessarily be because you didn't do your homework. Perhaps the person who hired you and with whom you expected to work is suddenly transferred to another division and the new boss has entirely different expectations. For a failure to qualify as intelligent, no recipe, blueprint, or instruction guide can have existed to solve the problem or precisely map the new ground in advance.

A crucial feature of new territory, whether you're a first-time parent or starting your first job, is uncertainty. That is part of the risk you assume when you try something new. It is not possible to predict exactly what will happen.

Mary and Bill grew up together in a close-knit neighborhood in New York City in the 1930s and '40s. Kids played ball on the street (unsupervised; without playdates) and parents chatted casually in courtyards. In the summer of 1953, when both Mary and Bill were back in New York after graduating from college, it seemed natural for Bill to set her up on a date with a friend he was confident she would like—the brother of a woman Bill was currently dating. But Mary, who would later become my mother, was skeptical—not only about a blind date, but about Bill's taste.

A year or so earlier she'd had a bad experience with a man Bill thought she'd like. As was done in the days of single-sex colleges in the 1950s, my mother had joined a busload of other young Vassar women to spend an event-filled weekend dining, dancing, and socializing with young Princeton men. Her date for the weekend? One of Bill's friends. Who drank too much, talked only about himself, and was too "forward," as Mom later put it. In her view, the weekend had been a waste of time. A failure. Even staying back at Vassar for the weekend to study would have been more fun. Bill had been wrong before, and my mother had little confidence that this new selection would be someone she'd like. If she followed Bill's advice, she risked another failed date. But she didn't want to be too hasty in dismissing his taste. There was no way to know for sure.

Meaningful opportunity

An intelligent failure occurs as part of what you believe is a meaningful opportunity to advance toward a valued goal. Jen Heemstra and Steve Knutson were pursuing a scientific discovery they hoped would result in an important paper in a top journal—they could almost see the entry on their résumés. It was disappointing to be wrong (at first). Jocelyn Bell saw—and then had to convince her professor of—an opportunity to identify something new about the solar system, even if she wasn't sure what that might be. My mother wanted to eventually meet someone to spend her life with. Finding a life partner, creating a new business, or making a scientific discovery can all embody meaningful opportunity. But the goal need not be lofty. Experimenting with a new recipe that looks delicious qualifies as an intelligent failure when it turns out to taste awful.

Learning to experience intelligent failure starts at an early age. A child taking her first step is well on her way to doing just that. But in elementary school, many children start to believe that getting the right answers is the only valued activity. This is why smart curricula in science, technology, engineering, and mathematics (STEM) that create opportunities for students to practice intelligent failure while mastering subject matter are so valuable. Brighton College, an independent school for boys and girls in Brighton, England, has taken this seriously. The school's philosophy, as described by Sam Harvey, director of the design and technology curriculum, maintains, "Pupils' creativity is not limited, we encourage them to create, trial, and test their ideas." In other words, to practice intelligent failure.

That's how five British teens at Brighton College saw an opportunity to advance not only their term assignment, but also to address a real problem: unintentional self-injury while opening an avocado, otherwise known as avocado hand. After one of their classmates accidentally cut his hand with a knife while slicing an avocado, the five thirteen- and fourteen-year-olds, encouraged by their teacher, Sarah Awbery, created a prototype paring tool to safely slice the avocado skin and remove the pit. One of over two thousand entries, the Avogo, as the teens named their invention, won the London Design Museum's Design Ventura competition in 2017 in the Independent Schools category. Later, the students raised money for manufacturing the Avogo through the crowdfunding website Kickstarter. New territory. Meaningful opportunity.

Brighton College provides just one example of teaching youngsters the habits and mindsets of intelligent failure. Hands-on exhibits in children's museums that, for example, give children the opportunity to place a ball in a chute and hypothesize about which of several directions it might fall offer early practice of the right kind of wrong. Play is integral to the spirit of intelligent failure. It doesn't always have to sting.

Do your homework

Intelligent failures begin with preparation. No scientist wants to waste time or materials on experiments that have been run before and failed. Do your homework. The classic intelligent failure is hypothesis driven. You've taken the time to think through what might happen—why you have reason to believe that you could be right about what will happen. My Harvard colleague Thomas "Tom" Eisenmann, an entrepreneurship expert, finds that many start-up failures are caused by the skipping of basic homework. For example, Triangulate, an online dating start-up, rushed to launch fully functional offerings that didn't fit any market needs. Eager to launch fast, founders skipped the research—customer interviews to probe for unmet needs. Giving short shrift to that crucial preparation, the company paid the price. Tom attributes this common failure, in part, to "the 'fail fast' mantra," which overemphasizes action, shortchanging preparation. Moreover, while this might seem self-evident, once you've done the homework, you must heed what it's telling you.

Take the tale of Crystal Pepsi, a soda launched in haste in 1992 in response to a market trend favoring clear and caffeine-free drinks. Why not offer a beverage that was both—and in a clear bottle to highlight its appeal? Early on, Pepsi scientists identified a rather large, intractable problem with the proposed new product: clear drinks in clear bottles deteriorate easily, soon acquiring a terrible taste. Early reports from bottlers confirmed this was a problem. In a hurry to get the product on the shelves, marketing executives ignored these indicators. No surprise if you've never heard of this soda. Crystal Pepsi has gone down in product-development history as one of the worst new-product failures of all time.

Jocelyn Bell could only notice that something was wrong with the data she collected because of her previous training in physics and radio astronomy. Someone without that background would only have seen squiggly lines. But Bell was able to confidently state, "I shouldn't be seeing something like that. I wanted to understand what it was." These two sentences reveal her high level of preparation. If she hadn't done her homework, she would have been ill-equipped to notice the unexpected. Only with an informed mental model about what *should* happen are you able to observe an anomaly.

The five British teens—Pietro Pignatti Morano Campori, Matias Paz Linares, Shiven Patel, Seth Rickard, and Felix Winstanley—armed themselves with knowledge by reviewing previous avocado cutters. "We plotted the daily routine," they said, "of what we thought a design enthusiast might get up to. . . . We explored a variety of products that already exist to help prepare fruit and vegetables. Many of them were cumbersome and large, and we wanted to create a sleek and stylish design. We experimented with different hook designs and then were ready to test our design for real." Jen's student Steve Knutson went to the scientific literature to get as much knowledge as he could about the problem he was trying to solve *before* investing time and chemicals in a new experiment—even though it meant tracking down an obscure paper from the 1960s.

Equally important is the desire to understand, as Jocelyn Bell exemplified, *why* the unexpected happened, or to anticipate what will happen in a new experiment. Gardeners, for example, want to understand why the same seedling may grow better in one location than another. Is it the soil? The number of hours the sun is overhead? The watering schedule? Or something else entirely? Teachers wonder why some students find it more difficult to learn. You may be curious about what challenges, opportunities, and experiences await when you begin a new job or move to a new location. Human beings are curious by nature, but over time we are at risk of losing our drive to understand new things. And it's hard to learn if you already know.

That's why outsiders to any existing system (a family, a company, a country) bring such a valuable new lens. They know that they don't know! Engineer-inventor Bishnu Atal remembers how frustrating it was to talk to his family back home in India when he first arrived in the United States in 1961 to work at Bell Labs. Why, he wondered, was the telephone audio reception so poor? Even simple conversations were difficult to comprehend. And why were overseas calls so costly? Those questions kept Atal and his colleagues at Bell Labs busy for the next twenty years. Atal's curiosity ultimately led to the development of "linear predictive coding," today the most widely used method in speech processing. Their technology allows you to conduct clear and inexpensive calls on your cell phone to people nearly anywhere in the world.

Keep it small

Eventually, with some persistence from her friend Bill, Mary agreed to the blind date. But this time, my practical mother intuited how to mitigate risk. The commitment was not to spend an entire weekend with the friend of a friend. It didn't even have to be an entire evening. She agreed to meet for a drink. At most, she'd lose a couple of hours and risk a boring or otherwise unsatisfactory experience. She was willing to try, given the minimal investment of time and energy.

Mary and Bill's friend Bob clicked in all the right ways. They eventually married—and the smart, serious, kind man she met that evening became my father. What's more, lightning, or Cupid, struck twice. My uncle Bill married the woman he'd been dating, my father's sister and later my beloved aunt Joan.

Because failures consume time and resources, you're smart to use both judiciously. Failures can also threaten reputations. One way to mitigate the reputational cost of failure is to experiment behind closed doors. If you've ever tried on a bold new style of clothing to see if it suits you, you probably did it behind the curtain of a store's changing area.

Similarly, most innovation departments and scientific labs are private, with scientists and product designers trying all sorts of crazy things without an audience.

Shutting down projects as soon as it's clear they are not working is another way innovators limit failure's size and cost. It's tempting for project teams to keep pushing the boulder up the hill. Tempting but wasteful. The smart, motivated people on most innovation projects could be better redeployed in the next risky endeavor. It's not easy to recognize, in real time, when you're throwing good money after bad—which is why I think analyzing progress should be a "team sport." You have to be willing to solicit input from people who have different perspectives on the project. To overcome the "sunk costs" fallacy, this helps to change the default incentive (to keep going) so people can feel good about saying it's time to stop. Astro Teller, head of the radical innovation company called X at Alphabet (Google's parent company), gives failure bonuses to employees who admit a project isn't working. He understands that it's no longer an intelligent failure when the faint writing on the wall starts to hint that a project is doomed.

When W. Leigh Thompson, then chief scientific officer at pharmaceutical company Eli Lilly, introduced "failure parties" back in the 1990s, his goal was to honor the thoughtful risks that are so necessary to advancing science. But, as important, he understood that these rituals helped scientists acknowledge failures in a timely way, freeing up resources for what came next. He was trying to keep failures as small as possible! I'd add to this that a "party" ensured that others in the department learned about the failure, to prevent repeating it—another best practice for keeping the costs of failure as small as possible. I hope it's clear by now that an intelligent failure is not intelligent the second time around.

Another best practice for keeping failure as small as possible is the design of smart pilots to test new ideas before the full-scale launch of an innovation. Pilots make sense: carry out small tests of something new to avoid big, expensive, visible failures. But too often this good idea goes wrong in practice: a seemingly successful pilot is followed by a major failure in the launch of the innovation to all customers. This happens when company leaders don't recognize how their incentives favor unfettered success, inhibiting intelligent failure. People are naturally motivated to have their projects succeed, including pilots, and formal and informal incentives reinforce that desire. As a result, those in charge of a pilot do everything in their power to delight the small group of customers participating, even if it requires extra resources or staff to get things right. Unfortunately, then the full-scale launch of the new product or service, no longer operating in the idealized context of the pilot, doesn't go well. A telecommunications company I studied underwent an embarrassing and expensive fiasco after a picture-perfect pilot of a new technology. The company's pilot *failed by succeeding* (instead of succeeding by failing)! By not doing the work to discover the vulnerabilities that needed to be fixed before a full-scale launch, the pilot failed the company and its customers.

The solution is to create incentives that motivate pilots not to succeed but rather to fail well. An effective pilot is littered with the right kind of wrong—numerous intelligent failures, each generating valuable information. To design a smart pilot in your organization, you should be able to answer yes to the following questions:

1. Is the pilot being tested under typical (or better yet, challenging) circumstances (rather than optimal ones)?
2. Is the goal of the pilot to learn as much as possible (not to prove the success of the innovation to senior executives)?
3. Is it clear that compensation and performance reviews are *not* based on a successful outcome for the pilot?
4. Were explicit changes made as a result of the pilot?

Let's review. To be intelligent, a failure must take place in new territory, in pursuit of a valued goal, with adequate preparation and risk mitigation (investing as little as needed to learn). With these criteria, summarized in Table 2.1, met, when you try something and it doesn't work, it's an intelligent failure. Now it's time to learn as much as you can from it.

TABLE 2.1: **How to Tell If a Failure Is Intelligent**

Attribute	Diagnostic Questions
Takes place in new territory	Do people already know how to achieve the result I'm pursuing? Is it possible to find a solution some other way, to avoid failure?
Opportunity driven	Is there a meaningful opportunity worth pursuing? What goal am I hoping to accomplish? Is the risk of failure worth taking?
Informed by prior knowledge	Have I done my homework? Before I experiment, do I have the available relevant knowledge? Have I formulated a thoughtful hypothesis about what might happen?
As small as possible	Have I mitigated the risks of taking action in new territory by designing an experiment that is as small as possible, while still being informative? Is the planned action the "right size"?
Bonus: you learned from it!	Have I mined the lessons from the failure and figured out how to put them to use going forward? Have I shared this knowledge widely to prevent the same failure from happening again?

Learn as much as you can

More than fifty years after my parents were set up, people were using the internet to organize what are essentially blind dates. That was how Amy Webb, who at age thirty was already well on her way to the successful career she's since established as a "quantitative futurist"—a career so successful that *Forbes* magazine listed her as one of fifty Women Changing the World—found herself rather cavalierly logging into a dating site and creating a profile to attract a life partner. She described herself on the site as an "award-winning journalist, speaker, and thinker" who had spent "12 years working with digital media and now advises various startups, retailers, government agencies and media organizations . . . all over the world." When prompted for what she liked to do for fun, she listed JavaScript and monetization.

One of her few dates was dinner with an IT professional. At the restaurant, he ordered multiple items from on and off the menu: appetizers, entrées, and several bottles of wine. Throughout their date, dish after dish arrived at their table. The conversation was bland. When the bill came, her date got up from the table, said he was going to the men's room, and never returned! Webb paid a bill nearly equal to an entire month's rent for her at the time.

Clearly, a failure. One from which she was determined to learn.

That night she reframed the failure as algorithmic. The dating algorithm the platform used for matchmaking had failed her. Or she had failed it. But how, exactly, did the algorithm work? Webb launched an extended experiment to learn where things had gone wrong.

Her goal: to collect data. Her method was to create ten fictitious online male profiles that contained the top qualities in the man she wanted to marry: smart, handsome, funny, family oriented, and willing to travel to far-off locales. Then she waited to see what kind of women these desirable men would attract. Careful not to deceive, she communicated minimally with her respondents. Entering her collected data on Excel spreadsheets, she also analyzed the profiles of the most popular women on the site.

Armed with new knowledge, she ran a second experiment, this time reverse engineering a new profile that, while genuine, was what she called "optimized" for the new ecosystem of online dating. Having learned that she was more than her résumé, she described herself as "fun" and "adventurous." She waited twenty-three hours before answering any messages. She posted new photographs of her wearing clothing that revealed rather than concealed her figure. This second profile was a smashing success. She found, met, dated, and married the man who became the love of her life and the father of their daughter. Webb maintains that her success was due to cracking the algorithmic code the site used. But she would not have cracked that code had she not first been willing to learn from failure and persevere.

Taking the time to learn from what went wrong is often the most cringe-inducing aspect of intelligent failure. Not all of us can remain as cheerful as Thomas Edison. You're not alone if you feel disappointed or embarrassed, and it's easy to want to push those feelings away. That's why it's important to reframe and resist blame and push yourself to be curious. It's natural to fall prey to self-serving analysis—"I was right, but someone in the lab must have altered something"—which takes us away from discovery. But a true desire to learn from failure forces us to confront facts more fully and rationally. You'll also want to avoid superficial analysis—"It didn't work. Let's try something else"—which generates random rather than considered action. Finally, avoid the glib answer "I'll do better next time," which circumvents real learning. What's necessary is to stop and think carefully about what went wrong so as to inform the next act. (Or decide to abandon the opportunity, which is itself valuable.) Table 2.2 shows some of the ways learning from failure is shortchanged in our lives and how to do better.

Analyzing results carefully to determine why a failure happened is paramount. Was it simply using the wrong chemical by mistake? Then the failure is basic, not intelligent. Was the hypothesis thoughtful but wrong? Then it's an intelligent failure. Analyze carefully. Ask, What went wrong? Why? It's *learning* from failure that leads, ultimately, to eureka. Learning to fail begins with the setup: recognizing an opportunity in new territory; doing your homework and designing small experiments that conserve time and resources. This is not the work of philosophers. It requires a bias for action—iterative action.

TABLE 2.2: **Practices for Learning from Failure**

To Avoid	Don't Say	Try
Skipping the analysis	*I'll just try harder next time.*	Thinking carefully about what went wrong and what factors might have caused it.
Superficial analysis	*It didn't work. I'll just try something else.*	Analyzing what the different causes of the failure suggest about what to try next.
Self-serving analysis	*I was right, but someone or something else messed it up.*	Digging in to understand—and accept—your own contribution (small or large) to the failure.

A Bias for ~~Action~~ Iteration

An intelligent failure is an episode with a beginning and an end. An *intelligent failure strategy*, practiced by inventors, scientists, and innovation departments around the world, strings multiple intelligent failures together to progress toward valued goals. When we experiment, we hope our hypotheses are right. But we must *act* to know for sure. You might be experimenting with a new hairstyle rather than a chemical to separate RNA, but there is no substitute for action. In most cases, your action will require follow-up action. If you had read the earliest drafts of this chapter, you would have seen an ugly mess! A willingness to confront shortcomings and trust iterative improvement—with ample access to a trash bin (electronic or physical)—allows a book to take shape and make it to press. In any uncertain endeavor, a bias for action gets you started, but progress will require iteration.

Back when my sons were young, we would spend snowy weekends on the slopes of Wachusett Mountain in Massachusetts. My sons' learning to maneuver their skis with increasing skill and grace—not to mention speed—was part of the fun. My younger son seemed to intuit the need for continuous improvement from an early age. Once, at about eight years old while still learning to ski, Nick asked me to watch him come down the slope. Dutifully, staring up the hill on an early-winter afternoon, I stood at the bottom and watched a small figure in a red parka carefully navigate the bumps and other skiers who sped by. When he reached me and asked, "How did I do?" I responded as I imagine many parents would, with an enthusiastic "You did great!"

His response threw me for a loop. Instead of the beaming smile I'd expected, he seemed puzzled. I saw the disappointment in his eyes as he asked, "Can't you tell me what I did wrong so I can get better?" Psychologist Carol Dweck calls this a "growth mindset," and it's rare, especially when children grow up being praised for their every step. Most children over time internalize a belief in fixed intelligence and natural ability. Maybe because he had an older brother naturally able to do so many things better, Nick had an unusual appetite for honest feedback. He relished the right kind of wrong. For him, each run was an opportunity to get better.

If you're wondering whether I, as a parent, had done anything right to nurture this attitude, I can only say that I was deeply familiar with Carol's research, and I did my best to comment on process ("I'm intrigued by how you're working with color") rather than outcome ("What a beautiful painting!"). Albeit not in this particular moment on the ski slope. In retrospect, I could have said, "You were in control of your speed, and you looked like you were enjoying yourself. If you bend your knees a little more and keep your chest facing downhill, your form will be better."

Learning from intelligent failure can be slow, whether in our lives or in the technology that shapes our world. Sometimes it takes decades, with multiple people building on others' failures. Take the traffic light, an invention that underwent a stop-and-go journey much like the traffic it now controls. First invented by railway manager John Peake Knight and installed in London in 1868, the system was powered by gas lamps and required a police officer to stand beside it and operate the signals. A month later, a police officer "was badly injured when a leak in the gas main caused one of the lights to explode in his face." Traffic lights were pronounced a public health hazard and the project stopped.

Forty years later, when automobiles hit the roads, the need for traffic lights became more urgent. A number of iterations were tried in the United States throughout the early decades of the twentieth century, with the first electric traffic signal—patented by James Hoge, whose design included the illuminated words *stop* and *move*—installed in Cleveland, Ohio, in 1914. But it fell to inventor and businessman Garrett Morgan to improve upon previous iterations with an idea in 1923 that brought the traffic light closest to the ones we have today.

The story goes that Morgan witnessed a spectacular accident at an intersection in downtown Cleveland that was already using a traffic light. The failure—as he saw it—was that the lights switched between stop and go without any interval between, giving drivers no time to react. Morgan's invention, which he patented and sold the rights to, to GE, was an automated signal with an interim warning light—the precursor to today's yellow light.

Other times, the time frame for experimentation is relatively short, even with several iterative failures on the way to success. Take Chris Stark, who wanted to find a use for the fallen apples he saw going to waste every autumn in New England. Make apple pies? Not a viable solution because the number of pies anyone can eat or store is limited.

Applesauce? Same issue.

Apple cider, he decided, was viable because the liquid could easily be stored and used for many purposes.

Now, to act. He engineered a drum with screws to break up the apples. But how to turn the device? First, he attached a bike crank. That failed because it required more effort than people were willing to exert. Next, he hooked up the drum to an old bicycle and used pedal power. That, too, failed; the chain flew off, making it dangerous to operate. In attempt number three, Stark attached an exercise bike to a platform, making it stationary, which was the charm in building his "exercider."

Attending to the results carefully to determine why a failure happened is paramount. Was it a simple matter of a chemical mix-up? Then the failure is basic rather than intelligent. If you had a hypothesis and it was wrong, remind yourself not to be too disappointed, but rather to be curious. Why was it wrong? What did you miss? Train yourself to care more about the new information the failure brought than about being wrong. You can take solace in the fact that it was an intelligent failure! But intelligent failures' lessons don't announce themselves. Take the time to diagnose the miss carefully. Ask, What did I hope would happen? What happened instead? What might explain the difference? This work can be painstaking, but it always points toward a better way. It clarifies what to try next.

Masters of Intelligent Failure

Who does intelligent failure particularly well? Scientists, as we have seen. Inventors, of course. Also, celebrity chefs and leaders of company innovation teams, to name a few. Despite superficial differences, elite failure practitioners have much in common, and these attributes can be emulated by any of us.

It starts with curiosity. Elite failure practitioners seem to be driven by a desire to understand the world around them—not through philosophic contemplation, but by interacting with it. Testing things out. Experimenting. They're willing to act! This makes them vulnerable to failure along the way—about which they seem unusually tolerant.

Driven by curiosity

James West's father wanted him to go to medical school. A doctor could never be without a job because there were always sick people in need. As a Pullman porter and a member of the Brotherhood of Sleeping Car

Porters, Samuel West told his son about the African Americans with PhDs whom Samuel worked alongside because they could not find any employment in their field. James's mother, Matilda West, who went from teaching high school math to working at the Langley Research Center as one of the "human computers" who used pencils, slide rules, and adding machines to calculate the numbers that would launch rockets and astronauts into space, was fired from that job for her activism in the NAACP. Evidently, a career in science, even working for NASA, was risky for an African American. Making a living as a doctor was as near zero a risk as one could get.

Yet despite his father's wishes and warnings, James majored in physics at Temple University. Perhaps the two Purple Hearts he was awarded for his military service in the Korean War signaled an appetite for risk, but his fascination with how the physical world functioned had been apparent from an early age. Like so many future engineers, as a child he was a terror with a screwdriver, constantly taking things apart to see how they worked; much to the adults' chagrin, he didn't always put those things back together. Once he took apart his grandfather's pocket watch, all 107 pieces.

One of West's favorite failure stories is about the old radio he rescued when he was about eight years old. Apparently, none of the adults in his large, close-knit extended family were there to make sure he didn't get into trouble that afternoon when, alone with the broken radio, tools in hand, he tinkered until he thought it was fixed. His house in Farmville, Virginia, like many houses in the 1930s, had only one electrical outlet in each room—from the light in the ceiling. West climbed up on the bed railing to plug in the fraying cord. He grabbed the socket and suddenly heard a loud buzzing sound.

Then he realized his hand was stuck to the ceiling.

What shocked him more than the electric current passing through his body (his older brother came into the room and knocked him down) was the nature and cause of that failure. The old radio was new territory to him. Getting it to play music provided a credible opportunity to advance. Preparation consisted of all the other items, mechanical and electronic, he'd already investigated. At eight years old, he figured that the risk mitigation was limited to whether the radio would transmit sound. Yet as can happen in any intelligent failure, an unintended consequence occurred. What caused his hand to stick to the ceiling? Why had that happened? He felt compelled to figure out how electricity worked.

Eight decades later, with more than 250 patents to his name, including one for the coinvention of the electret microphone that delivers the sound in our smartphones, James West reflected on the insistent curiosity he felt that day—an essential force to his later discoveries: "Why does nature behave in that way? What are the compelling parameters around the way nature behaves? And how can I better understand the physical principles that I'm dealing with?" When I shared a stage with West in 2015, the tiny beige headset microphones we each wore to give talks in the conference auditorium that day had been invented by him.

In 1957, West applied for an internship posted on a college bulletin board to work at Bell Labs, famous for its many groundbreaking inventions, then most notably the transistor. Bell Labs invited him out for the summer and somewhat arbitrarily assigned him to the acoustics research department, to work with a group trying to determine the millisecond interval between the moment when we hear a sound in the ear closer to a sound and when we hear it in the ear farther away (known as the interaural time delay). The problem was the headphones. At one inch in diameter, only a few people could hear the sound they generated. That led to a secondary problem: the difficulty of finding enough subjects to test. The assignment for the new intern was clear: "What can you do to help this group to be able to measure more people's interaural time delay?"

West went to the library and read a paper written by three German acoustic scientists about a different type of headphones that were dielectric and could be made in any size. A larger size might allow more test subjects to hear the clicking sounds the acousticians wanted to measure. The machine shop built the new headphones to West's speci- fications and—eureka! Hooked up to a large, five-hundred-volt battery, the larger headphones worked as he'd predicted they would.

Problem solved. The research project to measure interaural time delay could proceed. The summer intern earned a gold star. By Novem- ber, however, the headphones had failed. The acousticians called West, who was by then back at school, to tell him that the sensitivity of his devices was reduced to near zero. Something was very wrong.

West then reread the paper he'd found in the library and learned that, sure enough, after some time it was necessary to adjust the battery to change the direction of the electric current. That created a new problem. Reversing the polarity of the battery would not produce the correct pulse for the acousticians' test subjects. The problem couldn't be fixed over the phone. Bell Labs flew West out to New Jersey to take another look.

Still thinking about how to generate enough sound for the interaural time delay testing, West examined the headphones. He removed the battery and was surprised to find the headphones still worked. His first thought was that the capacitor was still charged—capacitors store and release energy over time. As an experiment, he discharged the capac- itor. But again, the headphones—still connected to an oscillator wire and a piece of polymer film—worked!

This was, however, no light bulb moment. Rather, it was a moment of darkness. Something was wrong because it wasn't supposed to work that way. Like Jocelyn Bell, who saw something in the radio telescope's data that she didn't understand, leading to the discovery of pulsars, West took notice of this unexpected event and, equally important, wouldn't let it go. It was just like when a frayed electrical wire had stuck his hand to the ceiling. He says, "I had to figure out—I couldn't do any- thing else until I figured out what the heck was going on in that piece of polymer." A less resilient failure practitioner might have walked away from this apparent mystery, but for West, curiosity and persistence won out. And that was how he realized the importance of electrets.

Now the real work, to solve a new set of problems, began. For the next couple years, West and his Bell Labs colleague Gerhard Sessler worked to figure out the physics of electrets. The breakthrough came when West and Sessler stopped thinking about how the electrical charge was generated and instead focused on the polymers that held the charge. Elite failure practitioners, as you will see again and again, are flexible in their thinking, willing to let go of one line of inquiry to consider another. The eureka moment came when West and Sessler figured out how to trap an electron in the polymer film. The ramifications (their invention rendered the battery unnecessary) were enormous and would eventually change millions of products that affect our lives. High-quality microphones could now be built in any size and shape and for a fraction of their previous cost. An electret microphone was first manufactured by Sony in 1968. Electrets' size, longevity, effectiveness, and minimal production cost mean that today they power 90 percent of microphones, smartphones, hearing aids, baby monitors, and audio recording devices.

Experimenting fearlessly

Born in Copenhagen in 1977, almost a half century after James West, René Redzepi burst on the global food scene in 2003, determined to create a new haute cuisine using only ingredients local to northern Scandinavia. At age twenty-five Redzepi was no novice. Bearded, scruffily handsome, with wide eyes that look steadily outward and a chef-size ego, the son of a Danish mother and a father who'd emmigrated from the Macedonian region of Yugoslavia, René had started culinary school at fifteen, after he was expelled from high school. He'd apprenticed in several restaurants, including El Bulli in Spain, famous for its innovations in molecular gastronomy and creative pairing of unusual ingredients. But cooking with only ingredients native to northern Scandinavia seemed *too* unusual, impossible. Even his closest friends derided the idea as "blubber" food.

Redzepi appeared to thrive on others' skepticism, shaking off negative reviews or turning them into badges of honor. Eventually, the restaurant he cofounded with Danish TV cooking host and entrepreneur Claus Meyer would be voted the best restaurant in the world five times. As you will see, success in haute cuisine depends in part on wild-eyed experiments.

"We are explorers of the edible world," Redzepi wrote in the published journal he kept from 2012 to 2013, "finding new methods and new treasures." Sourced new ingredients had long inspired Redzepi's creations; his curiosity about culinary oddities such as foraged vegetation, sea urchins, abalone, and ants, combined with experimental new methods such as fermentation and dehydration, led to many a radical new dish.

At first, Redzepi's experiments—cooking only with ingredients "farmed, fished, or foraged within 60 miles of the restaurant," for example—were relatively low risk. Over time, his range expanded to include such ingredients as turnips found in frozen tundra and a native plant that tasted like coriander. By 2013, during a pivotal year when he kept a journal, Redzepi wrote about his restaurant as a kind of laboratory where junior chefs spent weeks studying specific species, seeds, or growing areas to better capture the essence of some vegetable, say, a carrot, with which to concoct a dish for Redzepi to taste and decide whether it would make it onto the night's menu. Most didn't.

Restaurant kitchens have few rivals when it comes to intense, emotional, high-speed atmospherics. The stakes can feel high: personal reputation, ambition, hierarchy, and creative identity are at stake. This makes failure emotionally fraught for junior chefs, and Redzepi's initial attitude didn't help. "So many trials, so much shit," he wrote in his journal after some carrot experiments. "The guys became tense, almost scared, as they brought out one failure after another."

Eventually Redzepi learned to support failure explicitly and emphatically to make it more palatable, carving out a special time each week for junior chefs to experiment. The sessions fostered a culture in which failure was accepted as part of the innovation from which successful dishes emerge. Over time, he became a failure evangelist, viewing these behind-closed-doors sessions as a chance to "fail as much as you want, as long as you do it 100 percent." Seven years after the tense carrot failures, Stefano Ferraro, Noma's head pastry chef, embodied that new culture. "The key to my work," he explained, "is learning from every mistake, the premise for every improvement."

Only through normalizing risk-taking and failure could Redzepi continually push his craft. Food, he wrote, "has to stay relevant. It can't be static." Such a failure strategy can lead to stunning, surprising successes, such as the creation of a recipe based on live fjord shrimp that Redzepi exuberantly describes as "tiny, translucent, vibrating jewels, hopping around in the box 20 to 30 centimeters in the air." Where another chef might sauté or grill, Redzepi serves them, he explains, "on ice in small glass jars, with a side of brown butter emulsion" and describes what he calls the "captivating" sensation of biting into a live shrimp: "Your teeth feel a delicate crunch from the shell, then soft slightly sweet meat with a deep shrimp flavour in the head. It makes a memorable bite: predator against prey. The brown butter emulsion is really just for the timid, who want to cover the insect-like eyes and head with a quick, nervous dunk."

Although believing the experiment to have produced success, Redzepi worried that diners might not respond to a daring dish of live shrimp in brown butter. His worries were for naught. "The whole restaurant felt comradely," he wrote. "The early tables nodded appreciatively at later diners as they erupted in laughter and screams, and we became one big party where everyone felt they knew each other, like a family. . . . For as long as the sea gives us fjord shrimp, they will be on the menu."

Unlike inventing an electret microphone, cooking is fickle, mutable, and subjective. A great meal one night does not guarantee a great meal the next. When Noma's restaurant crew moved temporarily to Sydney, Australia, in 2016, Redzepi and his team experimented with bush tomatoes in a behind-closed-doors iteration of a dish made with clams. It was superb. However, when the team tried again the next day, the exciting flavors of the previous day remained elusive. The dish could not be served. "We are freaks," Thomas Frebel, the chef in charge of research and development, said. "We live for those amazing moments when we get it right. But most of the time is about failing, then standing up, and doing that again and again and again."

As with all innovators, the path toward success brought ups and downs. In November 2013, Redzepi faced a failure of another kind. Receiving "page after page of red numbers," he learned that the restaurant had "managed to lose a pile of money." With his commitment to locally sourced, in-season ingredients, he had spent lavishly obtaining them. Winter was especially difficult. "The frost is crippling," he wrote in his journal in February 2013. "With almost no products left to work with, we tried to tackle some broader concepts that could nudge us forward; we were searching for a way to outwit this fiendish weather."

His accountants warned that by January 2014 Noma would be unable to pay its rent. Considering his options, Redzepi didn't much like any of them: raise prices, fire staff, or accept an offer from an (unnamed) soft drink company to buy the restaurant. He instead hired a kitchen manager to monitor expenses and cut costs where possible. Soon, experimenting with radical new winter-menu projects—Trash Cooking and the Dried Kitchen—the restaurant lowered costs. Fish scales, dried turnips and horseradish, pumpkin; porridges made from whole kernels and grains; and toasted beechnuts formed unusual offerings that added to Noma's appeal. Despite the ever-present financial precipice, winter's challenges, and the possibility that a dish might not be successfully replicated, the restaurant continued to thrive.

Credited with increasing Copenhagen's tourism as people flew in specifically to eat at Noma, where a table had to be reserved a year in advance, Noma won three Michelin stars, all but unheard of for a Scandinavian restaurant. What explains this extraordinary success?

As Redzepi wrote, "We have to remember that everything we have achieved we have done by failing" and "by handling the failures we stumble over daily."

In January 2023, Noma surprised the culinary world by announcing that the restaurant would close for good at the end of 2024, bringing renewed media attention to Redzepi's successes and failures alike. Criticism of the elite restaurant scene in general, with its long hours and low wages, dominated much of the coverage, threatening to obscure the interesting pivot at the heart of the story. Noma would close its doors to diners, reinventing itself as a food laboratory for developing and selling new culinary inventions on the internet. Redzepi would pivot from chef to innovation leader. Only one thing was certain: a willingness to fail would come in handy in the next phase of the elite failure practitioner's journey.

Making friends with failure

Just as risk-taking behind the scenes is essential to success in haute cuisine, businesses around the world are similarly dependent on failure if they want innovation. Extolling failure in companies is less unusual today than it once was. But back in the fall of 2002 when I gave a lecture on failure at a design industry conference in Chatham, Massachusetts, I hadn't been sure how the talk would be received. Soon after I got offstage, a conference participant came up to me with a quizzical expression on his face. Douglas "Doug" Dayton, I learned, was a designer at IDEO and head of the company's Boston office. He struck me as serious and thoughtful, and something was clearly bothering him. Of medium height, dark haired, in his midforties, with a quiet, deliberate way of speaking, Dayton explained that a project carried out by one of his teams for Simmons, a mattress manufacturer that was over a century old, appeared to be floundering. He wondered if I might help him and the team make sense of what lessons to learn from it. I said I'd be delighted, especially if they'd let me write an official Harvard Business School case study about it.

That Doug said yes to my request to study and write about a company failure tells you a lot about his employer. Executives don't often open their doors to me when I say I like to study failure. No organization I know better epitomizes the ethos of intelligent failure than IDEO.

At the time, IDEO, a small innovation consultancy with an outsize global reputation, comprised twelve "studios" scattered around the world. Incorporated in Palo Alto in the heart of Silicon Valley, where the fail-fast philosophy was hard to miss, the company traces its history back to 1991, when Stanford engineering professor David Kelley and renowned industrial designer Bill Moggridge merged their small firms.

Since that time, IDEO employees, working in cross-disciplinary teams, have designed a remarkable range of household, commercial, and industrial products, services, and environments. Some of their most widely used innovations include the computer mouse (first designed and developed for Apple), the thumbs-up/thumbs-down interaction designed for TiVo's personal video recorder, now ubiquitous in social media platforms, and a disposable prefilled insulin injector for Eli Lilly. This short list nicely illustrates the company's range—from personal computers to medical devices to user interfaces. Although multiple factors contribute to IDEO's success—most notably the company's far-ranging technical expertise, which includes engineering (mechanical, electrical, and software), industrial design, prototype machining, human factors, architecture, and more—its cheerful attitude toward failure may be the most important success factor of all.

Employees are valued for their technical expertise but even more for their willingness to try new things that might not work. To encourage teams, one of the mottoes at IDEO is "Fail often, in order to succeed sooner," and David Kelley, CEO until 2000, was known to routinely wander the Palo Alto studio cheerfully saying, "Fail fast to succeed sooner." What Kelley understood was that, despite the need for failure in innovation projects being obvious, intellectually, the company's high-achieving young employees were hampered by the more subtle emotional aversion to failing. Too many of them had been straight-A students. "Failure's a fun idea, but not for me" might well describe how they were wired. Converting an intellectual appreciation into an emotional acceptance that allowed risky experiments required frequent repetition of Kelley's cheerful phrase. As Tim Brown, CEO from 2000 to 2019, explained in an interview with me in 2005, "The overriding spirit has been one of 'Go get on with it, figure it out, do well! We're here to support you, but we believe you can figure it out.'" The company's embrace of intelligent failure has long been the not-so-secret driver of its success.

But how does IDEO keep up its enviable reputation with all of that failure? The answer is simple. Most of IDEO's failures happen behind closed doors. And they happen through disciplined, iterative teamwork that draws on multiple areas of expertise. IDEO's also a place where company leaders—starting with the visible David Kelley exhorting teams to fail fast and often—have worked hard to build an environment of psychological safety for risk-taking.

In early November 2002, during my first visit to IDEO's Boston-area studio, then located in Lexington, Massachusetts, I stood at the top of the elevated, curved walkway known as the Island. From that vantage point it was easy to observe the chaotic activity within the expansive, messy, colorful space where designers, engineers, and human-factors experts worked together in small teams on innovation projects for corporate clients. Here, behind closed doors, they were free to make mistakes, take risks, fail, and try again. A space they called the prototyping lab, one of the few closed-off rooms in the office, was empty that day—not a good sign. Part of the reason was that the Simmons project had failed to give the machinists something tangible to build.

Any project that ends in successful innovation goes through multiple failures along the way because innovation occurs in new territory where a compelling solution is yet to be developed. Even the smartest experiments, as we see over and over, often end in failure. And just as in Jen Heemstra's lab or in Bell Labs, where James West invented, nearly all of these failures happen out of sight of the public. Put it this way: The corporate clients paying for those failures at IDEO aren't hovering over the designers' shoulders to watch the failures unfold. By the time the project is delivered to its eager customer, it's poised for success. This is part of the risk-mitigation strategy of any successful innovation department.

When I met Doug Dayton, he was trying to expand his company's offerings to include *innovation strategy services*—helping companies figure out product areas in which to innovate, rather than merely responding to design requests for a specific new product. These experiments would ultimately shift the company's business model, and business model experiments also bring failures along the way to success.

Doug explained that, in the past, "the typical project was initiated when a client came in with a three- to ten-page specification to describe the product they needed . . . and then [they'd] say, 'Okay, go design this.'" And IDEO would get it done. But by the early 2000s, clients had "started involving us earlier in their process, having us help create the context for the product."

Indeed, rather than asking for a new mattress design, Simmons hired IDEO to *identify new opportunities in the bedding industry*. Despite an enthusiastic response from Simmons executives during IDEO's final presentation of product ideas, months had gone by with no follow-up. Dayton had reluctantly concluded that the project was a failure. The team's ideas seemed creative and feasible, but Simmons was not acting on them. What had gone wrong?

The project had seemed a perfect test case for IDEO's new strategy services. It was just the kind of challenge that would intrigue a designer: take a mundane category (bedding) and blow it open to find new opportunities. The failure was not from lack of effort. Conducting interviews with customers of all ages, visiting mattress stores, and even shadowing mattress delivery people, the project team had learned a lot about beds and their associated spaces at different points in a sleeper's life. Their work identified an underserved group, "young nomads"— single eighteen- to thirty-year-olds who viewed bedding products as too unwieldy or expensive for their hypermobile lifestyles. They did not want to buy large, permanent items. They expected to move frequently. They lived in small apartments with roommates and used bedrooms for entertaining and studying, not just sleeping. With these insights, the team glimpsed radical new product ideas. A self-contained integrated mattress and frame. A mattress with visually distinct, foldable, lightweight modules that was easy to move. Yet Simmons had failed to implement any of the ideas.

Eventually, the Simmons failure taught Doug a crucial lesson: if strategic services were to help companies translate ideas into action (launching a new product line, for example), the work could no longer occur behind closed doors without the client. IDEO's recommendations would have to take into consideration what the client was capable of envisioning and executing. It became clear, as Tim Brown later put it, that IDEO had to learn how to usher ideas through corporate systems. This would only happen if the project team welcomed a client member or two.

Doug and his colleagues soon figured out how to turn failure into success. Expanding its strategy services, the company started to engage clients in the innovation process. The Simmons failure was partly explained by IDEO's lack of appreciation for what the client's manufacturing organization was set up to produce. The behind-closed-doors approach that served the company so well in *product innovation services*, shielding clients from failures along the way, backfired for *strategic innovation services*. To do better, IDEO began to hire more people with business degrees to complement the skills of the design, engineering, and human-factors experts. IDEO started to collaborate with clients to help *them* become better failure practitioners.

Consider how easily IDEO could have blamed the client for not appreciating the team's ideas. They could have made Simmons the bad guy. Instead, Dayton and his colleagues reflected on how they had contributed to the failure, and what they could have done differently. This willingness to learn helped the company expand its business model, to help clients innovate in new ways.

West, Redzepi, and Dayton, in such strikingly different contexts, give us a deeper appreciation for the common attributes shared by elite failure practitioners. As you have seen, these include genuine curiosity and a willingness to experiment and to make friends with failure. What motivates them to endure and befriend failure? An unrelenting drive to solve new problems that advance their craft.

Taking the Intelligence of Intelligent Failure to Heart

The stories and concepts in this chapter emphasize the twists and turns intelligent failure takes in lives, professions, and companies, to help you navigate failure. Once you appreciate the elements of intelligent failure, you can experience it more lightheartedly. Doing this starts with recognizing an opportunity you care about enough to be willing to risk failing. Then, it's about avoiding bad risks and embracing reasonable ones. This requires homework—making sure you've figured out what's known, what's been tried and not worked before, and designing experiments so that if you do fail, the failure is not overly large, painful, or wasteful. Today's elite failure practitioners such as Jen Heemstra, James West, René Redzepi, and Doug Dayton—as did Thomas Edison a hundred years ago—understand that failure is possible (even likely) when they're treading into unknown territory, but they're willing to take the risk because of the potential upside.

Internalizing a cognitive understanding of the principles of intelligent failure can help you develop healthy emotional responses that are constructive and enabling. Recalling the healthy attributional styles studied by Martin Seligman, we can see that it's wise to take the time to diagnose what went wrong, while reminding yourself that intelligent failures are *not* preventable. In new territory, the only way to make progress is through trial and failure. I believe that appreciating the elements of intelligent failure will help you feel better and be more effective at work and in life. Perhaps it also helps to remind yourself that intelligent failures are not caused by blameworthy acts. They are disappointing, but never cause for embarrassment or shame. Instead, intelligent failures should make you curious—eager to figure out why they happened and to sort out what to try next. Does that mean our amygdala welcomes intelligent failures with the praise and satisfaction they truly deserve? Not even close. We still far prefer success to failure, even the most intelligent failure.

In some cases, intelligent failures are especially worthy of celebration because they point us forward toward eventual success. They shut down one path and force us to seek another. The discovery of what doesn't work is sometimes as valuable as finding what does work. Here is where the failure parties in places such as Eli Lilly come into play: a pioneering team has brought valuable new information to the company, and they deserve appreciation for their work—and could do with some cheering up to help them cope with their disappointment. That's what happened when Lilly developed an experimental chemotherapy drug called Alimta in 2013 and spent a lot of money running clinical trials. Unfortunately, in Phase III trials the drug failed to establish what's called efficacy in treating patients' cancer. This was unquestionably an intelligent failure; no one could have known in advance what would happen, and the trial was only as large as needed to allow appropriate data analysis. A failure party was warranted.

The story might have ended there. But the physician who conducted the trial was intent on learning as much as possible from its failure. He discovered that some patients *did* benefit from the drug, and that the patients who *failed* to benefit had a folic acid deficiency. So he added folic acid supplements to the drug in subsequent clinical trials. This improved the efficacy significantly—and the product became a top seller with sales of nearly $2.5 billion a year.

Intelligent failure is the right kind of wrong. It should be clear by now that "embracing failure" becomes not just intellectually but also emotionally feasible when we limit it to intelligent failure. Embracing intelligent failure is a requirement for inventors, scientists, celebrity chefs, and company innovation labs. But it can also help the rest of us live fuller, more adventuresome lives.

The next two chapters explore failures that are not so intelligent. Nonetheless, neither basic failure nor complex failure is an event to hide or be ashamed of, but rather an inevitable part of life. So, we must learn how to confront them and how to learn from them.

CHAPTER 3

To Err Is Human

The only man who never makes a mistake
is the man who never does anything.

—Theodore Roosevelt

One of the most expensive banking failures in history occurred on August 11, 2020. Most failures in financial services are complex, resulting from varied combinations of company incentives, bad loans, economic conditions, misconduct, political events, or natural disasters. But not in this case. Here, three Citibank employees accidentally transferred $900 million—instead of the $8 million warranted—to several companies managing a loan for Revlon. As reported by Bloomberg, the senior manager who approved the wire transfer on the loan software failed to check all the boxes necessary to override an automatic default mode. Essentially, the bank wired the principal instead of the interest. This simple mistake triggered a basic failure. A large basic failure! When you experience a basic failure like this one, you want nothing more intensely than to rewind the clock for a do-over.

The Citibank employees who made the error tried to get that do-over.

But when they sought to regain the funds, some recipients refused to return them, despite receiving them by mistake. Understandably, Citibank sued. Then the judge made a controversial finders-keepers ruling that prevented Citibank from recovering the lost funds. Whatever you think of the judge's ruling, you probably have a lot of empathy for the employees whose mistake triggered the loss of hundreds of millions of dollars.

We all have days when everything seems to go wrong. Often, these small daily failures are nonetheless disruptive and wasteful. If only you had remembered to charge your cell phone. Why didn't you pay more attention when backing out of the driveway? Many slips occur due to *inattention*. Did you offend the friend because you didn't think carefully before you spoke? *Making assumptions* is another source of error. As for the job you'd expected to land—hadn't you impressed the interviewer? Your rapport, experience, and qualifications seemed perfect. Maybe you were *overconfident*, which can result in mistakes. Meanwhile, the clogged gutters on your roof that led to leaks into your basement and damaged the foundation? You were going to get those gutters cleaned as soon as you had a spare moment. *Neglect* is yet another common cause of failure.

These are basic failures. Unlike intelligent failures, which occur in unknown territory, basic failures involve errors in well-trodden terrain. Basic failures are not the right kind of wrong. In the continuum of failure types, they are farthest from intelligent failures. Basic failures are unproductive—wasting time, energy, and resources. And they are largely preventable. As shown in Figure 3.1, the greater the uncertainty, the lower the preventability. We can never be entirely rid of human error, but we can do much to minimize basic failure. To do that, we need to prevent the errors we can prevent and to catch and correct the rest. For those, we need to disrupt the link between the error and the failure it might trigger if it isn't caught in time.

Remember that errors—synonymous with mistakes—are by definition unintended. Errors often have relatively minor consequences, such as a tiny dent in a car bumper from backing out of the driveway too fast.

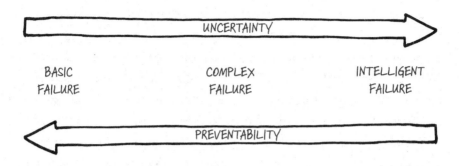

FIGURE 3.1: The Relationship between Uncertainty and Preventability

Call them the daily Oopses and Oh No's that we learn to brush off and to remedy. We'll apologize to the friend we accidentally offended. Clean the gutters this weekend.

In short, basic failures are everyday occurrences and many are not terribly consequential. But now and then a basic failure is catastrophic. Errors, even small ones, occasionally have serious repercussions. But none of them is the right kind of wrong, so why is learning about basic failures worth your time?

First, they offer us a chance to practice feeling okay about the fact that mistakes will happen. Beating ourselves up about them is unhelpful and unhealthy. Mistakes and the failures they trigger are a part of life. Occasionally they even bring eureka moments of discovery. A wrong turn on the road makes you late for a meeting but leads to a beautiful walking trail you didn't know was there.

Second, if we want to keep getting better at the activities and deepen the relationships we value most, we must be willing to confront and learn from our mistakes. We must overcome our aversion to them.

But the best reason to learn how basic failures work is to prevent as many of them as possible. A few insights and practices drawn from an extensive research literature on errors and error management can help you do just that.

Much of what we know about error management comes from decades of research and training in the aviation industry. Aviation has an impressive record of devising procedures and systems to reduce the errors that can trigger devastating basic failures. Indeed, preventing and reducing the "bad" failures that cause us trouble, rather than bringing discovery, is how to approach basic failure. For example, pilots and their crews found that confirming a verbal checklist of procedures and protocols before takeoff was effective in reducing preventable errors, a practice that has now become more widespread in fields such as medicine, thanks to Atul Gawande's bestselling book *The Checklist Manifesto*.

Checklists are not a guarantee against basic failures. They offer an enabling structure—but one that must be used with intention. On freezing-cold January 13, 1982, Air Florida Flight 90, headed for Fort Lauderdale, crashed into the ice-covered Potomac River shortly after takeoff from National Airport in Washington, DC. Investigators, drawing on an audio recording of the pilots in the cockpit, pinpointed the simple human error that led to this catastrophic basic failure. Here's an excerpt from that recording as the pilots go through a routine preflight checklist. As is typical, the first officer read each item off the checklist, and the captain responded after checking the appropriate indicator in the cockpit:

> First Officer: Pitot heat.
> Captain: On.
> First Officer: Anti-ice.
> Captain: Off.
> First Officer: APU.
> Captain: Running.
> First Officer: Start levers.
> Captain: Idle.

Do you notice anything wrong with any of the captain's responses? You need no technical knowledge of flying an airplane to spot the error, but it helps if you're accustomed to a cold climate. Because that was exactly where the Air Florida pilots' human error lay.

Accustomed to flying in warm climate conditions, their checklist routine usually called for the anti-ice instruments to be *off*. That particular check on the list had become second nature. They did it *in their sleep*, as the saying goes. Failing to stop to think that the to-them-unusual wintry conditions called for a departure from their routine—the deicing instruments should have been *on*—the crew triggered a devastating failure, complete with the loss of seventy-eight lives. Much like the software mistake made by the Citibank managers, they failed to enact an override to habitual practice.

The Basics of Basic Failure

Nearly all basic failures can be averted with care and without need of ingenuity or invention. The important thing to remember about errors is that they are unintended—and punishing them as a strategy for preventing failure will backfire. It encourages people not to admit errors, which ironically increases the likelihood of preventable basic failure. This is as true in families as in companies.

While basic failures don't have the thrill of intelligent failures, they still present opportunities for learning. And despite lacking the intricacy of complex failures, they can be equally catastrophic.

Not all mistakes cause basic failure. This may seem obvious, but many errors do not lead to failure. Mistakenly putting the cereal in the refrigerator and the milk in the cupboard is an error, but only if left uncorrected will these errors lead to the (still-small) basic failures of spoiled milk and soggy cereal. Sometimes a patient is mistakenly given the wrong drug without any consequences at all. You might call that a lucky dodge.

We all make mistakes. Forgetting to charge your cell phone does not cause a basic failure if you find somewhere to plug it in while continuing your call. Accidentally adding too much or too little sugar to the batter means the cake will taste more sweet or less sweet than intended but won't render the cake inedible. A baseball team can win the game though some players strike out. Never making a mistake is not a realistic or even desirable goal for any of us.

Yet all basic failures are caused by mistakes. Missing a phone call scheduled to provide necessary information on a time-sensitive issue is a basic failure that could be caused by forgetting to charge your phone. A cake will fail to be edible if you accidentally substitute salt for sugar. A baseball team fails if they only strike out and never score a run. Error is always the precipitating event for a basic failure.

What about deliberate errors? A deliberate error is an oxymoron and is better labeled mischief or sabotage. The prankster who deliberately mislabels your kitchen's sugar and salt canisters is causing mischief. An organized sports event in which a team underperforms to intentionally lose for a perceived gain is sabotage. When it comes to errors, intent matters.

How to Recognize a Basic Failure

The bus driver walked away from the accident in Prospect Lefferts Garden in a daze, his wrist aching and bloody. He had thirteen years of experience as an operator with the Metropolitan Transportation Authority in New York City. Now his forty-foot blue-and-yellow bus was crammed into the bottom of a Brooklyn brownstone. He told witnesses congregated on the sidewalk that his foot had caught between the brake and the accelerator, and he'd lost control of the bus. It had lurched forward, crashing into other vehicles and then the side of the building, shattering the glass windows on a first-floor doctor's office. Sixteen passengers were injured, none seriously. A video released later showed that the driver had held shopping bags between his feet.

The accident was a classic basic failure.

Although it was against the rules to store any items near the pedals, on the afternoon of June 7, 2021, the fifty-five-year-old driver took a chance with the shopping bags. Investigators found no mechanical defects in the vehicle. The bus had been traveling along its normal route. Weather and visibility were fine. The accident was attributable to a single, easily identifiable cause—the driver's stuck foot.

The accident presents two characteristic features of basic failures: They occur in known territory. They tend to have a single cause.

Known territory

To be classified as a basic failure, the mistake must occur in an area where knowledge already exists about how to achieve a desired result. The driver whose bus crashed into the side of the building broke the safety rules by placing the shopping bags between his feet. Similarly, when a chair collapses because you didn't follow the assembly instructions, the broken legs on the floor attest to a basic failure. Guidelines, rules, previous research, and knowledge gleaned from someone you know are illustrations of known territory. If you can find instructions on the internet, it's known territory. In short, existing knowledge can be put to use without magic or miracle. Access or training is available. Building codes and safety regulations codify known territory to prevent failure and are often put into place in response to a prior failure.

Simply put, a failure is basic when errors happen because we do not *use* knowledge that was available—whether due to inattention, neglect, or overconfidence.

What if you make a mistake the first time you bake cookies or build a coffee table? Get lost in a city where you do not speak the language? The failures that might ensue are basic because knowledge of how to bake cookies, build coffee tables, or get around the city was available. Get a recipe, follow the instructions, use a map. Of course, my classification system has an element of judgment. For instance, in some situations you might not know that prior knowledge exists. Fair enough. In that case, it's fine to classify your failure as intelligent—occurring in new territory for you. Children experience many errors and basic failures (toddlers tipping over, kids losing their homework) because the world, not new to adults, is new to them. Parents who try to shield their children from experiencing any errors or failures deprive them of valuable learning that is crucial to their development.

Single cause

The bus accident was a basic failure with a single cause—the driver's stuck foot. A phone died because it ran out of battery power. A cake was inedible because salt was substituted for sugar. A plane crashed because the deicer was turned off on an icy day. A bank lost money because the correct boxes were not checked.

Sometimes, failures that initially appear to have a single cause turn out to be embedded in a complex web of causes. For example, the tragic port explosion that devastated Beirut in 2020 was initially attributed to a simple cause: 2,750 tons of chemical fertilizer improperly stored. However, further information implicated poor safety procedures, lack of oversight, and possible government involvement. As you will learn in the next chapter, when multiple errors, sometimes enhanced with a pinch of bad luck, line up, they cause complex failures.

Human Drivers of Basic Failure

The *New York Times* headline on March 31, 2021, said it all: "Factory Mix-Up Ruins Up to 15 Million Vaccine Doses from Johnson & Johnson." Much of the world, after anxiously waiting for a vaccine for over a year, was now fervently sourcing venues for a lifesaving jab. Within the United States, doses were released to the public in quantifiable batches and doled out to individuals according to strict guidelines based on occupation, age, health issues, and location.

How could 15 million doses be ruined?

Workers at the plant had accidentally contaminated a Johnson & Johnson batch with a key ingredient used to produce another vaccine, from AstraZeneca. The manufacturer, Emergent BioSolutions, had contracted with both pharmaceutical companies and allowed, at its location in Baltimore, ingredients meant for one account to be used in the other. As the story continued to unfold, by June 2021 the wasted doses had climbed to about 60 million. This basic, excruciatingly wasteful failure was the result of inadequate vigilance. More simply, inattention.

Inattention

Careless mistakes resulting from inattention are one of the most common causes of basic failure. I've learned this the hard way. Most memorably, on May 13, 2017, I found myself lying flat in a hospital emergency room while a physician's assistant put nine stitches in my forehead near my right eye. A careless mistake by me had caused the basic failure that brought me there.

Just two hours earlier, I'd been racing a sailboat in Boston's Charles River Basin, having signed up for a special alumni regatta. I'd anticipated a casual fun event with people like me who'd raced on the college sailing team decades ago. Arriving on the dock, I quickly realized that most of these alumni were recent graduates—young, athletic, and competitive. Some of them national champions. But I was game. After all, my crew, Sandy, and I were experienced sailors. We'd raced together in the summers (in somewhat larger boats) for years.

Not coming in dead last in the first couple of races thus felt like a win, especially since I hadn't sailed a high-performance sailboat in thirty-five years. These small boats catch the wind and practically skim across the surface of the water. Designed for speed, they call for skill and vigilance—and Sandy and I had used both to keep up with the fleet.

So when everyone headed to shore for a short break before the next race, I felt relaxed, enjoying the sun that was starting to warm the cool spring morning. With the dock dead downwind, our sail was out as far as it could go. As any experienced sailor knows, when a sailboat is heading downwind, the smallest shift in wind direction—and on the Charles River shifts are incessant—can send the boom flying over to the other side of the boat.

Heading toward the dock, chatting with Sandy, I looked away from the sail for a second. Long enough for the boom to fly across the boat and knock me overboard. Stunned to find myself swimming in the frigid river, I managed to stay afloat as he grabbed the tiller, turning to rescue me. Hauling myself in across the stern, hampered by heavy wet layers of clothing, I saw blood. A lot of blood. Pooling in the sailboat's hull. (Head wounds bleed a lot.)

Shivering and bleeding, I made it to the dock, feeling deeply embarrassed and ashamed. Who was I to think I should be out here sailing against these young athletes? Once in the hospital, wearing dry borrowed scrubs, I had more time to fall into a deeper feeling of shame: I felt bad about the waste. The mess. About taking up several clinicians' valuable time. About disappointing my crew. The injury seemed a punishment for the hubris of signing up for the regatta. I wanted desperately to turn back the clock.

Mine was an old-fashioned error in an analog world. But living in the digital age increasingly creates competing demands on our attention that only exacerbate our human tendency to slip up. Back at Johnson & Johnson, although none of the contaminated batch was shipped, the error went undetected for days until uncovered by a quality-control check. Still, it was a colossal embarrassment for the manufacturers and a setback for Johnson & Johnson—not to mention for people waiting for a vaccine dose. It's easy to forget, but back in the early spring of

2021, the urgency of receiving the COVID vaccine was acutely felt around the world. For many, a longer wait would be life-threatening.

Like many theoretically preventable failures, the basic failure at the Emergent BioSolutions plant was not an isolated incident but reflected a problematic safety culture, as suggested by the following reported events: Earlier vaccine lots had also been thrown out for contamination. Mold was a persistent problem in areas that were supposed to be kept immaculately clean. Supervision and training were scant for the many new hires needed to handle the mammoth vaccine production. Although vaccine manufacturing is known as a "fickle" business and some error is inevitable, the reports suggested a pattern of lapses had led to the high-profile contamination of millions of doses. When inattention becomes a cultural feature in an organization, you have a breeding ground for producing basic and complex failures alike.

Fatigue plays a role in slips due to inattention. The U.S. Centers for Disease Control and Prevention (CDC) reports that a third of adult Americans do not get enough sleep. Such alarming sleep deprivation not only leads to an array of health concerns, but also to accidents and injuries. To cite one example, investigators found that 40 percent of highway accidents identified human fatigue as a "probable cause, a contributing factor, or a finding," despite the fact that the National Transportation Safety Board (NTSB) has made 205 fatigue-specific recommendations since the early 1970s.

Another study found that sleep-deprived medical interns made 5.6 percent more diagnostic errors than well-rested interns. Relevant for almost everyone, a 2020 study found a 6 percent increase in fatal car accidents the week after we "spring forward." The jump was even higher—about 8 percent—for those who live on the western edge of the time zone.

We are all vulnerable to sleep difficulties stemming from a variety of factors, and, yes, more sleep may help reduce the daily mistakes in your life. But it's also important to step back and consider what causes sleep deprivation. Medical errors or accidents by long-haul truck drivers related to fatigue may be the result of overly long shifts assigned by headquarters personnel or, worse, scheduling algorithms that maximize efficiency over common sense. It's always good practice not to stop after identifying the first, most proximal, cause of a failure. Tracing a seemingly simple cause (a tired worker) back further (a problematic schedule) is part of systems thinking, a key practice in the science of failing well, discussed in chapter 7. It matters because the most superficial cause may not point to the best lever for preventing similar failures in the future.

Inattention is all too human. It's hard to stay vigilant, to pay close attention in those moments that need it most. Relatedly, sometimes we're aware that something requires our attention, but we put it off. And nothing bad happens, at least not for a while.

Neglect

A damaged floor caused by a leak from a sink that persisted for too long is a simple example of the human tendency to neglect situations with the potential to reach a breaking point. Neglect tends not to produce instant harm but rather allows the buildup that ultimately results in failure. Because we are forgetful and busy, it's easy to put things off. In retrospect, it's easy to see what went wrong. You would have done better on the test if you had studied harder. You should have brought an umbrella when rain was predicted. Fortunately, most of these "would have, should have" errors in our daily lives do not cause undue harm. Other times, however, neglect can have serious consequences.

Just ask Jack Gillum, who was the engineer of record for the Hyatt Regency Hotel in Kansas City, Missouri, a building originally designed with a soaring atrium that featured four suspended walkways made of concrete and glass. About a year after the hotel's completion, on July 17, 1981, a dance was held in the atrium. Partygoers thronged on the ground floor. People gravitated to the airy walkways and peered down on the dancing couples far below. Suddenly, the second- and fourth-floor walkways began to sway—then they collapsed, crashing with full force into the crowd below.

Twenty years later, Gillum reflected that the design flaw for the walkways was so obvious that "any first-year engineering student could figure it out." The use of existing knowledge could have prevented the accident. The original design drawings called for one long vertical steel rod to run the height of the fifty-foot atrium. Midconstruction, the metal fabricator, Havens Steel Company, proposed two shorter steel rods to replace the one long rod. A hasty shop drawing configured the bolts and washers that would be necessary to install the shorter rods to the walkways' crossbeams, and the change was approved by a project engineer in a brief phone call. The changed design connected the second-floor walkway to the fourth-floor walkway rather than to the roof, doubling the intended load. At that moment, and in the months that followed, everyone supervising the building of the grand hotel neglected to check the safety ramifications. No one acted to halt construction based on what even an engineering student could have figured out: the physics of the new two-rod design made the walkways "barely able to support their own weight."

It was a basic failure waiting to happen. That fateful night, the added weight of the revelers on the walkways proved to be too much.

Gillum, with whom the ultimate responsibility lay, took the blame in the later investigations. His license was revoked for gross negligence. However, earlier warning signs that should have prompted a closer look into the rod and beam construction were also neglected. Over a year prior to the walkways' collapse, when the hotel was still under construction, the atrium roof collapsed. Later, when the walkways were up, and construction workers pushing heavy wheelbarrows reported the walkways to be unsteady, the workers were simply rerouted. Many opportunities to look more closely into the safety hazards of the architecturally ambitious design were missed. The hotel owner, Crown Center Redevelopment Corporation, pressed for time and reluctant to increase expenditures on an already extremely expensive building project, ironically ended up paying out over $140 million in damages.

Years later, Gillum confessed about the Hyatt collapse, "This is a tragedy I think about 365 days a year." By then he was in his seventies. When speaking at engineering conferences, he emphasized, "Engineering societies need to talk about failures. That's how we learn." The Hyatt Regency Hotel collapse has become a classic example of a structural-engineering failure, taught in many modern classrooms. The loss of 114 lives made this one of the deadliest structural-engineering failures to date. But it's by no means a singular catastrophe. As we will see in chapter 4, similar conversations about design flaws, ignored early warnings, and last-minute changes occurred when the Champlain Towers South condominium in Surfside, Florida, collapsed on June 24, 2021. The causes of that collapse were more numerous and slow moving, however; that (complex) failure offers a more obvious mix of factors—some related to organizational behavior and others to engineering design.

Overconfidence

Although some basic failures stem from misplaced steel rods or ignored regulations, simply not reflecting on the implications of a decision is a common underlying cause. People fail to draw on available information or even common sense. *What was I thinking?* is the vernacular: What was I thinking when I booked two important meetings at the same time? What was I thinking when I forgot to pack a sweater, or socks, when traveling to a cold climate? Often, the answer, as you may have experienced, is *I wasn't thinking*. As in, when scheduling a meeting, I didn't check my calendar. When packing, I didn't consult the weather reports, I was preoccupied with other thoughts, or both.

At the turn of the millennium a talking, singing, joking sock puppet was the mascot of a new pet food company that had invested heavily in an award-winning advertising campaign that eventually included ads during the Super Bowl broadcast. Generous venture funding from investors who included Jeff Bezos at Amazon.com for what promised to be the biggest pet food supplier on the internet allowed the start-up to, among other things, purchase large warehouses and buy its biggest online competitor.

In February 2000, the company's wildly successful IPO raised $82.5 million. What were they thinking? Apparently, no one had done the most rudimentary market research to assess the actual size of the market for pet food and pet products. Nor did the business plan account for the company's selling merchandise for a third *less* than what it cost to acquire it. Not even a year later, CEO Julie Wainwright was forced to liquidate Pets.com. Despite its infectious charm, a talking sock puppet was not sufficient grounds on which to run a business. A case can be made that this was a basic failure. Fortunately, Wainwright learned from it, heading into what she described as a "journey of self-discovery." "The days and years that followed Pets.com," Wainwright recalled, "were some of the most transformative of my life. I desperately sought normal. I never achieved that. I landed someplace richer and stronger." Later recognized as one of the 2021 *Forbes* 50 over 50 (influential entrepreneurs, leaders, and scientists), Wainwright appears not to have been crippled by her very public failure.

Leaders who ignored or hid the glaring early evidence that COVID-19 was highly contagious and potentially deadly were making some of the mistakes that allowed the pandemic to spread as quickly as it did in the early part of 2020. Decision makers' unwillingness to act on available information with appropriate public health measures constitutes a preventable error of judgment. The consequences of the failure to act included almost two hundred thousand preventable deaths according to one report in the *Lancet*.

This is not to say that the COVID pandemic did not also bring many complex failures. Indeed, it did. For example, the opportunity to limit the spread of infection was hampered by supply-chain challenges that prevented masks and other protective gear from getting to those most in need. Some leaders' unwillingness to authorize additional production of that equipment when asked to do so in the spring and summer of 2020 is easily designated an error (knowledge existed that made the urgent need for masks unambiguous). This error added to the immense complex failure that manifested as a worldwide pandemic.

COVID-19 had it all: basic failure, complex failure, and ultimately even intelligent failure. The stunningly fast and successful vaccine development relied on scientists who knew how to work with hypothesis-driven failures in the lab. But avoiding the grave error committed by many leaders—of ignoring available expertise—might have greatly mitigated the spread and death toll of the virus.

Faulty assumptions

Assumptions, by definition, take shape in our minds without explicit thought. When we assume something, we're not directly focusing on it. We fail to challenge assumptions because they seem to us self-evidently true. Assumptions thus leave us with erroneous confidence that our model or our way of thinking is correct, often because it has worked before and has become part of our belief system. *We've seen this before. We've always done it this way.* Our first child was a great sleeper so the second baby will also sleep through the night. We always traveled along this route so why check to see if the bridge is washed out? Faulty assumptions, based on scant evidence or poor logic, are a breeding ground for basic failures. (All children are alike. The storm wasn't that bad.) We've always used fossil fuels so the evidence about its negative effects on the environment must be false or exaggerated. Yesterday someone won the jackpot at the casino, so wins are likely. Unlike judgment errors (I didn't enjoy the movie I thought would be great), which are human and inevitable, faulty assumptions drive decisions invisibly.

Consider the revelations about the shocking lack of due diligence of many high-profile investors—content to assume that others had vetted the technology—that came to light in the trial of Elizabeth Holmes. Holmes, charged with promising a revolutionary and potentially profitable method of blood testing at Theranos while knowing it to be fraudulent, stands as a lesson in the ease with which assumptions can be made from superficial signals.

Assumptions are taken-for-granted beliefs that feel like facts. Because we aren't consciously aware of them, we don't hold them up for scrutiny. Many assumptions are harmless; we can safely assume our car is parked where we left it the night before. If we stopped to challenge every assumption we make, we'd never get out the door in the morning. But our everyday lives present countless small basic failures caused by relying on faulty assumptions. When we assume our friendly new neighbors agree with our political views and criticize a public figure they admire, we cause chilly relations across the fence. When I assumed (inexcusable in retrospect) that I was prepared for the final exam in multivariable calculus because I'd done well on the midterm, I short-changed studying and failed the exam. Although it could have shattered my confidence, the failure instead led to new, better study habits. By now it's clear that faulty assumptions can lead to failure—and that assumptions are hard to avoid. Let's take a look at some best practices for when, and how, to pause, identify, and challenge assumptions, along with other strategies for reducing basic failure in our lives.

When not to fail fast and often

You get the picture. We all make mistakes. To err is human. Often the consequences are harmless, other times unfortunate, and occasionally they're catastrophic. The failure craze—the "fail fast, fail often" culture that wants us to embrace failure seemingly indiscriminately—takes inspiration from the intelligent failures inherent to innovation but risks glossing over the vast and varied failure landscape, which also includes basic and complex failure. Some failures *are* bad, not in the sense of immoral but in the sense of wasteful. Whether tragic (a lost life) or silly (spilled milk), waste can be reduced through the diligent application of good failure practices. Basic failures are the most preventable of the three types. Excellent companies strive to prevent as many basic failures as they can. The chances are that you wish to do so as well.

This is why we cannot afford to ignore mistakes. Basic failure's ubiquity serves as an invitation to strive to minimize it. My goal is to make basic failures fewer and further between. (It's the opposite of how we think about intelligent failures, which I believe we should strive to increase, to accelerate innovation, learning, and personal growth.) But behaviors and systems that prevent basic failure can save lives, create immense economic value, and bring personal satisfaction.

How to Reduce the Basic Failures in Your Life

Research on error management has expanded considerably in recent years. Although generally focused on high-risk organizations, this work offers practices that you can put to work to reduce basic failures in your own life as well. These include making safety a priority, expecting and catching errors, and learning as much as you can from them. But it starts with making friends with error—and with our fallibility.

Befriending error

What complicates the quest for friendship is our aversion to errors. We hate to be wrong. We feel embarrassed or ashamed. But we *can* do better. Not too long after my sailing accident, aware of the research on healthy attribution skills, I recognized that making a mistake was not cause for deep shame. A better way to think about the situation was that, yes, it had been adventurous to sign up for the regatta—a thoughtful decision related to doing something just for fun. I challenged my belief that signing up for the race had been wrong and stupid. My mistake had been inattention in a dangerous situation—pure and simple. Now the only thing left was to learn the right lessons from it.

Our aversion to errors prompts people to make sense of them in delightfully creative ways. My husband, for example, dismisses his minor errors with the spontaneous phrase "Anyone would have done that." Anyone would have tripped on the uneven sidewalk. Anyone would have taken the wrong turn onto that dead-end street that came right before the one the navigation system wanted you to take. The failure was due to some external factor. *I* didn't screw up; the sidewalk or the navigation app did. Mistakes were made, but not by me! Yes, these factors contributed—each unquestionably increased the chances of the screwup. But human error played a starring role. Auto insurance companies routinely hear people explain away their accidents by saying things like "The stop sign jumped out in front of my car."

When presented with the choice between admitting our mistakes or protecting our self-image, the decision is easy. We want to believe we are not at fault, so we find every reason to justify what we did as correct. That makes it hard to learn! A psychological bias known as the *fundamental attribution error* exacerbates the problem. Stanford psychologist Lee Ross identified this fascinating asymmetry: when we see others fail, we spontaneously view their character or ability as the cause. It's almost amusing to realize that we do exactly the opposite in explaining our own failures—spontaneously seeing external factors as the cause. For example, if we show up late for a meeting, we blame traffic. If a colleague is late for a meeting, we may conclude he is uncommitted or lazy.

This cognitive bias complicates the vital analytic task of failure diagnosis. You always contribute *something* to the failure, even if other factors also play a role. But, because you are more able to alter your behavior than to, say, fix the sidewalk, focusing on what you might have done differently is more practical and powerful than bemoaning the shortcomings of your environment. A *Texas News Today* article entitled "Colin Powell's Wisdom," written soon after the death of the legendary general and former secretary of state, highlighted Powell's willingness to confront and own up to failure. As Powell said in 2012, "Disappointment, failures, and setbacks are a normal part of the life cycle of a unit or a company, and what the leader has to do is constantly be up and say, 'We have a problem, let's go and get it.'" It's simple!

But not easy.

Befriending vulnerability

Owning our errors becomes easier when we accept human fallibility as a fact and put that acceptance to use in learning and improving. In the most successful teams in my research, people, especially team leaders, talk about the ever-present chance that things will go wrong. They are honest and good-humored about mistakes, which nurtures the psychological safety you need for people to speak up quickly about them. This is a best practice—in families, too, not just work teams—if you want to reduce basic failures.

I find it helpful to think about it this way: Vulnerability is a fact. None of us can predict or control all future events; therefore, we are vulnerable. The only real question? Whether you acknowledge it! Many worry that doing so will make them appear weak, but research shows that being open about what you know and don't know builds trust and commitment. Admitting doubt in the face of uncertainty demonstrates strength rather than weakness.

Another best practice is acknowledging your own contributions—no matter how large or small—to the failures that do occur. This is not only wise, it's practical, for two reasons. First, it makes it easier for others to do the same, making the analytic work of diagnosing failures easier, and second, other people will then see you as approachable and trustworthy and will be more enthusiastic about working with or befriending you.

Putting safety first

Although it's easy to think of basic failure as mundane and thus not likely to yield a return on investments of time or money, in fact the potential upside of error reduction is large. Paul O'Neill understood this when he became the CEO of aluminum manufacturer Alcoa in October of 1987. After starting his career in the U.S. Department of Veterans Affairs and the U.S. government's Office of Management and Budget, O'Neill seemed an unlikely candidate to lead the global corporation, an impression that only deepened at his first press conference in a hotel ballroom near Wall Street. Charles Duhigg, in his inspiring book *The Power of Habit*, recounts that O'Neill opened his remarks to investors and analysts by saying, "I want to talk to you about worker safety." Perhaps expecting to hear about inventories, market outlook, capital investments, or geographic expansion plans, the room fell into a stunned silence as O'Neill continued, "Every year, numerous Alcoa workers are injured so badly that they miss a day of work." Duhigg reports with amusement that one investor bolted for a phone, telling his client, "The board put a crazy hippie in charge and he's going to kill the company." The investor advised his client to sell the stock immediately, "before everyone else in the room started calling their clients and telling them the same thing."

It's worth noting that Alcoa did not have a "safety problem" in 1987. The company's safety record was better than that of most American companies, "especially considering," as O'Neill explained that day in the hotel ballroom, "our employees work with metals that are fifteen hundred degrees and machines that can rip a man's arm off." With that graphic image in mind, O'Neill set an ambitious target: "I intend to make Alcoa the safest company in America. I intend to go for zero injuries."

What O'Neill knew was that worker safety could only be achieved when people at the company (at all levels) committed themselves to what he called "a habit of excellence"—a habit that would positively affect production quality, uptime, profitability, and, yes, ultimately stock price. Attention to detail would be central to this excellence, as would every employee's willingness to push back against unsafe practices and to point out others' seemingly small errors. (Yes, this does mean that O'Neill had to create a psychologically safe workplace if he wanted to achieve his goal.)

How? For starters, O'Neill invited employees to speak up with all suggestions for safety or maintenance. He also sent a note to every worker, with his personal phone number, telling the workers to call him if their managers didn't adhere to safety practices. When one did, he thanked him and acted on it. To help managers build psychologically safe environments, he encouraged all of them to ask themselves, daily, whether every member of their teams could respond yes to three questions:

1. Am I treated with dignity and respect by everyone, every day, in each encounter, without regard to race, ethnicity, nationality, gender, religious belief, sexual orientation, title, pay grade, or number of degrees?
2. Do I have the resources I need—education, training, tools, financial support, encouragement—so I can make a contribution to this organization that gives meaning to my life?
3. Am I recognized and thanked for what I do?

Finally, by showing that he cared more about worker safety than profits, O'Neill removed a major barrier to speaking up. When a safety incident happened, small or large, he made it an instant priority. He spoke directly with workers at the plants where such events had occurred to get their perspectives on what had happened. He took responsibility when, six months into his new role, a worker was killed on the job—telling executives, "It's my failure of leadership. I caused his death." O'Neill believed that employees who were given respect and support were more likely to follow safe practices, to push back against unsafe requests, and to speak up about errors and safety violations.

If you're wondering how well the panicked investor's client was served, the answer is not well at all. When O'Neill retired at the end of 2000, Alcoa's safety record had experienced a significant improvement, annual net income had grown to five times 1987's performance, and the company's market capitalization had risen by $27 billion. Duhigg calculates that had you put a million dollars into Alcoa that October day in 1987, you would have earned another million in stock dividends, and you could have sold the stock for $5 million on the day O'Neill left.

This enormous accomplishment required a first step of befriending human error, then putting systems into place so people could routinely catch and correct it before anyone was harmed on the job.

Catching error

The boy Sakichi was born in 1867 in rural Japan. His mother wove cotton that was grown in the region. He learned carpentry from his father, but he had an inventor's inquiring, curious mind and an appreciation for intelligent failure. He liked to tinker with wood in an old barn, where he was not afraid to destroy his first, failed efforts at building a better weaving machine. By age twenty-four he'd received his first patent, for a wooden loom, and promptly opened a business to manufacture looms. After a year, his factory failed. Undeterred, he continued to invent, innovate, and improve his looms; by age thirty he had invented

Japan's first steam-powered loom. This time, his business venture was a success. By the 1920s, the Toyoda Automatic Loom Works was manufacturing 90 percent of the looms in Japan, and in 1929, a leading British textile machinery manufacturer, Platt Brothers, bought the patent rights. Toyoda insisted to his son, Kiichiro Toyoda, that the future lay in manufacturing cars; using the patent sale as seed money, the son founded what became the Toyota Motor Company.

What might be Sakichi Toyoda's most enduring legacy, however, was his loom's error-management technique—when a warp string accidentally broke, the machine automatically stopped. To prevent destroying precious material, the loom would not start again until a person fixed the thread. To describe this function, Sakichi Toyoda coined the term *jidoka*, which translates to "automation with a human touch."

Today, *jidoka* in Toyota's automotive factories can best be seen in the company's much-lauded Andon Cord. When a team member spots a problem, or even an indication that there *might* be a problem, on the manufacturing floor, she pulls a cord above her workstation to prevent the problem from compounding.

Although Toyota's Andon Cord is famous—and at one time seemed absurd to executives in U.S. automotive companies, who could not imagine giving that kind of power to frontline workers—most people do not appreciate a vital nuance in how it works. Pulling the cord immediately sends a signal to a team leader that there might be a quality problem. It does *not* immediately stop the assembly line but instead stops the line after a delay (of approximately sixty seconds, or what's called the cycle time for each assembly task). During that brief window the team member and the team leader together diagnose the situation. For most (eleven out of twelve) pulls of the cord, the problem is quickly resolved, and the cord is pulled a second time. The second pull prevents a line stoppage. When a problem cannot be quickly resolved, no second pull occurs, and the line automatically stops until the problem is corrected. Waste has been avoided, and a perfect car is set to emerge from the end of the assembly line.

Although elegant and practical, the Andon Cord, for me, embodies simple leadership wisdom. It conveys the message "We want to hear from you." *You* refers to those closest to the work—those best positioned to judge its quality. Not only are employees not reprimanded or punished for reporting error, they are thanked and recognized for their close observation. This may explain how it's possible for someone to be pulling an Andon Cord every few seconds in one of Toyota's many worldwide factories. It also explains how quality improvements continued to accumulate, ultimately turning the tiny Japanese loom company into a global automotive powerhouse.

The genius of the Andon Cord lies both in how it functions as a quality-control device to prevent defects and in its embodiment of two essential facets of error management: (1) catching small mistakes before they compound into substantial failures, and (2) blameless reporting, which plays a vital role in ensuring safety in high-risk environments.

Learning from error

Mastery in any field requires a willingness to actually learn something from the many mistakes you will necessarily make. When Tanitoluwa Adewumi, a ten-year-old in New York, became the United States' newest national chess master, the boy's words, like his title, were well beyond his age: "I say to myself that I never lose, that I only learn. Because when you lose, you have to make a mistake to lose that game. So, you learn from that mistake, and so you learn [overall]. So losing is the way of winning for yourself."

Chess is a game of practice as well as skill and intelligence. It's not enough to simply show up for ten hours per day and shuffle pieces across the board. You will make countless mistakes (and lose numerous games), but if you don't study *why* that specific mistake led to a loss, you will not achieve mastery.

Professional athletes similarly fall off balance beams, miss shots, strike out, stumble, lose, and come in last. But they watch videos of themselves and their teammates making mistakes to figure out what went wrong and which skills are weak. Coaches advise how to improve and make those mistakes less often. With practice, rowers learn how to twist the oars at the correct angle. Divers learn how far to bend before they leap. Golfers learn how to hit the ball with precision. As golf champion Yani Tseng puts it, "You always learn something from mistakes." What can we take away from the practices of elite athletes? It seems to me that they learn how to confront their mistakes by focusing instead on possibility—on the achievements palpably within reach even if they eluded you today. They show us how to care more about tomorrow's goal than today's ego gratification.

Fostering a healthy attitude about human fallibility is the first and possibly most important step for helping us catch and correct mistakes. But to complement and support these behavioral practices, implementing failure prevention systems can dramatically increase your chances of success.

Prevention Systems

None of these failure prevention systems is revolutionary. All reflect common sense. Yet few companies or families take the time to get them in place. My favorite of these is *blameless reporting*—an explicit system to enable early detection of potential harm.

Blameless reporting

Recognizing that bad news doesn't age well, many thoughtful organizations and families have explicitly (or sometimes implicitly) implemented blameless reporting. Does such a policy imply a tolerance for bad behavior or low standards? Anything goes? Not even close.

The policy requests that people speak up quickly about errors and problems, so as to prevent them from turning into larger problems, or serious failures. The promise is that reporting will not be penalized. It does *not* promise, however, that if subsequent investigation uncovers deliberate disregard for standards, or unethical or illegal conduct, that these violations will not be punished. The policy thus implies—and sometimes formalizes—a separation between systems of learning and systems of evaluation. In some institutions, including the U.S. Air Force, the policy goes so far as to punish people for *not* reporting a problem in a timely way.

Blameless reporting also applies in families. Parents of teenagers, for example, can make sure their children know to call at any time of day or night if they need a ride home. No questions asked. The risks created by the combination of alcohol, driving, and adolescence are best managed, such parents believe, by ensuring that the lines of communication are open. They want their children to understand that "no questions asked" is truly a viable, nonpunitive option. Learning and safety are thereby prioritized above evaluation in dangerous situations.

Psychological safety both enables and is enabled by blameless reporting. The policy sends the message "We understand that things will go wrong, and we want to hear from you quickly so we can solve problems and prevent harm." Recall that the most effective hospital teams in my medical-error study could report errors without fear of being blamed. Compared to those who were reluctant to report errors, these teams were better able to learn from errors and take measures to prevent them.

When Alan Mulally arrived as the new chief executive officer at the Ford Motor Company in 2006, he quickly recognized that people were not speaking up about the many problems plaguing the company (so deep in debt that it anticipated a loss of $17 billion that year). To begin understanding and remedying the problems, Mulally instituted a simple structure for blameless reporting. He asked his team to color their reports green (on track), yellow (possible issues or concerns), or red (stalled or off track). "The data sets you free," Mulally told his executive team with a smile. By emphasizing that real problems existed and needed to be confronted, Mulally hoped the executives would start actively managing problems, as a team, rather than avoiding them.

But it's one thing to institute a new system for truthful reporting of what's going on, and it's another for people to believe that they won't be punished or shamed. This is why initial responses—whether from a boss or a parent—to bad news are critical.

At Ford, red reports indicating problems were in short supply for far longer than Mulally had hoped. To encourage truth telling, he reminded the team of the anticipated billions in losses. Finally, an executive named Mark Field courageously revealed that an upcoming launch of the new Ford Edge was badly sidetracked. The Edge was meant to be Ford's next "big thing." The team fell silent, anticipating the emotional rebuke or termination that would follow this news. To their surprise, Mulally applauded and said, "Mark, that is great visibility." Then Mulally asked, "Who can help Mark with this?"

Shocked, but relieved, several executives shared ideas, identified prior experiences, and volunteered engineering staff to help fix the problem. According to Mulally, the entire "exchange took twelve seconds." Sharing bad news with a team—or a family—is the first step to making things better.

Mulally argued that transparency increased performance pressure. "You can imagine the accountability!" he exclaimed in an interview, presenting a hypothetical scenario to clarify: "Are you going to be red on an item, and then are you going to go through the week and come back and say to all your colleagues, 'I was really busy last week, I didn't have a chance to work on that.'" Mulally understood that blameless reporting does not mean low standards, nor does it lower the pressure to get the job done. Quite the opposite. With greater transparency comes a sense of mutual accountability, which drives people to solve problems together.

Blameless reporting is an essential component of the comprehensive and extended Aviation Safety Reporting System (ASRS) developed in the United States by NASA in a partnership with the Federal Aviation Administration (FAA) and later adopted internationally. Flight attendants, air traffic controllers, and maintenance staff, as well as pilots, can report errors without the name of the person who made the error. Even airport names and flight numbers are excluded. Moreover, regulations guarantee that information is "confidential, voluntary, and non-punitive." Reports are made in writing, on an official form, and include prompts to describe the chain of events that caused the problem, how it was corrected, and the human factors involved, such as judgments, decisions, and actions.

The goal of anonymity is to encourage people to report error without fear. Many of the errors are relatively minor near misses that did not result in damage or failure; for example, taking too long to spot the runway lights. And compiling a sizable database of error reports is valuable because it can be analyzed to reveal the most common errors and problems, to inform training scenarios for pilots, and to guide aircraft manufacturers in future development.

In short, blameless reporting is part of a coordinated learning system. Only by discovering errors can they be addressed and prevented. A study of 558 accident reports made in the United States between 1983, when the error training was first introduced, and 2002 found a 40 percent drop in the pilot errors that could have contributed to accidents. What's more, according to aviation journalist Andy Pasztor, in the twelve years between 2009 and 2021, U.S. airlines carried more than 8 billion passengers without a fatal crash.

Preventive maintenance

What do dentistry and cars have in common? Here's a hint: just as brushing your teeth after meals prevents painful and expensive decay, so does changing the oil in your car at regular intervals prevent engine damage. In both domains, preventive maintenance is essential. This practice is as dull as it is valuable. So what is it about human beings that makes it so easy for us to neglect preventive maintenance?

Part of the answer is found in what psychologists call temporal discounting, the tendency to discount or devalue the significance of delayed responses to actions. Studies show that people give less weight to outcomes that will occur in the future compared to events in the present. Just as the offer of a dollar next week is less exciting than a dollar right now, we have trouble taking seriously the bad outcomes that will happen when we fail to perform a tedious task today. Our tendency to discount the future explains the prevalence of many unhelpful behaviors—whether eating that extra piece of chocolate cake or procrastinating on studying for an exam—and the failure to keep up with preventive maintenance is similarly problematic. It's hard for us to take seriously the car breakdown that didn't happen. We don't experience joy because our car engine didn't seize today, whereas investing time and money in maintenance creates palpable inconvenience.

A delightful episode of the popular *Freakonomics* podcast in October 2016 explained the drag on the economy from our unwillingness to invest in preventive maintenance. Stephen Dubner and his guests focused on cities and infrastructure rather than personal habits, but the principle of discounting the future applies equally. Politicians, as Dubner's guest, economist and cities expert Edward Glaeser, pointed out, are motivated to limit spending in the present, while society benefits from today's investments that support communities into the future. Ironically, governments in ancient Rome, investing extensively and wisely in building and maintaining the vital systems upon which communities depend, fell prey less often to temporal discounting than modern cities and states. Without its infrastructure investments, Rome could not have been as populous, nor as lasting. Despite our greater knowledge, technology, and ability to model and predict decay, the speed of change in our modern world seems to exacerbate our hyper-focus on the present.

Codification

Restaurant kitchens rely on detailed lists of tasks for closing and open-ing the next day. By codifying the procedure, it can be followed by anyone. Fast-food restaurants rely on process steps to ensure efficiency and uniformity, often posting graphical step-by-step recipes on the kitchen wall.

Whether consciously or not, most of us have adopted at least a semicodified process in some areas of our life. Before leaving the house, we make sure the stove and lights are turned off. Lock the door. Check for wallet, keys, phone. A friend keeps a folder in her computer with detailed and individualized lists of what each of her four children needs to pack for the family's annual summer camping trip. Because a five-year-old cannot pack with the same independence as a twelve-year-old, she's organized the lists by age; that way, she only has to write up a new list every couple of years for the oldest child. Before each trip, she prints out the packing lists for each child and tapes it by the child's bed. In addition to saving time, such codification reduces the likelihood that anyone will forget to pack a toothbrush or favorite stuffed animal. She has lists for her husband and herself as well. She is not alone. Highly organized people tend to codify many aspects of their domestic and professional lives. I am not one of them. Productivity organizers, many of them software based, essentially help you codify to boost efficiency, reduce waste, and prevent error.

No discussion of codification is complete without reference to the book *The Checklist Manifesto*, by my Harvard colleague Atul Gawande. Since its publication in 2009 it's helped to popularize and establish the habit of drawing up a series of process steps to ensure consistency and attention to detail and to reduce careless error. Gawande credits Dr. Peter Pronovost, who wanted to reduce or prevent infection in patients in the intensive care unit at the Johns Hopkins Hospital in Baltimore, as having written a checklist of five things doctors need to do when inserting a central venous catheter:

1. Wash hands with soap.
2. Clean patient's skin with antiseptic.
3. Put sterile drapes over patient's body.
4. Wear a sterile mask, hat, gown, and gloves.
5. Put a sterile dressing over the site of the inserted catheter.

Though such steps seem simple and obvious, the checklist has become a proven method to ensure against the haste and the memory slips endemic to human error. To cite one example, doctors and nurses in Michigan who followed Pronovost's checklist for eighteen months saved fifteen hundred lives and $100 million for the state. Checklists, however, are not foolproof. Medical errors continue to be an enormous challenge for hospitals and the health-care professions. According to Raj Ratwani, director of MedStar Health's National Center for Human Factors in Healthcare, medical checklists "have gotten us only 20 percent of the way" toward reducing error. Mistakes in U.S. hospitals are estimated to cause at least a quarter of a million unnecessary deaths of patients annually. The vast majority of these are complex failures, as you will learn in chapter 4.

Like the Air Florida pilots in the beginning of this chapter, so accustomed to flying in warm weather that they did not stop to *think* about the deicer, we need to make sure checklists are used with our brains turned on. Additionally, checklists need to be updated when knowledge evolves or rules change.

Required training

In the early 1970s, airplanes began to be fitted with a "black box" that recorded data about the flight, such as speed and altitude and, equally important, the voices of the crew in the cockpit. Because the black box data could be physically retrieved from the scene of airplane crashes, investigators could reconstruct what had happened in the last minutes of a flight, which too often were also the last minutes in the lives of pilots, crew, and passengers. Investigative reconstructions were conducted to root out causes, and as crash after crash occurred, it became increasingly clear that the majority of accidents were attributable to human errors made by the cockpit crew. These were often simple mistakes, and they led to basic, but tragic, failures.

Take, for example, Eastern Air Lines Flight 401 in December 1972. The pilot and his crew in the cockpit were highly trained and experienced professionals; they'd amassed over fifty thousand flight hours combined. The weather on this routine flight from John F. Kennedy Airport in New York to Miami was favorable. What brought the plane down was the pilot and crew's fixation on a burned-out light bulb on the nose gear. Several times the captain told the others in the cockpit to find the problem with the light bulb; but while they tried to fix that problem, neither he nor anyone else noticed a much more urgent problem until it was too late: the plane was fast losing altitude. The Lockheed L-1011 crashed into the Florida Everglades. One hundred and one people lost their lives.

By the late 1970s, it was clear to many that something needed to be done about airline safety. Like medicine and nuclear reactors, considered in chapter 4, aviation is a high-risk field where small errors can have catastrophic results. The NASA Industrial Workshop held in 1979 brought together aviation experts from private industry and government with psychologists and academic researchers. In the decades since, several iterations of a training called crew resource management (CRM) brought down the accident rate. My dissertation adviser's role in that training led ultimately to my research on hospital errors in the early 1990s. In addition to blameless reporting and error management, CRM has evolved to include training in leadership, communication, situation awareness, and hazardous attitudes. Many of CRM's core tenets have been adopted by business and, increasingly, by the health-care professions.

Failure-proofing

Prior to 1967, parents who left pill bottles accessible to young children risked a trip to the emergency room. So many children were becoming accidentally poisoned that Dr. Henri Breault, chief of pediatrics and director of the Poison Control Center at a hospital in Windsor, Ontario, came home at 3:00 a.m. one day and, according to his wife, said, "You know, I've had it! I am tired of pumping children's stomachs when they're taking pills that they shouldn't be having! I've got to do something about it." That was the impetus for the invention of a cap too complicated for children to open. First called a Palm N Turn when introduced in the Windsor area, the invention reduced poisoning accidents by 91 percent.

That's one example of failure-proofing—taking measures to reduce a known risk factor. Today, childproofing one's home and car is commonplace. Not only medicine bottles that require reading and strength to twist and pinch, but self-locking car doors, covers for electrical outlets, straps to anchor tippy furniture, gates around swimming pools, and much more.

Poka-yoke, which means "error-proofing" in Japanese, a term that originated with the Toyota Production System (TPS), is a valued practice in modern manufacturing. That so many of the objects we use benefit from *poka-yoke* is evidence of basic failure's ubiquity. We all experience instances of inattention. We can all hold faulty assumptions and be overconfident. The goal is to take measures to reduce the number of basic failures these tendencies cause.

Eminent design researcher Don Norman has been thinking and writing about the relationships between humans and the things we use since the 1980s. His work laid the foundation for the field now called human-centered design. Norman argues that much of what we call human error can be attributed to poor design. He cites as an example the online drop-down menu that asks users to select from an alphabetical list of the fifty states when filling in an address. Too easy, Norman claims, to select Mississippi instead of Minnesota because of their adjacency. The design has not been error-proofed.

Norman's deep understanding of how humans think is tightly woven into his ideas about design. For example, he points out that we are likely to give familiar tasks less attention, thus increasing the risk that we will slip up. That's what happened to the experienced pilots who forgot to turn on the deicer when flying in cold weather; as experts they gave the checklist less attention than it warranted. Software designers who accept the inevitability of human error can provide contextual error warnings (Twitter warns before you reach the character limit), provide safety nets (the undo function for documents), and support short-term memory loss for information-heavy tasks by saving a person's previous entries.

Much as with codification, we can all think of creative ways to failure-proof our everyday lives. Install a light on that stone wall at the end of the driveway to reduce the chances that you will back into it. Keep an umbrella near the door to encourage you to bring it along if it looks like rain. Make a study date with a friend to increase the chance that you will adequately review for the exam. Become mindful of assumptions. Consciously work against temporal discounting. The possibilities are endless.

Finally, keep an open mind in case your basic failures are opportunities in disguise.

Eureka! When Basic Failure Converts to Success

Lee Kum Sheung, a twenty-six-year-old chef at a small restaurant serving cooked oysters in Guangdong, a coastal province in south China, did not intend to vary the preparation that fateful day in 1888. Lee mistakenly left a pot of oysters to simmer too long, only to come back to a sticky brown mess. Tasting the result, he discovered that it was delicious! It did not take him long to decide to make his "oyster sauce" on purpose, selling it in jars under the Lee Kum Kee brand. Eventually his "brilliant mistake" would make Lee and his heirs extremely wealthy. When Lee's grandson died in 2021, the family was worth more than $17 billion. Even if most basic failures don't yield valuable new products, many of today's favorite foods, including potato chips and chocolate chip cookies, were discovered by accident.

Although most basic failures don't generate billion-dollar businesses, those that do had to be noticed—and reframed as opportunities. This only happens when you bring an open mind and a good-natured response to mistakes.

To Err Is Human, to Prevent Basic Failure, Divine

Errors will always be with us. Often, they're harmless. Other times they cause basic failures that range from a funny story to tell friends (a dented bumper) to a devastating loss of life (the Kansas City Hyatt Regency Hotel collapse). All of us confront daily opportunities to disrupt the causal chain linking error to failure. What makes basic failure hard to prevent is our instinctive aversion to error, especially our own. But by befriending error so we can catch, report, and correct it, consequential failures can be avoided.

Equally valuable is embracing preventive tactics of all kinds—from training to error-proofing. This is not the sexy part of failing well—not the part that gets social media likes or hailed as the latest management fad. Given its enormous value (just ask Alcoa stockholders or commercial airline passengers!), this is a shame. A vital part of failing well is preventing basic failures. If you aspire to zero harm and failure-free work at the point of delivery, it's essential to make friends with human error.

Yes, to err is human. And to forgive (ourselves, especially) is indeed divine. But adopting simple practices to prevent basic failures in our lives and organizations is both possible and worthwhile. You might even say it's empowering.

CHAPTER 4

The Perfect Storm

Unfortunately, most warning systems do not
warn us that they can no longer warn us.

—Charles Perrow

Captain Pastrengo Rugiati was a sturdy, congenial man who loved
the sea and the ships on which he'd served. He had a reputation for
kindness. When one of his officers received notice of the birth of a
child, Rugiati would order the ship's whistle blown, fly a blue or pink
ribbon from the mast, and order a party for all men not on duty. That
Friday night in March 1967, he lingered on deck after midnight as the
Torrey Canyon sailed northward, nearing the end of its monthlong
journey from Kuwait to Milford Haven, Wales. The sea below was calm;
clear sailing was predicted for the next several days.

Rugiati had stayed up late to go over the details of the especially
challenging operation that lay ahead: unloading the approximately
119,000 tons of crude oil his ship was carrying. Things had to go right;
the ship was pressed for time. If Rugiati didn't make Milford Haven by
11:00 p.m. the following day, he'd have to wait another six days for a

comparable high tide that would allow a ship of *Torrey Canyon*'s size to unload. Neither he nor the crew nor the Liberian shipping company that employed them could afford such a delay. He took special care with the calculations because the ship was missing a copy of *The Channel Pilot*, the standard maritime manual and best available knowledge for navigating the waters ahead. When he finally turned in to his bunk, he requested to be called when the notorious Isles of Scilly—an archipelago off England's southwestern coast—was sighted starboard (on the ship's right).

Around 6:30 a.m. the first officer woke the captain. He reported that ocean currents and wind had pushed the ship off course. Hoping to correct for this, the first officer had reset the ship's direction. Rugiati was annoyed that the first officer had changed course without permission. Even more vexing, the rerouting would add time to their journey. Rugiati put the ship back on its original course, which he'd worked out so meticulously the night before. Although they would now have to pass close to Seven Stones Reef, a legendary danger to sailors, Rugiati believed the ship and her crew would be safe. In retrospect, that would prove debatable, even a judgment error.

Still, Rugiati might have safely steered his ship to harbor save for two additional unexpected small events that followed each other in close succession. First, two lobster boats suddenly appeared in the fog, blocking forward movement and forcing the captain to turn away. With little room to maneuver, seconds counted. Second, a mechanical problem in the steering wheel prevented the rudder from responding immediately to Rugiati's attempted turn. That tiny delay would matter.

Rugiati was paying close attention. But he was too late. Too close to the reef. He was out of luck. Around 8:50 a.m. the *Torrey Canyon* hit the reef at full speed. The bottom of the massive ship was torn out. Fourteen cargo tanks were ripped open, triggering a devastating oil spill of 13 million gallons. That Saturday, March 18, 1967, was only the beginning of what would turn out to be a tremendous failure, to this day Britain's biggest oil spill.

As Captain Rugiati later said at the official inquiry, "Many little things added up to one big disaster." The deadline, the currents, the fog, the lobster boats, and the steering control—on another day, all might have gone well. Take out any of these factors, and the accident would likely have been averted. Rugiati would most likely have continued for many years doing what he loved best: sailing tankers across the world. Instead, he became as broken as his boat—shamed and blamed—his career dashed. "For a ship's captain, his ship is all, and I have lost mine," he confessed. To most people, including the ship's owners and insurers, and especially in his own eyes, the highly skilled captain had become an abject failure.

Many Little Things

The *Torrey Canyon* tragedy provides a classic example of a complex failure. The "many little things" adding up to produce a failure, whether large or small, captures the essential feature of this third type. As in so many stories, "little things" that regularly occur without mishap happen to line up in the wrong way—allowing a failure to sneak through the guardrails that normally prevent it.

This chapter digs into the nature of complex failures and why they're on the rise in nearly every facet of contemporary life. But first, this story serves to remind us to treat the topic of failure soberly. Not all failures qualify as the right kind of wrong! Some are downright catastrophic. Some are tragic. Others are merely a source of chagrin. The science of failing well starts with a clear-eyed diagnosis of failure type—so as to better understand, learn from, and most important, prevent as many destructive failures as possible. Like basic failures, complex failures are not the right kind of wrong.

Still, to say that complex failures are not the right kind of wrong is *not* to call them blameworthy. Some are, but most, as you will see, are not. Like intelligent and basic failures, complex failures can be powerful teachers if we are willing to do the hard work of learning from them.

Looking for the Culprit

Although in excellent health when he'd set out, the physical strain and psychological shock of what would become Captain Rugiati's last journey impaired his health. He lost twenty pounds and developed a lung infection and was now under strict doctor's orders to see no one but his wife, Anna, who visited daily. But the paparazzi found him in Genoa when the Liberian-appointed Board of Investigation, before which Rugiati and several other crew members had testified, reached its conclusion: Captain Pastrengo Rugiati was solely responsible. His license was rescinded, and he would never sail again. A photographer snapped an image of the terrified man under the bed.

Afterward, the decision was perceived as hastily reached. A crew member testified that the navigational measurements he'd taken and reported in the last hours before the accident had been inaccurate. Also, someone on deck, it was unclear who, had mistakenly moved a side lever on the steering wheel, slowing Rugiati's maneuvers in those final, crucial seconds. And then there was the missing copy of *The Channel Pilot*, which could have provided navigational guidance. Placing the blame on one person, the captain, was not only a relatively easy response to what had gone wrong, it was also good news for the ship's owners and insurers; according to at least one estimate, the verdict saved them nearly $17 million.

The reflex to blame someone, to pin the fault on a single individual or cause, is nearly universal. Unfortunately, it reduces the psychological safety needed to practice the science of failing well. CEOs are fired when a company underperforms. Spouses blame each other for that late day-care pickup. Children routinely point the finger elsewhere to escape blame. It's easy and natural to look for single causes and single culprits, but for complex failures this instinct is not only unhelpful, it's inaccurate. And it makes it harder to talk openly and logically about what really happened and how to do better next time. Later I'll talk about approaches to reducing complex failure, but for now I want to emphasize that a psychologically safe environment in which people know they will not be blamed for mistakes or disappointing results is the bedrock that allows organizations and families alike to experience less of the wrong kind of failure and more of the right kind.

What about accountability? Executives in industries as varied as hospitals and investment banks have asked me this question. Surely individuals must face consequences for failure to avoid an overly lax culture? If people aren't blamed for failures, how can they be motivated to improve? This concern is based on a false dichotomy. In actuality, a culture that makes it safe to admit failure can (and in high-risk environments *must*) coexist with high performance standards. A blame culture primarily serves to ensure that people don't speak up about problems in time to correct them, which obviously doesn't help performance. This is why blameless reporting is so valuable. As you will see, uninhibited, rapid reporting of anomalies is vital for high performance in any dynamic context.

The Complexity of Complex Failure

Although basic failures are occasionally devastating, complex failures are the real monsters that loom large in our lives, organizations, and societies. While basic failures present reasonably solvable problems with single causes, complex failures are archetypically different. They're prevalent in settings such as hospital emergency rooms and global supply chains because multiple factors and people interact in somewhat unpredictable ways. Increasingly volatile weather systems are another breeding ground for complex failure. My years of studying complex failures in health care, aerospace, and business have produced a set of remarkably disparate examples that nonetheless share common attributes. Above all, they have more than one cause. Complex failures happen in familiar settings, which is what distinguishes them from intelligent failures. Despite being familiar, these settings present a degree of complexity where multiple factors can interact in unexpected ways. Usually, complex failures are preceded by subtle warning signs. Finally, they often include at least one external, seemingly uncontrollable, factor.

Familiar settings

Unlike intelligent failures, which take place in new territory—such as choosing never previously combined ingredients to innovate in cuisine, dating to find a life partner, or conducting acoustics experiments that result in a game-changing electret microphone—complex failures occur in settings where you can find plenty of prior knowledge and experience. Although on his last voyage Captain Rugiati may not previously have sailed that exact route in those exact weather conditions, basic knowledge for a successful voyage was well established. A social event, vacation trip, or semester in school are examples of familiar settings in which we all may have experienced a complex failure or two. Most of the accidents, tragedies, and disasters that appear in the daily news are complex failures in reasonably familiar settings.

Consider the *Rust* film set in New Mexico where cinematographer Halyna Hutchins suffered a fatal gun wound on October 21, 2021. Bonanza Creek Ranch had previously been used by other filmmakers and was reasonably familiar to the crew, who had been working there for several days. Everyone on production was reasonably familiar with the necessary processes and precautions their industry had established for making a movie that used firearms. Yet actor and producer Alec Baldwin somehow held a gun that accidentally discharged the fatal bullet with "what sounded like a whip and then a loud pop." Director Joel

Souza, standing beside Hutchins, suffered a shoulder wound. A tragic complex failure.

In the investigation that followed, it became clear that established safety procedures for handling firearms on set had not been strictly followed. Twenty-four-year-old armorer Hannah Gutierrez-Reed, in charge of overseeing gun safety and usage on set, told investigators that earlier on the day of the accident she had followed protocol by checking that the ammunition intended for shooting scenes that day included only "dummies" and no "hot rounds," or live bullets. However, assistant director David Halls, the last person to inspect the gun for safety before handing it to Baldwin and announcing it was "cold," told investigators that he had made an error by not checking all the rounds that day—a major breach of safety protocol. What's more, it was unclear how live ammunition, ordinarily banned on a movie set, had even arrived on the premises in the first place. Worse, a week earlier, "accidental discharge" occurred twice without leading to increased scrutiny of safety practices on the film set.

It's this familiarity that makes complex failures so pernicious. In familiar situations you feel more in control than you actually are—say, driving home (familiar) despite consuming alcohol at a party—making it easy to be lulled into a false sense of confidence. Captain Rugiati felt in control of his ship because of his meticulous planning the night before and his years of experience. I'm sure you can think of examples from your own life where this has been true. Maybe you felt confident in your ability to lead a team project, having done it many times before, only to find yourself beset with unexpected challenges whose difficulty you'd underestimated. Maybe you or someone you know felt reasonably immune from COVID because of precautions that seemed adequate and then became infected. More generally, when you find yourself thinking, "I can do this in my sleep," watch out! Overconfidence is a precursor to complex failure, just as it is to basic failure.

Complex failures are not always catastrophic. We've all had experiences in which a mini "perfect storm" derails our plans. You set your alarm for p.m. not a.m., making you late getting out the door; your gas tank hovers on empty, so you stop to fill it. Then an accident on the highway creates unusually heavy traffic, making the drive to the doctor's office take longer than anticipated. You arrive thirty minutes past your scheduled appointment time, and the doctor, having rushed off to an unexpected emergency at the hospital, is no longer available. Although relatively benign, the missed appointment is a complex failure.

Multicausal

Complex failures have more than one cause, none of which created the failure on its own. Usually a mix of internal factors, such as procedures and skills, collides with external factors, such as weather or a supplier's delivery delay. Sometimes, the multiple factors interact to exacerbate one another; sometimes they simply compound, as with the straw that broke the camel's back. In the lawsuits and blaming that proliferated following the shooting accident on the Bonanza Creek Ranch, one thing was clear: if any *one* of the smaller errors had been caught or avoided, the tragic failure could have been averted. Maybe the bullet would have missed Hutchins had she stood behind the camera at a slightly different angle. If Baldwin had pulled the revolver more slowly or less forcefully, it might not have discharged. If the ammunition had never been allowed on set. If the handler hadn't loudly announced that the gun was cold. In this case, as in so many others, the system, with its intended protocols, was weak, its execution lax.

Called "one of the deadliest engineering failures" in U.S. history, the collapse of Champlain Towers South on June 24, 2021, was a tragic complex failure that took ninety-eight lives. To search for causes, we might even go as far back as the 1890s when ambitious developers decided to build a city on a stretch of swampland known as Miami Beach. Next, consider their eradication of the mangrove forests that served as "natural storm walls, mitigating tidal damage and blocking high winds," leaving the resulting buildings vulnerable from the start, and even more so with today's intensified storms and rising sea levels. Add to this the condominium owners' likely reluctance to fund expensive—and to them unexpected—maintenance costs as the thirty-nine-year-old building aged. Because local regulations required recertification of such structures after forty years, an engineer inspecting the Towers a year and a half earlier noted that the design of the concrete slab underlying the pool deck allowed water to collect in the building's foundation. He also saw small fissures and erosion that did not seem to create immediate risk. The estimated cost of $9 million to correct the deck problem—well beyond what the building had in its reserves—led to delay, heated arguments among tenants, and resignations of some board members. Although tempting, seeking to identify a single culprit—developers, owners, city government, or climate change—will come up short.

External factors

In complex failures, an external or uncontrollable factor often enters the mix. You can think of this as bad luck. The *Torrey Canyon* failure was brought about by a tragic combination of unpredicted external (lobster boats that unexpectedly appeared) and uncontrollable (ocean currents) factors. A live bullet is found in the armorer's storage facility. Rising water levels in the Miami area exacerbates structural aging in the Champlain Towers. A teenager drives home from a party, his impaired judgment amplified on a road turned suddenly icy. A virus with a previously unknown chemical makeup becomes as uncontrollable as human behavior.

At times the line between a basic failure and a complex failure blurs. What seems at first a basic failure, such as mistakenly loading a real bullet instead of a blank, turns out, upon further examination, to be complex when that initial obvious single cause reveals causes of its own.

Take, for example, the tiny but fateful mistake made by a thirty-five-year-old naval officer named Brian Bugge who loved to scuba dive. Although he was ordinarily meticulous and attentive, on the last dive of an advanced training class, he stepped off the boat and into the ocean waters near Honolulu without having turned on the oxygen supply to his rebreather. Within minutes, he became hypoxic and drowned, his instructor and classmates just feet away.

Although his error in not turning on the oxygen supply suggests a basic failure, zoom out and we can see the multiple causes that make this failure complex. For one, the instructor was new in a hectic training program where schedules changed frequently and at the last minute. And why were buddy checks not done? Why wasn't Brian's equipment double-checked before he dove that day? Perhaps it was overconfidence. Brian was an experienced diver, and the dive took place in literally familiar territory—the class had previously dived in that exact location. Another external factor: most of the students were military officers, accustomed to respecting hierarchies, and reluctant to speak up to question the instructor's authority. Finally, according to Brian's widow, Ashley Bugge, he had felt conflicted about completing that early-Sunday-morning dive. The night before, he'd offered to forgo the dive altogether and instead spend the day with Ashley and their two small children. An avid diver herself, she'd encouraged him to go. "I looked him in the eyes and I told him to just do it," Ashley later recalled. "I told him I know [you don't] really want to quit the class."

Understandably, Ashley has since often thought about how differently things would have turned out if only she had not pushed Brian to go on that final dive and instead insisted he stay home. But, she says, "For me, it's not about who is to blame and who did this or who did that. This is not a blame game for me." This is an important point. Blaming's solitary focus takes us off the hook. It means we don't need to examine contributing factors carefully, which is essential for preventing future complex failures. This is especially true when the goal is ensuring safe operation in inherently complex settings, as explored later in this chapter.

Warning signs

Finally, complex failures are generally preceded by small warning signs that get missed, ignored, or downplayed. On the *Rust* set, although no one had been hurt when the prop guns accidentally went off the previous week, crew members who had spoken up about safety had not been taken seriously—evidently no additional safeguards or precautions had been implemented. Instead, crew members described feeling rushed to complete the movie within the required shooting schedule. Other working conditions were also suboptimal. The crew had been promised—and requested—hotel rooms in nearby Santa Fe but were instead forced to commute an hour each way from Albuquerque after working twelve- to thirteen-hour days on the movie set. Paychecks did not always arrive on time. Fed up and frustrated, five members of the camera crew composed emails the night before the shooting stating their intention to resign.

No doubt you've looked back after a significant failure to see how it could have been prevented. If only you hadn't ignored that clunky sound in the car engine before embarking on a long drive where repair shops were few and far between, you might not be standing by the side of the road. If you'd talked to your professor after doing poorly on the midterm about how to improve *and* had not had a family emergency that took up your time and attention, you would have studied more for the final exam and passed the course. Understanding why we often miss signals that warn of failure is crucial to their prevention—and will be addressed later in this chapter.

A thorough diagnosis of a complex failure usually identifies missed signals, along with giving us a deeper understanding of who and what were accountable. The engineer inspecting Champlain Towers South saw small fissures in the concrete and mild erosion in the rebar—neither clearly signaling immediate risk. Too often failure analysis is superficial, and steps taken to remedy the situation end up making it worse.

Making Matters Worse

The days and weeks that followed the *Torrey Canyon*'s breakup on the Seven Stones Reef turned a tragic failure into something much worse and even more complex. As Stephen J. Hawkins, a scientist who studied the impact of the resulting oil spill from the tanker on wildlife, put it, "The cure was worse than the malady." Looking at the chain of events—as well as the thinking—that went into what would become a series of failed attempts to halt the ongoing tragedy is instrumental. The way a multicausal failure can become twisted and difficult to uncoil, like a knotted rope that becomes more resistant to straightening the more you pull, is not unique to the *Torrey Canyon* disaster. Understanding complex failures' architecture is part of finding the keys to their prevention.

At first, *Torrey Canyon*'s owners thought the ship could be salvaged. They hired a Dutch company, which sent tugboats and rescuers on board to unload the oil into the water and pull the lightened tanker free from the rocks. Captain Rugiati and the crew bravely stayed with their ship. But the supertanker was lodged into the rocks too deeply to be pulled out; its jumbo hull continued to break apart, and oil continued to leak dangerously, threatening fire, forcing everyone ashore. Next, the British Petroleum company dumped into the water seven hundred thousand gallons of an industrial detergent called BP1002, in some cases rolling barrels of detergent off cliff tops.

No one knew how dangerous the chemicals were to ocean life. Beaches in West Cornwall were covered by what a reporter described as "a thick carpet of black goo." About fifteen thousand seabirds eventually died. The British government and the Royal Navy equivocated about how to handle the disaster, refusing at first to admit its severity, adding to the chaos. The ship was in international waters, making it unclear exactly who was in charge and what was entirely legal. Finally, ten days after its initial grounding, the Royal Navy bombed the super-tanker. Only twenty-three of the forty-one thousand-pound bombs dropped hit the target; napalm was also dropped, sending up three-mile-high plumes of black smoke that could be seen a hundred miles away. Finally, on March 30, nearly two full weeks after oil first leaked, the *Torrey Canyon* began to sink.

Large-scale crises such as that of the *Torrey Canyon* that make headlines often combine multiple smaller failures and a mix of failure types. No one knew how to control the breaking ship and the leaking oil; nor did anyone know how to cope with the tons of crude oil as it spilled across hundreds of miles of pristine coastline. One thing went wrong, followed by another and another. "Many little things added up to one big disaster." Whereas basic failures present reasonably solvable problems, complex failures, as this tragedy exemplifies, are archetypically different. Unfortunately, these perfect storms are not a thing of the past. And sometimes they unfold over decades.

Unfolding over Decades

Thirteen minutes after takeoff from the Jakarta, Indonesia, airport on October 29, 2018, Lion Air Flight 610 crashed into the Java Sea. The initial inquiry found an engineering problem with one of the Boeing 737 MAX jet's two sensors, which had mistakenly triggered an automatic system that pushed the plane's nose down hard and fast. Having descended at over five hundred miles per hour, the plane had no survivors. Back in the United States, the FAA informed Boeing that the safety risk was low enough to continue flying the 737 fleet of airplanes. Boeing was given seven months to test and revise the automatic software system and was asked to inform pilots about how to handle the malfunction should it happen again.

Problem solved?

Unfortunately, no. A mere five months later, in March 2019, another 737 MAX crashed for exactly the same reason. Ethiopian Airlines Flight 302 departed from Addis Ababa, the capital of Ethiopia, and within minutes plunged into the ground at 575 miles per hour, disintegrating upon impact. This time, the FAA grounded the entire 737 MAX fleet. Deeper and more extensive investigations would soon find multiple causes for this complex failure. Certainly, the engineering design and the new software system were suboptimal—significant causes in understanding how these failures occurred. But if you look harder, Boeing's culture along with its broader industry environment played crucial roles in these failures, presenting a classic case of complex failure.

I read these headlines in 2019 with a grim sense of familiarity. My academic career had been devoted to understanding preventable failures in complex organizations. As with the gun that misfired on the *Rust* set and the scuba diving oxygen tank that was not properly set, it's tempting to chalk up the two crashes to software bugs that led automatic sensors to malfunction. Idiosyncratic failures in complex technology. But as before, look more closely and you will see some of the usual culprits defining complex failure: multiple causes in a reasonably familiar setting, with its false sense of security; missed signals; and interactive complexity in a shifting business environment. At times I simply cannot bear the frequency of this recurring story. My research has shed light on why it happens—on the cognitive, interpersonal, and organizational causes that make complex failures so thorny. This multiplicity of factors also means you have many levers with which to interrupt the otherwise inexorable flow toward failure. It means that any one of us can become a complex-failure *preventer*.

The silver lining in every perfect storm is this: each complex failure contains multiple opportunities for prevention. Think about that missed doctor's appointment: all you needed was either to double-check your alarm clock is set for a.m. or to fill the gas tank the night before. One fix would have prevented the failure. With that in mind, think of all the complex failures you've likely prevented.

Sometimes, one must go back decades to understand the origins of a complex failure—and thereby to identify the many opportunities for prevention. For causes of the 737 MAX crashes, we can point to a significant factor back in 1997, the year that Boeing acquired its chief American competitor, McDonnell Douglas, for $13.3 billion in stock. Soon, leadership changes accompanying the acquisition (another cause) resulted in a company culture shift from Boeing's historical emphasis on engineering (valuing invention and precision) to McDonnell Douglas's historical emphasis on finance (prioritizing profits and shareholder value). Before the acquisition, Boeing's top executives tended to come from engineering backgrounds, sharing a common technical language and sensibility with Boeing employees. Not incidentally, the shared engineering sensibility helped engineers throughout the organization feel safe enough to raise concerns about, for example, problems with an aircraft's speed, design, fuel efficiency, and, especially, safety. Engineers and executives could and did interact informally outside of work to discuss new ideas or suggestions. Post-acquisition, top executives tended to have backgrounds in finance and accounting; journalist Natasha Frost derisively described them as "bean counters" for their lack of technical understanding of how aircrafts function. Exacerbating this change in culture, corporate headquarters moved from Seattle to Chicago in 2001. Senior executives now worked more than two thousand miles away from the engineers designing the planes, further estranging the two groups.

Fast-forward to 2010. That was the year Airbus, Boeing's largest European competitor, unveiled its new A320 jet (fourth cause), promising a significantly more cost-effective aircraft due to its improved fuel efficiency. Boeing's top management were stunned—Airbus had developed its new jet in complete secrecy—and rightly feared that Boeing could lose loyal customers. You can see how the scene was set for the disaster that followed. Stage right: a culture that disempowers engineers and empowers the bean counters. Stage left: a competitive threat that could lead to negative financial consequences for shareholders and thus to reputational damage. From here, the script is maddeningly predictable.

In response to the unexpected Airbus threat, Boeing executives decided against expensive and lengthy research to design an entirely new model in favor of updating their existing 737 airplanes. Suddenly, speed to market mattered most. The executives promised that the new 737 MAX would be 8 percent more fuel efficient than the new Airbus. In theory, the executives' idea—to adapt an existing design in reasonably familiar territory rather than risking the inevitable intelligent failures that brand-new innovation would entail—was a prudent use of resources. In reality, the engineering challenge of modifying the 737 was considerable. To accommodate the newer, more fuel-efficient engines, the engineers had to shift the engines' location "farther forward and higher on the wing," which affected the way the plane handled when climbing at a steep angle. To compensate for the new aerodynamics, the engineers created an automated stall-prevention system, called MCAS.

Here's where the conflicts between Boeing's engineers and management became consequential. FAA regulations required pilots to undergo simulator training when an aircraft design differed considerably from prior models. Simulator training was expensive, a problem for airlines (those loyal customers), because it took valuable resources (pilots) offline. To circumvent the regulation, Boeing managers came up with a clever, if ethically problematic, strategy to downplay the 737 MAX's design differences by deemphasizing the MCAS software and its difficulties for pilots. They did not mention the new MCAS stall-prevention system in the pilot manual. The chief technical pilot felt pressured to state that simulator training was unnecessary. Only after the second crash did previous emails between engineers who had expressed safety concerns become public. One employee had written, "Would you put your family on a MAX? . . . I wouldn't." Another engineer claimed that managers had turned down his proposed design upgrades due to "cost and potential [pilot] training impact." In a classic description of what it's like to work in an organization with low psychological safety, an engineer wrote, "There is a suppressive cultural attitude towards criticism of corporate policy—especially if that criticism comes as a result of fatal accidents."

As is often the case in large organizations, a "suppressive cultural attitude toward criticism" was not limited to those directly involved with the malfunctioning 737 jets. Intense scrutiny after the two fatal crashes found that workers in the Boeing 787 Dreamliner plant in South Carolina felt pressure to stick to an overly ambitious production schedule and were fearful of losing their jobs if they raised quality concerns. Although they did not work at the facility where the ill-fated 737s were produced, the South Carolina workers' experience presented a textbook case of a widespread belief among employees that speaking up would trigger retribution rather than appreciation. In December 2019, a little over a year after the first Lion Air crash, Boeing fired its CEO and halted production of the 737 MAX. Its stock dropped; the company's worth plummeted. Worse, three years later, the U.S. Department of Justice charged Boeing with criminal fraud, costing the company more than $2.5 billion in fines and compensation to victims.

It's tempting to look at the *Torrey Canyon* and 737 MAX failures and feel angry. But keep in mind that hindsight is twenty-twenty. How to do better is obvious in retrospect. What each of us must take to heart is that uncertainty and interdependence in almost every aspect of our lives today means that complex failure is on the rise. Academic research can help us understand why. It can, as you will see, also help us do better. Once you understand the factors and what they mean for your organization and your life, it may at first feel daunting—but it is in fact empowering. Seeing the world around you for its *complex-failure propensity* sets you up well to navigate the uncertain future ahead.

Complex Failure on the Rise

The most obvious cause of modern complex failures is the increasingly complex information technology (IT) that underlies every aspect of life and work today. Factories, supply chains, and operations in many other industries rely on sophisticated computer controls where a small glitch in one part of a system can spiral out of control. You may remember when a credit-reporting company named Equifax reported that the Social Security numbers, addresses, and credit card numbers of nearly 150 million Americans had been stolen from the company's software platform. According to CEO Richard Smith's congressional testimony in October 2017, the "breach occurred because of both human error and technology failures." Hackers gained log-in credentials for three servers, which enabled access to forty-eight additional servers. The complex failure escalated because the breach went undetected for seventy-six days, giving hackers ample time to roam the system, extracting personal information as well as high-level information about Equifax's data design and infrastructure.

Maybe you've lost valuable information stored on a personal computer because you neglected to back up data even though you knew a backup was important. Hopefully the consequences of losing the data are not as dire as those experienced by a Welsh systems engineer named James Howells. In 2013, he accidentally threw away a hard drive belonging to an old computer (the hard drive extracted after a spilled lemonade had destroyed this gaming laptop of his), only to realize, too late, that he'd lost the sixty-four-character private key that would unlock what had begun as his modest bitcoin investment. Despite his relentless efforts for permission to retrieve his precious hard drive from the municipal landfill, eight years later he had not been able to claim the half billion dollars the bitcoin was then worth.

Social media has altered business, politics, and friendships, making *going viral* a household term. The global financial industry links every bank, and countless households in every country, making us vulnerable to human error taking place on the other side of the world. As my friend Columbia University strategy professor Rita McGrath explains, years ago most of our institutions were separate and thereby buffered from the effects of errors outside their walls. No longer. The digitization of massive amounts of information has continued to grow exponentially as the cost of computing power has decreased. The development of smart systems that communicate independently gave rise to an infinite variety of potential breakdowns. This interdependence is a breeding ground for complex failure. As Rita puts it, when "things that used to be kept separate bump up against other each (in other words, when once-*complicated* systems become *complex*) it becomes far more difficult to predict what's going to happen next." IT creates new vulnerabilities because interconnectedness instantly spreads the impact of small failures.

We don't have to look any further than the 2019 coronavirus that originated in Wuhan, China, and spread quickly around the world to find examples of how global interconnectedness makes complex failures more likely. Consider this small example. In early 2020, when the demand for protective masks suddenly spiked worldwide, factories in China began ramping up production, loading them onto cargo boats, and shipping them far and wide. As a result, empty shipping containers piled up in those far-flung countries right when China needed them most to export more masks.

Contact tracing, the attempt to limit the virus's spread by locating the people with whom an infected person has had contact so as to isolate all parties, stems from the recognition of complex failures. Each infected or exposed person is potentially one in a multitude of causes for the failure that is an ongoing pandemic. My friends Chris Clearfield and András Tilcsik literally wrote the book on complex failure and why it's on the rise. *Meltdown*, their engaging, and at times terrifying, book explains the "shared DNA of nuclear accidents, Twitter disasters, oil spills, Wall Street failures, and even wrongdoing." Like me, Chris and András were influenced by sociologist Charles Perrow, who identified risk factors that make certain kinds of systems vulnerable to breakdowns.

How Systems Spawn Complex Failures

The thinking that eventually developed into my framework for categorizing failure began to take shape thirty years ago. My research had been asking why medical errors persisted, even in top-notch hospitals—and even after expert and public attention to the problem had exploded. The discovery of the prevalence of unintended harm in hospitals came as a shock to the public and medical professionals alike in the late 1990s. Such errors in U.S. hospitals have been estimated to cause a quarter of a million unnecessary patient deaths annually. How could so many well-trained and well-intended health-care workers who professed to do no harm persist in doing so? Much of the reason, I found, lies in the nature of complex failure.

My engineering background had made me a fan of Perrow's groundbreaking book *Normal Accidents*, first published in 1984, which had a lasting influence on experts' thinking about safety and risk. Perrow focused on how *systems*, rather than individuals, produce consequential failures. The importance of that distinction cannot be underestimated. Understanding how systems produce failures—and especially which kinds of systems are especially failure-prone—helps take blame out of the equation. It also helps us to focus on reducing failure by changing the system rather than by changing or replacing an individual who works in a faulty system.

I turned to Perrow's work to help me figure out the persistence of medical accidents. Perrow described a *normal accident*—a term intended to provoke—as a predictable (that is, normal) consequence of a system with interactive complexity and tight coupling. *Interactive complexity* means multiple parts interact in ways that make the consequences of actions difficult to predict. For instance, slightly altering his ship's course put Captain Rugiati on a path where the sudden appearance of two lobster boats required a subsequent sudden and difficult-to-execute turn, culminating in a fatal accident. *Tight coupling*, a term borrowed from engineering, means that an action in one part of the system leads inexorably to a reaction in another part; it's not possible to interrupt the chain of events. When a bank ATM's mechanical hardware takes your bank card, the software that controls the machine and the banking application are tightly coupled, working together to complete your transaction. If any one component fails, so does the entire system. Tightly coupled systems have no slack.

For Perrow, calling an accident *normal* meant that certain systems function as accidents waiting to happen. Their design makes them dangerous. It is simply a matter of time before such systems fail. In contrast, a system with low interactive complexity and loose coupling—say, an elementary school—would not be prone to normal accidents. If a system had high complexity but lacked tight coupling (say, a large university with many academic departments that operate relatively independently), things could go wrong in one part without automatically triggering a major failure in the whole system.

As Perrow's students Chris and András pointed out in *Meltdown*, over time more and more of our institutions have moved into Perrow's danger zone: "When Perrow published *Normal Accidents* in 1984, the danger zone he described was sparse. It included systems like nuclear facilities and chemical plants and space missions. Since then, all kinds of systems—from universities and Wall Street firms to dams and oil rigs—have become more complex and tightly coupled."

Perrow was writing in the aftermath of the near meltdown at Pennsylvania's Three Mile Island nuclear power plant in 1979, a highly visible failure that got people's attention. As a sociologist rather than a nuclear engineer, Perrow may have missed some technical nuances when he assessed nuclear power plants as tightly coupled and inter-actively complex, making them inherently unsafe—an assessment later experts have challenged. But his framework helped many of us who were interested in safety and accidents to think about the con-texts we studied in new and useful ways. Figure 4.1 presents Perrow's classic model, with new labels I created for each quadrant. The upper right captures Perrow's core idea that interactive complexity and tight coupling, such as are found in nuclear power plants, create a *danger zone*. Perrow used railroads to illustrate the combination of tight cou-pling and linear interactions in what I call the *control zone*. A typical

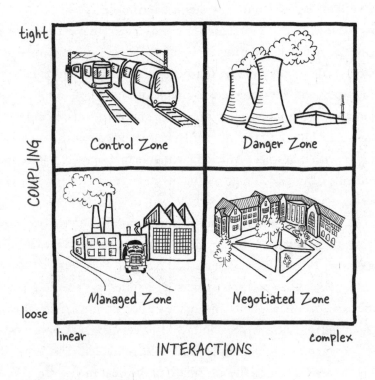

FIGURE 4.1: Perrow's Model Revisited

manufacturing plant presents loose coupling and linear interactions. Because classic management works extremely well in such contexts, I refer to this as the *managed zone*. Lastly, complex interactions combine with loose coupling in a university, with its ongoing negotiations to keep things organized and functioning, giving rise to what I call the *negotiated zone*.

In my study of medical accidents, I wondered if systems of patient care in hospitals were interactively complex and tightly coupled. If the answer to both was yes, then according to Perrow's framework, patient care failures in hospitals were simply inevitable and irreducible.

Loose coupling in hospitals

Back in 1996, my answers to these questions were yes and no. Today, my answers remain unchanged. Hospital-based patient care offers considerable interactive complexity. For example, a physician writes a prescription that gets filled by a pharmacist, delivered to the floor by someone else, and administered by several nurses during the hospital stay. I determined, however, that the links in this chain are loosely coupled. A failure in one part of the system can be caught and corrected at any time. This is the silver lining for complex failure here: the handoffs are human. I concluded that hospitals did not fall into Perrow's worst-case quadrant. That meant that it should be possible to achieve zero harm.

Nonetheless, system failures continued to happen, so 1 decided to look more closely into this. I learned that loose coupling doesn't preclude systems from breaking down. It just means it's possible to catch and correct errors before a complex failure occurs. Let's take a real example from my research in hospitals. A ten-year-old boy, whom I'll call Matthew, is mistakenly given a potentially fatal morphine dose. Matthew becomes the victim of a complex failure created by a handful of individually innocuous factors.

A complex failure unfolds

In my analysis, I identified seven factors that contributed to the accident. Overflow conditions (first factor) in the ICU meant that Matthew was placed after surgery in a regular medical unit, with less specialized staff. A newly graduated (second factor) nurse on duty in the unit leaned in to program the electronic infusion pump, located in a dark corner of the room (third factor), to release the prescribed amount of morphine to help reduce postsurgical pain. Unfamiliar with the device (fourth factor), the nurse asked a colleague for help. The colleague, an experienced nurse, was in a rush (fifth factor) but stopped to help, studying the machine's dials. Programming the pump required entering two values correctly: the morphine concentration and the rate of infusion. The label had been printed in the pharmacy and wrapped around the drug's cassette container in a way that partly obscured the concentration (sixth factor). The experienced nurse used the visible information to calculate and program the machine with what she believed was the correct concentration. The first nurse looked over the shoulder of the second to check the numbers, rather than independently carrying out his own calculations (seventh factor). Each of these seven factors presented a unique prevention opportunity.

Within minutes, Matthew's face began to turn blue, his breathing visibly distressed. The first nurse turned off the infusion machine, called for the doctor, and began ventilating the child with a breathing bag. The doctor arrived within minutes and confirmed that Matthew had been given a morphine overdose—several times more than was appropriate. The quick-thinking doctor administered a drug to reverse the effect, and within seconds Matthew's breathing returned to normal.

Removing any one of the contributing factors could have averted this nonfatal, but still consequential, medical failure. This tiny perfect storm of slightly unusual events lined up to allow a failure despite the well-intended hard work of all participants. Health-care error experts today use what's called the Swiss cheese model to explain this kind of system failure.

Swiss cheese

Introduced in 1990 by Dr. James Reason, an error expert at the University of Manchester in the UK, the Swiss cheese model calls attention to the defenses that normally prevent consequential failures in complex systems such as hospitals. Holes in the Swiss cheese are likened to small process defects or errors. A hole in your block of Swiss cheese can be seen as a flaw—an empty space that does not contribute to your nutrition. Fortunately, the holes in the cheese are discrete and contained, says Reason, leaving the cheese intact. But occasionally, the holes line up, creating a tunnel—a line of defects that compound and end in a consequential accident. If a nurse hadn't immediately noticed Matthew's distress, the sequence of causal events might have ended in a far worse failure, one that could not have been reversed.

Picturing the cheese with its holes helps us appreciate the role of chance and the ever-present opportunity to catch and correct small defects before they accumulate in a catastrophic way. Reason emphasized that system failures are common but can be (and usually are) prevented by a system's many defensive layers. If you go into the office of a hospital executive today, don't be surprised if you see a little spongy replica of a Swiss cheese wedge. It's there to remind everyone that things can go wrong and so must be noticed and stopped before harm occurs.

To aim for zero harm in complex systems such as hospitals is not the same as aiming to erase human error. To err is human. Error will always be with us. But we can design social systems that make everyone aware of the inevitability of error and poised to catch and correct it before it causes harm. That means understanding that Swiss cheese holes sometimes line up—despite being separated by time or distance—to create a tunnel through which complex failure flows unimpeded.

Complex failures range from the small to the catastrophic. Their complexity, along with their increased prevalence, may make us pessimistic about preventing them. But a growing body of knowledge can help. It starts with an academic theory introduced in 1989 as an explicit rebuttal to Perrow's notion that certain systems are simply too dangerous to operate safely.

How to Reduce Complex Failures

The problem with Perrow's idea that organizations could not safely function with interactive complexity and tight coupling was that so many such organizations did in fact function without mishap for years, even decades. Nuclear power plants operated without incident nearly all the time. So did air traffic control systems, nuclear aircraft carriers, and a host of other inherently risky operations. A small group of researchers led by Karlene Roberts at the University of California, Berkeley, set out to study how they did it. What they discovered was more behavioral than technical.

The term *high reliability organization*, or HRO, captures the essence of the theory. HROs are reliably safe because of how they make everyone in them feel accountable to one another for practices that consistently catch and correct deviations to prevent major harm. *Vigilance* is one word for it. But it's more than that.

To me the most interesting part of HRO research is the observation that rather than downplaying failure, people in HROs are *obsessed* with failure. My colleagues Karl Weick, Kathie Sutcliffe, and David Obstfeld wrote a seminal paper highlighting the culture of HROs as preoccupied with failure, reluctant to simplify, acutely sensitive to ongoing operations (quick to detect subtle unexpected changes), committed to resilience (catching and correcting error, rather than expecting error-free operations), and valuing expertise over rank. In other words, HROs are weird places. Rather than holding back to see what the boss is thinking, people there don't hesitate to speak up immediately. A frontline associate, to avert a crisis, can tell the CEO what to do. Failure is clearly seen as an ever-present risk that can nonetheless be consistently averted.

From the research on complex systems, human error, and HROs, I take away that complex failure is a worthy foe. We should not underestimate the challenge that lies ahead—but nor should we shy away from it. Whether you're more intrigued by the Swiss cheese model or the cultural attributes of HROs, the consistent message that runs through these expert perspectives is that we *can* reduce the occurrence of complex failures in our lives by following a set of simple (not easy!) practices, starting with learning as much as you can from the complex failures that have already occurred.

Learn from past complex failures

Catastrophic complex failures often become the wake-up calls that spark investigation and change in training, technology, or regulations. Shortly after the *Torrey Canyon* disaster, international emergency entities set new rules that required more protection for oil tankers in both construction (double hulls instead of single hulls) and new equipment to better control the oil. Shipowners became strictly liable, where previously they had been liable only through negligence. The Oil Pollution Act the United States passed in 1990 set up legal processes for responding to catastrophic oil spills, regulations around oil storage, and requirements to plan for emergencies. Today, we know much more about cleaning up oil spills with less toxic ingredients and when to leave affected areas alone, in part because of what was learned from how France handled the *Torrey Canyon* oil slicks that reached their shore: detergent was not used, marine life was not as badly affected, and the oil was broken up more effectively.

The *Torrey Canyon* spill spurred awareness and activism in the 1970s that led directly to today's environmental movement. Volunteers flooded beaches in attempts to rescue and clean oil-covered birds. Reporters and marine biologists drew public attention to the deaths of not only seabirds, but to most of the marine life from the south coast of Britain to the Normandy shores of France. Fifty years later, Martin Attrill, director of the Marine Institute at Plymouth University, explained how the failure changed how we think about natural resources: "At the time the *Torrey Canyon* went down we were still considering the sea as the main place to put all our waste. It was 'the environment can deal with this,' and the main concern was for the ship and whether it could be salvaged." Likewise, Halyna Hutchins's accidental death invigorated discussion in the film industry about stricter rules and oversight for handling firearms on set. Today, people in the scuba diving community are actively building a stricter safety culture to prevent drownings like Brian Bugge's.

Although post-catastrophe investigations are important, the rise in frequency and severity of complex failures means we can't afford to act only in their aftermath. Reducing complex failures starts with paying attention to what I call *ambiguous threats*. Whereas clear threats (a Category 5 hurricane will hit your neighborhood tomorrow) readily trigger corrective action (evacuate your house), we tend to downplay ambiguous threats—missing chances to prevent harm. Downplaying ambiguous threats is the opposite of what occurs in high reliability organizations. I've observed this downplaying in settings ranging from the NASA Space Shuttle program to Wall Street to pharmaceutical drug development. What do to these disparate settings have in common in addition to complexity? High stakes and a drive to succeed—a drive so powerful it blinds people to subtle warning signals.

Pay attention to early warnings

On February 1, 2003, *Columbia*, the oldest orbiter in NASA's Space Shuttle program fleet of five, broke apart reentering Earth's atmosphere, killing all seven astronauts. Later investigation found that a large piece of insulated foam had dislodged from the shuttle's external tank at launch, hitting the shuttle and creating a large hole in the wing, which doomed the mission. Maybe some of you remember where you were when you heard this news—or that of the *Challenger* launch fiasco, seventeen years earlier. I remember those moments vividly, in part because of a dawning sense of dread that these were the kinds of failures that might have been prevented.

Sometimes, as you have no doubt experienced, failures come out of the blue—meaning no one saw them coming or even worried a little about the possibility. The *Columbia* failure was not one of those.

On January 17, 2003, the day after *Columbia*'s seemingly successful launch and fifteen days before it broke apart, Rodney Rocha, a NASA engineer, pored over launch video. Something didn't look right. Seeing a grainy speck in the video, Rocha could not be sure what it was, but he worried that a chunk of insulating foam might have fallen off the shuttle's external tank and struck its left wing. In short, he'd identified an ambiguous threat. An early warning signal. To find out more, he wanted images of the shuttle's wing from spy satellites, which could only be obtained by asking the Department of Defense for help. Rocha's request for images was turned down by NASA managers, largely because of a general conviction that small bits of foam were not dangerous. Had those wing images been obtained, disaster might have been avoided.

An ambiguous threat is just that: ambiguous. It *could* be a real threat of failure, or it could be nothing. Your car may run without mishap, your teen may act responsibly, and the stock market dip may be nothing. In retrospect, the erosion seen in the engineer's Champlain Towers South inspection seems a clear signal of imminent collapse—but at the time it was undeniably ambiguous. Ambiguous threats are problematic because of the natural human tendency to downplay them. It's natural, and more pleasant, to assume nothing's wrong and to adopt a wait-and-see attitude. Perhaps you've heard of confirmation bias—our tendency to see what we expect, thereby reinforcing an existing belief or prediction by paying attention to confirming data and failing to notice disconfirming data. Becoming more self-aware, as you will see in the next chapter, is one element of learning to notice early warnings—and to actively seeking disconfirming data, just in case. But it's natural to adopt a wait-and-see attitude instead of getting curious and taking a closer look at some subtle signal of irregularity. The financial industry turned a collective blind eye to the risk of mortgage-backed securities, composed of shaky loans granted to people with neither assets nor income to ensure repayment. When the housing bubble burst, it triggered another perfect storm as a vast web of financial assets linked to mortgages collapsed in value. Boeing executives downplayed the risk of new software's malfunctioning to evade costly pilot training. In my research, I've found that it's natural to downplay subtle signals of risk, but that doesn't mean we don't care. Our confidence that things won't fail is reinforced by hope, expectations, and prior experiences that things mostly operate as they should.

An advantage of studying failures in the public sector is the availability of information. After the U.S. government's *Columbia* Accident Investigation Board (CAIB) released a lengthy and detailed report on August 26, 2003, my colleague Mike Roberto and I set out to analyze the shuttle failure from an organizational perspective. We soon added another colleague to the team, physician Richard Bohmer, and spent many months studying transcripts and email correspondence surrounding the *Columbia* disaster. Eventually we identified (and named) the phenomenon of ambiguous threats as essential to understanding what had happened. An ambiguous threat emerges when at least one person detects a potential risk—one that is by no means clear-cut. Your car engine is making a funny sound, which might mean it will break down soon or might mean nothing. Your teenager is attending large parties where alcohol may be present. A rise in housing foreclosures might signal a financial collapse. Rodney Rocha saw a grainy speck in a video.

The Space Shuttle program's many years of success—a streak of more than 110 successful missions in the seventeen years since the *Challenger*'s launch failure—leading up to the *Columbia* mission contributed to the ease with which NASA management downplayed the ambiguous threat. The engineers lacked adequate data but thought the video might indicate a larger and later (that is, faster) piece of foam hurtling toward the shuttle's wing. Senior managers viewed foam strikes as maintenance issues that were annoying but not catastrophic. The strength of management's shared belief effectively blocked further exploration.

Human cognition and organizational systems both conspire to suppress subtle signals of danger, making complex failures more likely. NASA managers dismissed the engineers' concerns because the managers' brains and protocols reinforced the conviction that foam strikes were, at worst, a nuisance. Shuttle missions had returned safely to Earth for years despite small foam strikes. The same cognitive factors explain why so many leaders failed to grasp that a novel coronavirus could bring the world to a standstill and cause millions of unnecessary deaths. Had they been able to recognize the threat of COVID-19 more readily, they could have instituted preventive public health measures sooner and with greater conviction.

Given the inherent challenge of responding to ambiguous threats, what can we do to prevent the complex failures in our lives? To answer that question, let's take a look at some unusual organizations that do it well.

Leverage the recovery window

To counteract our tendency to downplay ambiguous threats, think about the window of opportunity in which recovery is still feasible before a complex failure occurs. The window opens when someone detects a signal—however weak—that a failure may lie ahead. It closes when the failure occurs. Recovery windows can last anywhere from minutes to months. When recognized, they present crucial opportunities to identify, evaluate, and respond—first to learn more about what's happening and then to take corrective action. For example, had NASA requested satellite images, it would have been clear that foam-strike damage posed a real danger to the crew. Instead, NASA squandered the recovery window. Similarly, the week between the first time a firearm went off accidentally on the film set of *Rust* and the tragic accident that resulted in Halyna Hutchins's death presented a recovery window that was squandered. Ditto for the months between the first and the second Boeing MAX crashes, despite pilots filing four reports of concerns to NASA's anonymous reporting system, ASRS. Simulator training for pilots subsequently flying the new Boeing 737 MAX would have provided experience with malfunctions of the MCAS system to help pilots respond when the plane began to nosedive.

Recovery windows can be seen as valuable opportunities for fast learning. This is true even when a threat turns out to be benign. For example, parents' frank discussion with their teens about the dangers of drinking and driving and letting them know that it's okay to call anytime for a ride home with no questions asked is a smart response to an ambiguous threat and may prevent a tragic accident. But these windows depend on a willingness to speak up without certainty that a failure may lie ahead. This is one way that a psychologically safe environment helps prevent the wrong kind of wrong.

Welcome false alarms

How can we sense complex failures before they happen? The very nature of complex failures—their multiple factors interacting in unique, unprecedented ways—makes that idea seem a fool's errand. Yet there are simple, elegant ways to try.

It starts with changing your attitude about false alarms.

Recall that any worker in a Toyota factory can pull an Andon Cord to alert a team leader of a possible error before it turns into a production failure. The team leader and team member examine the potential problem, however small, and together either fix or dismiss the threat. If only one of twelve pulls of the Andon Cord stops the assembly line for a genuine problem, you might think the company would be upset by wasting supervisors' time chasing the eleven false alarms.

It turns out that the opposite is true. A pulled Andon Cord that does *not* identify an actual error is framed as a useful drill. The false alarm is instead experienced as a valuable learning moment, a welcome education on how things go wrong and how to adjust so as to reduce that possibility. This is not a cultural nuance. It's a practical approach. Every Andon Cord pull is seen as a valuable episode that in the long run saves time and promotes quality.

A similar approach is at work in a fascinating health-care innovation called the rapid response team (RRT). Designed to respond to calls for assistance from a bedside nurse who observes a subtle change in a patient (say, in skin pallor or mood) that might—but equally might not—indicate an imminent danger such as a heart attack, RRTs bring specialized physicians and nurses together at the bedside within minutes to assess the situation and intervene if necessary. Prior to the introduction of RRTs, nurses would only request an external team for actual emergencies, such as a real heart attack—triggering a full code blue response to revive a patient in serious medical distress.

Initially implemented in Australia two decades ago, RRTs reduced the frequency of heart attacks. Ten years later, Mike Roberto, David Ager, and I supervised an award-winning undergraduate honors thesis at Harvard, carried out by Jason Park, on four hospitals in the United States that were early adopters of rapid response teams. We began to see RRTs as a tool for amplifying ambiguous threats. Just as people speaking to crowds through a megaphone amplify their voice, so do RRTs and Andon Cords amplify ambiguous signals of a complex failure. Amplify does not mean exaggerate; it just helps a quiet signal be heard.

Amplifying an ambiguous threat that something might be amiss for a patient ultimately led to a reduction in heart failures. First, it made it less likely that nurses—frontline workers with relatively less clout in the hospital hierarchy—would be ignored if they reported an early warning signal about, for example, changes in a patient's breathing or cognition. RRTs legitimized such calls. Second, even inexperienced nurses felt more secure about speaking up if something about a patient didn't look or feel right—even a change in mood might be enough.

You probably remember "The Boy Who Cried Wolf," Aesop's fable in which a shepherd boy warns frequently but falsely of an arriving wolf. When a wolf finally does show up, no one listens, and all the sheep (and in some versions the boy) are devoured. The message to countless generations of children? Maybe it was supposed to be "don't lie," but it seems to me many of us internalized the message as "don't speak up unless you're sure."

No one wants to be viewed as stupid for calling attention to a feeling that turns out to be nothing. I'm sure you can think of a time when you held back from mentioning a concern for fear it was a false alarm. Perhaps you thought that people would laugh or think you were naïve for bringing it up. It's always easier to wait to see if someone else mentions it. To help overcome this ubiquitous tendency, best practices for RRTs included a list of early warning signals nurses could consult to legitimize their calls. This list helped nurses build on their vague hunch—because they'd simply be following the protocol. When the RRT showed up, it brought more trained eyes to the bedside to assess whether the patient was failing.

This is more than vigilance. When people are given permission to amplify and assess weak signals (such as with an Andon Cord or a rapid response team), they are invited to engage wholeheartedly in the work—to embrace its inherently uncertain nature, to believe that their own eyes and ears and brains matter. Well-designed RRT systems err on the side of inclusion to emphasize that the time taken to diagnose is a worthy investment if fatalities can be reduced. The sooner a problem in the making is noticed, the more leverage you have for solving it and averting harm. A Stanford study found a 71 percent reduction in code blues (a code blue is a tortuous and often unsuccessful process to rescue patients suffering cardiac arrest) following RRT implementation, along with a 16 percent reduction in risk-adjusted mortality.* Interestingly, other studies have failed to find an improvement. Why the difference?

It is not enough to simply announce an RRT program. It matters how the effort is framed. If hospital staff expect RRTs to uncover a hidden fatal threat every time one is called, everyone will soon tire of the false alarms and the program will peter out. However, if false alarms are celebrated as useful training sessions that build teaming skills, then, just as at Toyota, false alarms not only don't feel wasteful, they feel valuable. In his insightful book *Know What You Don't Know*, Mike Roberto has described the mindset shift underlying RRTs as one of detecting smoke rather than fighting fire.

How would you apply this idea in your team—or family? It's as simple as learning to appreciate others for speaking up with a concern—whether that concern turns out to be real or imagined. Thanking people for taking the micro-risk of speaking up without certainty reinforces the behavior and periodically averts serious accidents.

Think beyond the thing

Catching and correcting mistakes to make truly safe workplaces, whether in a factory, hospital, or aircraft, requires a culture of vigilance. Adopting Andon Cords to prevent small mistakes from becoming big

---

*In health care, risk adjustment takes the severity of patients' conditions into consideration when comparing quality performance across groups in a study.

mistakes helps build such a culture, as do consequences for sleeping on the job. Because we know for sure that things do go wrong.

I recently interviewed Aaron Dimmock, a former navy pilot, about a time when he successfully avoided a complex failure. As a retired Naval Air Training and Operating Procedures Standardization instructor pilot, Dimmock flew countless operational and training missions, including those designed to assess aircraft readiness. He told me about a routine maintenance flight in Puerto Rico some years ago, when he and his team had to check whether the aircraft was working well enough to be operational. In addition to Aaron, the crew consisted of a second pilot, a flight engineer, and an observer.

Four unexpected problems occurred on the flight: (1) after takeoff, the landing gear wouldn't go all the way up; (2) an engine that was supposed to restart after shutdown did not restart; (3) a second engine began to malfunction; and (4) the landing gear malfunctioned on the way down. Had these deviations lined up, Swiss cheese fashion, the resulting complex failure would likely have meant a crash, a massive loss of equipment, or even crew fatalities. Instead, Aaron and his crew landed safely because they took corrective action at each of the Swiss cheese holes. How, I asked, did they do that?

Aaron explained that in each of the instances where something had gone wrong, he and his team were able to "think beyond the thing." Instead of getting stuck in "the thing," or the immediate error, they were able to "think beyond" and work together to do what's called catch and correct.

Let's break that down. First, they noticed in each instance that something had gone wrong—with the landing gear or the engines. That's the *catch* part of the operation. Second, they responded to each error systematically and carefully as it occurred. "We feel confident, but not overconfident," he continued, "and we are able to keep calm in the aircraft so that all four of us are able to contribute to the conversation. 'What is the engine looking like? What do you hear?' All four of us share as accurately as we can what we are seeing, and then we put those pieces of information together to make a decision. We have a safe space within which we challenge each other and share."

That's the *correct* part of catch and correct.

"I have to ensure that everyone has a voice," Aaron said when I asked him about his most important responsibility as a team leader. "There were times when it was awesome to have the flight engineer's opinion, but there were a couple times where he treated his perspective as the end-all be-all." That was when Aaron intervened. He asked others on the crew to offer their view. "Tom, what do you think?" "Petty Officer Robbins, what about you?" This is an important point about psychological safety: it needs to be cultivated lest crucial voices be lost. Making sure that everyone is heard is not a matter of good manners or inclusivity for its own sake. Rather, it's what helps to keep an aircraft in the air and to safely land it.

In contrast, in the lead-up to the *Columbia* shuttle launch, compounding the risks of space travel was an organizational culture that made it hard for engineer Rodney Rocha to speak up. Meeting transcripts show clearly that NASA managers did not actively seek dissenting views. Engineers reported feeling all but unable to talk candidly about potential threats, to raise tough questions, or to express views at odds with their bosses'. Ditto for engineers at Boeing before the MAX failures.

Embracing the Possibility of Failure to Reduce the Occurrence of Failure

My decades-long fascination with error, harm, and failure has left me humble about the complexity of these topics. The mix of factors—technology, psychology, management, systems—means none of us can master every aspect of the relevant knowledge to feel "we've got this." But a few simple practices have emerged from my work that can help prevent complex failures. With these, we all have the power to make that kind of difference—in our own lives and in the organizations we care about.

It starts with *framing*. Explicitly emphasizing the complexity or novelty of a situation helps put you in the right state of mind. Otherwise, we tend to expect things to go right. "I've never done a perfect flight," said Captain Ben Berman, whom you will meet again in chapter 6. Understanding that subordinates in his crew may hesitate to speak up because of his rank, he reduces that risk by letting them know he expects that he will make mistakes. He frames the arguably routine flight that lies ahead as anything but.

Next, make sure to *amplify*, rather than suppress, weak signals. Imagine standing in front of a crowd and trying to be heard. Your lone voice is caught in the wind. Your words are lost. You need a megaphone for people to hear you. The same is true in any team, organization, or family. Given what we know of the human tendency to ignore (on the set of *Rust*) or downplay (with Boeing's 737 MAX jets; with the *Columbia* foam) weak signals that can portend complex failures, it's up to us to amplify them just long enough to hear what they have to say. Amplify doesn't mean exaggerate or dwell on it endlessly; it simply means *make sure a signal can be heard*. And if its message ends up being "all is well," we must learn to be nonetheless glad we asked.

Finally, make a habit of *practicing*. Musicians, athletes, public speakers, and actors all rehearse before a performance to be as prepared as possible. In organizations with spectacular safety records—such as Alcoa under Paul O'Neill—don't be surprised if you see people routinely doing dry runs, drills, or practice sessions. They don't have great records because they somehow figured out how to eliminate human error. No. They have great records because they catch and correct error. That takes practice. It also helps to build a culture that celebrates it. Aircraft simulators, fire drills, active-shooter drills, and rapid response teams are all examples of rehearsing so as to be better prepared to respond to problems when they do occur. It's not possible to develop contingency plans for every failure. But it is possible to build the emotional and behavioral muscles that allow us to respond to human error and unexpected events alike with speed and grace.

All three of these practices are enabled and enhanced by competencies I refer to as self-awareness, situation awareness, and system awareness—the topics we turn to next.

PART TWO

PRACTICING THE SCIENCE

OF FAILING WELL

CHAPTER 5

We Have Met the Enemy

Between stimulus and response there is a space. In
that space is our power to choose our response. In
our response lies our growth and our freedom.

—Attributed to Viktor E. Frankl

He bet every penny he had on an economic prediction that turned out to be entirely wrong. An entrepreneur with enviable energy and brains, armed with an MBA from Harvard, Ray Dalio had learned to expect success. Bridgewater Associates, the investment business he founded at the age of twenty-six, had enjoyed seven years of phenomenal returns, making Dalio a frequent guest on national business news programs discussing the economy or the stock market. He was especially proud of his ability to accurately predict long-term trends. Now, in 1982, at the age of thirty-three, he suddenly found himself unable to pay his family's bills.

Dalio had been convinced that the U.S. economy was headed toward crisis because of continued turbulence in a handful of economic indicators. He had been well aware that his prediction was controversial but had nonetheless been extremely sure he was right. Most people, he had convinced himself, were simply wrong. So, he took an enormous risk, investing everything on a bet he expected to reap vast returns. Then, instead of entering a recession, the U.S. economy began one of the longest periods of growth in its history.

By now, readers of this book will appreciate that being wrong is part of being alive in a complex and uncertain world. There is no shame in being wrong about the future. No matter how well we do our homework and no matter how much thought goes into our predictions, some of them will turn out to be wrong. Just ask Thomas Edison. Or Jennifer Heemstra. Nothing ventured, nothing gained, especially when it comes to intelligent failure. It's worth noting, however, that Dalio's failure doesn't meet all the criteria to qualify as intelligent. Yes, he was pursuing an *opportunity*, in *new territory*, and he had done his *homework* (few were better students of market behavior than Ray Dalio). However, by betting everything he had, Dalio missed a crucial criterion of intelligent failure—take *small* risks. His bet was simply too large to be smart, given the inherent uncertainty of the economy.

"Losing this bet was like a blow to my head with a baseball bat," recalled Dalio. "I went broke and had to borrow four thousand dollars from my dad just to pay my family bills." Worse, Dalio continued, "I was forced to lay off the people I cared so much about—until my company was left with just one employee: me." Dalio's is one of the more public failure stories I've come across. It's also one that triggered one of the more dramatic personal turnarounds.

Today, Dalio credits this failure as a major cause of his subsequent extraordinary success, including his firm's becoming the largest and most profitable hedge fund in history: "In retrospect, that failure was one of the best things that ever happened to me. It gave me the humility I needed to balance my aggressiveness and shift [my] mindset from thinking, 'I'm right,' to asking myself, '*How do I know* I'm right?'"

How do I know I am right?

It's a powerful question. Failing well, perhaps even living well, requires us to become vigorously humble and curious—a state that does not come naturally to adults. Psychologists and neuroscientists have discovered that, far too often for our health and success, a kind of automatic sense that we're right blinds us—the confirmation bias again. We literally fail to see disconfirming evidence. Other times, we're privately aware that we've failed but reluctant to admit it. Ray Dalio ultimately saw his large and public failure as a gift for this very reason: it was impossible to ignore: "Being so wrong—and especially so publicly wrong—was incredibly humbling and cost me just about everything I had built at Bridgewater."

He had no choice but to learn from it.

Most of us are not as lucky. We go about our work and lives hampered by, and partly oblivious of, some well-documented human tendencies that make it difficult to learn the valuable lessons failures offer. Part of the problem is that we are reluctant to share our failures with others—an old truth, today exacerbated by social media—and this reduces everyone's ability to learn from them. Important information is lost—and we become doomed to repeat failures that could have been prevented.

For some, to begin learning from failure takes one large enough to be undeniable. We need to be hit over the head with our wrongness to make us stop in our tracks and start to wonder where we went wrong. Dalio's failure, which fit the bill, was devastating financially, but also intellectually and emotionally. He had only himself to blame. He'd too often been the smartest person in the room, which made it all the more painful to be wrong. But it was all the more helpful in shaping his subsequent approach to his work.

We all don't need a public fiasco to change how we think to help us better navigate the inconvenience and embarrassment of ordinary, not-so-large failures in our day-to-day lives. We just have to learn a new way of thinking—one that favors learning over knowing.

Who Me? Couldn't Be!

Overcoming the instinct to find someone—something—to blame for even the smallest blip is a good start. Maybe you remember the cookie-jar song from childhood—an infinite-loop sing-along, each verse feeding directly into the next in a never-ending chorus. Someone sings out, "Who stole the cookie from the cookie jar?" and we're off and running, child after child enthusiastically rejecting the accusation ("Who me? Couldn't be!") and sending it forward, until everyone tires of the song. The ritual of denial and passing the blame brings laughter and recognition. We dodge blame instinctively. Remember my friend Sander's three-year-old, who instantly protested his innocence after his father's minor collision with a parked car.

Earlier chapters depicted people who learned from all kinds of failures—many of which were intelligent—with curiosity and resilience. People such as James West and Jennifer Heemstra and Clarence Dennis skillfully applied the lessons they gleaned from painful setbacks as part of building successful and fulfilling lives. But we're not hardwired to confront failure thoughtfully; *we have to learn to do it*. This chapter digs into how our spontaneous thinking makes it hard to confront even the most intelligent failures constructively and describes practices that can help. These can be used by anyone who wants to join the ranks of the elite failure practitioners we've gotten to know in this book. They apply equally to your personal and professional life. They've been developed or practiced by psychologists, artists, athletes, scientists, and physicians. And they have one thing in common: no one can do them for you.

How We're Wired

Our aversion to failure is studied in fields ranging from neuroscience to organizational behavior. I first learned about the interrelated dynamics of our brains and social systems back in 1987 from Daniel Goleman's thoughtful book *Vital Lies, Simple Truths: The Psychology of Self-Deception*. I was immediately hooked. Goleman wrote about mechanisms at three levels—cognition, group dynamics, and institutional systems—that reinforce one another and blind us to unwelcome truths. Failure is surely an unwelcome truth. These multilevel self-protective mechanisms boost our mood in the moment but harm our lives and relationships in the longer term.

Believing is seeing

To begin with, our brains are wired in ways that make it easy to miss our failures, often leaving us blissfully unaware we've come up short. I am not talking about willful denial—but rather about how we literally miss crucial signals that point to the need for corrective action. Even if you were familiar with the concept of confirmation bias, chances are that you rarely stop to consider the role it plays in your day-to-day life. Have you ever found yourself driving along, convinced you're heading toward your intended destination, then suddenly realizing you're lost? Possibly you dismissed puzzling signals along the route ("How weird, they moved that sign") that could have enlightened you? I know I have. For me, it's somewhere between embarrassing and laugh-aloud funny when the truth of my error suddenly becomes undeniable (maybe the location of the sunset tips you off).

Even experts in data interpretation can be fooled by their beliefs. All of us readily notice signals that reinforce our existing beliefs and unconsciously screen out signals that challenge them. This is true both for specific situations (the direction I'm driving right now) and for general opinions about the world (climate change is a hoax). To see how this works, you don't have to look much further than how you gravitate to news feeds that supply updates reaffirming your existing interpretation of certain events. Think about how Ray Dalio must have missed signals that could have challenged his interpretation of where the economy was heading. He was vulnerable to noticing signals that reinforced his prediction. As you read this chapter, where might the confirmation bias be playing out in your life? Chances are good that each of us will never become aware of some failures of our own making (the remark that lands poorly at a meeting) and will be surprised (having missed the signals) by other failures that can't be missed (say, getting fired from a job).

The sunk-cost fallacy—the tendency to persist in a losing course of action after investing time or money in it when stopping would be more beneficial—is a type of confirmation bias. We can't quite believe we were wrong in our initial assessment, don't want to reconsider, and thus dig in, becoming even more wrong—throwing good money after bad, as the saying goes. An unwillingness to believe our initial assessment is wrong is one of the ways otherwise intelligent failures in new territory—such as in a company innovation project—become less intelligent: teams continue to push forward despite a growing unspoken awareness that the project is doomed.

Confirmation biases are fueled by our natural motivation to maintain self-esteem, which helps us tune out signals that we might be wrong. Those who score high in narcissism experience a greater confirmation bias. Alas, as my colleague Tomas Chamorro-Premuzic notes, "Narcissism levels have been rising for decades." But everyone—not just the irrationally self-centered and overconfident—is prone to letting ego get in the way of something that is clearly rational and in our best interest: learning to improve. Rational, yes, but effortful.

Taking the low road

Neuroscience research identifies two basic pathways in the brain—the low road and the high road. Daniel Kahneman, the psychologist who showed that our aversion to loss outweighs our attraction to gain, popularized this distinction in his 2011 book *Thinking, Fast and Slow.*

Slow (high road) processing is thoughtful, rational, and accurate, while fast (low road) processing is instinctive and automatic. Why are these distinctions important? It's easy and natural for us to process a failure through fast, instinctive, automatic low road pathways in our brain. The problem is that low road cognition triggers an immediate response to failure in the brain's amygdala (that *fear module* for self-protection that in today's world sometimes holds us back from risk-taking). As we have already seen, how we interpret events affects our emotional responses to them. Fortunately, we can learn how to reinterpret events in our lives to avoid persevering in unproductive negative feelings. To do that, you must override the amygdala, with its superfast pathway from perceived threat to fear, to challenge its automaticity with information and reasoning.

To see how this might work, think about a time when you experienced an intense emotional response to an unexpected event at work. Perhaps you saw your team members all heading off at lunchtime and assumed you'd been deliberately excluded. If you then learned that one had a dentist appointment, another had a parent-teacher conference, and the third was running out to grab a sandwich, you would probably feel better immediately. Often you don't receive information fast enough to contradict your initial reaction and regain your equilibrium, but you can learn to pause and challenge your initial response. By way of contrast, if you're driving down the street and a car suddenly appears in an intersection, you'll slam on your brakes to avoid an accident, in part aided by an amygdala-triggered intense fear reaction. In this case, the fast pathway was lifesaving. But today, the chances are that you're more often activated by a perceived threat than a true threat.

The amygdala, which protected us from many real threats in prehistoric times, operates according to a "better safe than sorry" logic. Imagine walking through the woods at night and seeing a large, hulking shape ahead. Is it a bear? Or a boulder? From a survival perspective, an organism is better off overreacting to a false positive—running or hiding because the shape might be a dangerous bear—than failing to react to a false negative by continuing on blithely, only to be mauled by a bear. But today, that same fear module makes us unwilling to take career- and life-enhancing interpersonal risks that no longer threaten our survival.

Held back by prepared fears

We are saddled with what psychologists call prepared fears. These include fears of dangerous animals, loud noises, and sudden movements. To this list of prepared fears add that of being expelled by the tribe. University of Virginia professor James "Jim" Detert and I consider being rejected by a group as a survival-based prepared fear. The risk of coming up short in the eyes of an authority such as one's boss triggers a prepared fear in the brain related to being expelled from the tribe, a reality that might long ago have resulted in death from exposure or starvation. But today when we're afraid to speak up about failure, our colleagues lose valuable opportunities to learn vicariously. Also, we miss out on opportunities to avoid preventable failures.

Meanwhile, distracted by irrational prepared fears, we miss signals of longer-term peril that require slower thinking but constitute *true* threats to survival, such as the impact of climate change on food supplies and sea levels. Fast, automatic low road processing feeds the confirmation bias, encourages complacency, and hides failure's useful lessons. Slow high road processing happens when we stop to question the automatic to wonder what is happening and what it might mean. Most important, it happens when we stop to ask ourselves, How might I have contributed to the failure?

What fascinates me about the distinction between automatic and considered thinking is that the solutions experts have devised to override habitual human cognition are, at their core, similar. Coming from fields as varied as psychiatry, neuroscience, and organizational behavior, these strategies consistently identify the possibility of *pausing to choose how we respond.* This chapter showcases a few of my favorite thinkers who've developed practices for making these vital acts of choice possible. But first, another trip wire in our path to navigating failure needs a closer look: even when we know we've failed, we may not learn what we need to learn to avoid doing it again.

Failing to Learn from Failure

We live in a society that espouses celebrating failure for its valuable lessons. Yet, in practice, it's hard to learn from failures we ignore or hide. What if a common response to failure is to stop paying attention rather than to learn anything valuable? Behavioral scientists Lauren Eskreis-Winkler and Ayelet Fishbach say that's exactly what happens.

Eskreis-Winkler and Fishbach conducted five studies to test the hypothesis that failure, rather than promoting learning, actually *undermines* it. In one study they asked participants a series of questions starting with identifying which of two symbols from a fictional ancient script represented an animal. Afterward, one group of study participants was told, "You are correct" (success feedback). The other group was told, "You are incorrect" (failure feedback). To see how well they learned from each type of feedback, participants were given a follow-up test. This time they were asked to look at the exact same symbols and asked to identify which one represented a nonliving entity. Sounds pretty straightforward, right? Yet those who had been told they were correct in the first round scored higher in their second test than those told their answers were incorrect. Over and over, people learned less from being given information about what they got wrong than about what they got right.

Was this because success feedback was simply easier to apply? To test this explanation, the next study designed the failure feedback to require fewer "mental inferences" and procedural steps to put it to use in the next tasks. That is, the researchers made the failure feedback less cognitively taxing to apply than the success feedback. Nonetheless, failure-feedback participants continued to do worse! The results also showed that even with financial incentives that favored using the failure feedback, the pattern didn't change. Success feedback was *still* more effective, compared to failure feedback, in helping people learn.

The researchers concluded that failure is "ego threatening, which causes people to tune out." Further support for this explanation came from the fifth study, where participants observed others take similar tests—rather than taking them themselves. This time they learned equally from the failures (and the failure feedback) as from the successes. Without the ego threat, the shortcomings of failure feedback were erased. It seems we're pretty good at learning from other people's failures! In real life, however, we often don't hear about them.

Eskreis-Winkler and Fishbach also showed that, unsurprisingly, people are less likely to share information about their failures compared with their successes. The first reason is obvious: people don't want to look bad in front of others. But the second reason was more subtle. When they asked fifty-seven public school teachers if they would prefer to share stories of a past failure or a past success, 68 percent of the participants opted to share success. Even though the stories would be shared anonymously, removing the risk of looking bad in front of others, the teachers still opted for success stories. Why? They believed that failures told them what *not* to do but not necessarily what to do to succeed the next time. Eskreis-Winkler and Fishbach concluded that unawareness of failures' useful information made learning from failure difficult. So they designed an experiment in which participants were helped to identify the useful information in their failures, and this made them more likely to share them.

In a very different study with similar conclusions, my colleagues Bradley "Brad" Staats and Francesca Gino—then professors at the University of North Carolina—studied how seventy-one surgeons learned from failure versus success on a total of 6,516 cardiac surgeries in ten years. The surgeons learned more from their own successes than from their own failures, but learned more from others' failures than from others' successes. This effect—again ego protecting—was less pronounced if a surgeon had a history of personal success. Failures presumably stung less sharply with that cushion of prior success.

Note that the work of Eskreis-Winkler, Fishbach, Staats, and Gino, like that of all researchers who publish in academic journals, underwent peer review, being evaluated by colleagues for weaknesses and shortcomings. From my own experience I know how psychologically brutal this particular "learning process" can be. Well-intended criticism meant to improve a paper is a kind of failure feedback. It's easy to tune out with thoughts such as Why revise the paper if it's so bad? Or, even more counterproductive, They don't know what they're talking about! Eventually, painfully, I've learned to pause the unhelpful thoughts so I can use criticism in improving my papers.

You've probably experienced near misses in your life—those close calls that fortunately don't end badly. You swerve just in time to avoid hitting the other car. Another five minutes and you would have missed your flight. You almost committed a serious social faux pas but quick thinking saved you at the last minute. It's easy to see how a near-miss event would be far less ego threatening than an actual failure. You didn't have to suffer embarrassment or worse. Does this mean we're able to look more dispassionately at near misses than at actual failures and are thus more able to learn from them? A growing body of research—some of which I've contributed to—explores this idea. What you can take away from this research is that *framing matters*. For instance, how did you think about that close call? Did you see it as a failure (a miss that almost happened) or as a success (a good catch)? If you've framed the close call as a success, you're more likely to tell your colleagues or family about it, making all of you more able to learn from it.

What should we take away from this academic research on learning from failure? Learning from failure is difficult for a host of reasons. Sometimes we miss the failures, other times they threaten our self-esteem or don't seem to contain valuable information or we don't speak up about them. These largely cognitive barriers are exacerbated by the unpleasant emotions failure evokes, especially in relation to how we measure up to others.

The Quiet Power of Shame

In a world obsessed with success, it's easy to understand how failure can be threatening. Many live not so much lives of quiet desperation but of quiet shame. No one has done more to explain and lessen the emotional pain this causes than Brené Brown.

Driving out shame

A professor at the University of Houston, Brown has popularized her research about shame, vulnerability, and empathy in a series of books, podcasts, and TED Talks. We've all experienced what Brown calls "the warm wash of shame" when we've failed in the eyes of ourselves or others. She defines shame as "an intensely painful feeling or experience of believing we are flawed and therefore unworthy of acceptance and belonging." Some researchers see shame as "the preeminent cause of emotional distress in our time." No one wants to remain long in that intensely painful warm wash.

When we see failures as shameful, we try to hide them. We don't study them closely to learn from them. Brown distinguishes between shame and guilt. Shame is a belief that "I am bad." Guilt, in contrast, is a realization that "what I did is bad." "I am bad because I didn't do my homework" engenders feelings of shame. But if I see my actions as bad (guilt), it fosters accountability. It is thus better to feel guilty than ashamed; as Brown tells us, "Shame is highly, highly correlated with addiction, depression, violence, aggression, bullying, suicide, eating disorders . . . [while] guilt [is] inversely correlated with those things."

What happens if we rethink failure in this way? We can help ourselves learn from failure if we simply reframe a situation from "I was not promoted because I am a failure" to "I failed to get the promotion." Our relationship to failure improves when we *un*learn the belief that "I am a terrible nurse because I made that mistake" to understand instead that "I made a mistake" and to ask, "What can I take away from it that will help me avoid making the same one in the future?"

Likes and shares

Social media, as a relatively new communication phenomenon, capitalizes on our age-old reluctance to share our failures. Social media's relentless visuals make it easy to focus on how we appear to others and to feel ashamed if we don't somehow match up to the group's ideas of perfection. Here's how one college student described her feelings about using Instagram:

> I just didn't fit in to what Instagram standards were at that point, and so that caused a lot of uneasiness. . . . I would post a picture, and I would gain likes. And the more I edited my picture, the more likes I found that I would get. If I get this amount of likes, then I'm worthy. . . . And if you don't get the certain amount of likes that you think that you're going to get, it makes you feel a little rejected. . . . Instagram is supposed to be a place where you can share different points in your life, but that's not exactly what it is anymore. It's just you share what looks good. You share the ups. You only see the ups.

Multiple studies have concluded that social media usage is harmful for teenagers'—especially teen girls'—sense of self, aggravating body image issues and contributing to feelings of low self-esteem. Facebook conducted internal research for two years—before it was leaked and shared with the world in 2021—about its Instagram app's effects on body image issues. Company researchers consistently found Instagram use harmful, particularly for teenage girls. A 2019 internal presentation put it bluntly: "We make body image issues worse for one in three teen girls." A subsequent internal report noted that 32 percent of "teen girls said that when they felt bad about their bodies, Instagram made them feel worse."

One college student wrote of "overwhelming feelings of inadequacy" as she "scroll[ed] through images of girls with toned, flat stomachs" and "trendy outfits and constant vacations in the world's most glamorous locales." You could say that it's yet another incarnation of our innate fear of being rejected by a group, where you feel that avoiding rejection depends on your ability to manipulate how others see you.

Academic studies confirm what firsthand accounts convey. Research on social media use, mental health, and body image is extensive and growing. A 2018 study in the *Journal of Social and Clinical Psychology* found that reducing the amount of time you spend on social media makes you feel better. Discussing the paper in a *Forbes* interview, the lead researcher, Melissa Hunt, from the University of Pennsylvania, commented, "It is a little ironic that reducing your use of social media actually makes you feel less lonely."

Social comparison is natural. One of the most ubiquitous and enduring features of human society, social comparison has helped people behave in ways that contributed to cooperation and health for countless generations. But this natural human tendency is transmogrified by the ease with which social media expands the comparison set, while systematically biasing the content toward unrealistic standards. The voyeuristic nature of social media, which allows us to study others' posts privately without being seen, also distorts the functionality of social comparison. Interacting with people directly, whether friends or coworkers, gives you a relatively clear-eyed view of their behaviors, hopes, and worries. That you naturally compare yourself to them is functional in part because it's mutual! Everyone is calibrating in an ongoing way what's acceptable and desirable, helping the group function. In contrast, studying others' sanitized posts without being seen loses the authentic give-and-take of real life and leaves you with distortions. Staring at others' deceptive images and updates of success threatens our sense of well-being. As Hunt put it, echoing statements from teenage girls, "When you look at other people's lives, particularly on Instagram, it's easy to conclude that everyone else's life is cooler or better than yours."

It stands to reason that social media is shaping our behavior in ways that make sharing problems, mistakes, and failures harder than ever. Both research and firsthand accounts focus on the harmful effects of constant exposure to others' success, fun, and photoshopped perfect looks. Explicit mentions of failure, or failure avoidance, are rare, and social media's emphasis on unblemished successes further inhibits healthy attitudes toward failure. Spending considerable time on social media creates a risk of seeing ourselves as failures by comparison to the edited lives that others are living.

Embracing vulnerability

Given what we know about the pressure to only share the "ups" so as to look perfect in the public eye, the willingness of a handful of superstar athletes to come forward and admit their vulnerability is all the more admirable. Swimmer Michael Phelps, "the most decorated Olympian ever," has openly discussed his struggles with serious depression. More recently, twenty-four-year-old Simone Biles, "the most decorated gymnast of all time," didn't compete in the Tokyo Olympics in 2021 due to the "twisties"—a mind and body failure to connect and a loss of air sense. Biles described what happened to her during a practice session: "It's basically life-or-death. It's a miracle I landed on my feet. If that was any other person, they would have gone out on a stretcher. As soon as I landed that vault, I went and told my coach, 'I cannot continue.'" After a lifetime of pushing through physical and mental limits, Biles chose to stop. Having grown up exposed to worldwide media as well as social media's endless likes, she shared a "down." She was not perfect. What's more, she admitted defeat with her head up and used the opportunity to wholeheartedly support her teammates' success.

Biles's exceptional ability to embrace defeat stands out for her triumph over the success messages society sends us from birth. As Brené Brown says about parents, "When you hold those perfect little babies in your hand, our job is not to say, 'Look at her, she's perfect. My job is just to keep her perfect—make sure she makes the tennis team by fifth grade and Yale by seventh.' That's not our job. Our job is to look and say, 'You know what? You're imperfect, and you're wired for struggle, but you are worthy of love and belonging.'"

Choosing Learning over Knowing

Whether from the research or your own life experiences, it is probably clear by now that the deck is stacked against us having a lighthearted, learning-oriented relationship with failure—a relationship this book seeks to nurture. The fears and defensive habits that buffer us from some of failure's unpleasantness and bolster our self-esteem also place limits on our ability to grow and thrive. The good news is that we *can* learn to think differently—so as to find more rewarding and joyful ways of navigating life in an uncertain and constantly changing world. Wharton professor Adam Grant devoted his compelling book *Think Again* to the idea that, with conscious effort, we can indeed learn to challenge our automatic thinking. A few research-backed suggestions for stretching your boundaries and for feeling better about your inevitable failures follow.

The overarching skill that ties the self-disciplines of failing well together is framing—or more precisely, *reframing*. Framing is a natural and essential cognitive function; it's how we make sense of the continuous, overwhelming, confusing information coming our way. Think of a frame as a cluster of assumptions that subtly direct attention to partic- ular features of a situation—just as a physical frame around a painting draws attention to certain colors and shapes in the artist's work. We experience reality filtered through our cognitive frames, a fact that is neither bad nor good. But it gets us in trouble when we fail to challenge frames that don't serve us well. When confronting failure, most of us automatically frame it as bad, triggering self-protective reflexes and shutting down curiosity.

Fortunately, *reframing* is possible. This means learning to pause long enough to challenge automatic associations. Realizing you will be late for an important meeting, you can challenge the spontaneous panic response—taking a deep breath and reminding yourself that it will be possible to make amends, and your survival is not at stake. In a far more dramatic example, Nazi concentration camp survivor Viktor Frankl elucidated the power of reframing for readers of his timeless book, *Man's Search for Meaning*. Enduring concentration camps, in- cluding Auschwitz, in part by imagining himself in the future sharing stories with those on the outside of the courage he saw in others, Frankl deliberately reframed the meaning of the horrors he was experienc- ing. Trained as a psychiatrist and psychotherapist, he recalls this as a moment of transformation—a shift from minute-to-minute suffering and fear to hope grounded in a plausible vision of the future. Frankl's remarkable story of resilience shows how seeing the same situation in a new way can be life enhancing.

Reframing

Modern psychologists have identified a handful of opposing cognitive frames in which one frame is healthier and more constructive but the other is more common. Essentially, the more constructive frames em- brace learning and accept setbacks as necessary and meaningful life experiences. The more common and natural frames, in contrast, interpret mistakes and failures as painful evidence that we're not good enough.

One of the most popular and powerful of these frameworks, identified by Carol Dweck at Stanford University, contrasts a fixed mindset with a growth mindset. In numerous experimental studies, Dweck and her colleagues showed that people, especially school-age children, holding a "fixed" (sometimes called performance) mindset are more risk averse and less willing to persevere through obstacles than those with a "growth" mindset. For example, a performance mindset believes, "I am not good at math so I won't even try to get better at it." A growth mindset believes, "Math is difficult, but if I pay attention and ask questions about my mistakes, I can learn to do better." The growth mindset, which views challenging tasks as opportunities to learn and grow, leads children to persist longer in difficult tasks. Moreover, these children learn more than their counterparts. Unfortunately, after a few years of socialization in most school systems, the performance frame becomes the default.

I had the chance to talk with Carol Dweck in Washington, DC, when we were both invited to meet with Arne Duncan, secretary of education under President Barack Obama, to explore the implications for schools of our respective areas of research. Sitting around a long rectangular mahogany conference table in a conference room adjacent to Secretary Duncan's office, each of us spoke briefly about our work before the conversation turned to a shared exploration of the challenges that today's students face in the information age. I was excited to realize that Carol's work on how a growth mindset helps students take on and persevere in challenging tasks complemented and overlapped with my work on how a psychologically safe environment makes it easier to ask questions and admit mistakes. Both of us studied how people learn amid challenge and adversity, rather than shy away from it. As Secretary Duncan listened intently, asking many good questions, his commitment to making a difference in the education of the next generation was palpable. I've thought a lot since that day about how learning mindsets and learning environments reinforce each other—in schools, companies, and families.

A business leader who has taken Carol's work to heart is Microsoft CEO Satya Nadella, who worked hard to change the culture at his company to embody a growth mindset. Speaking in a prerecorded video for a course I taught in January 2022, Nadella recalled, "I was lucky that I picked a metaphor that spoke to what people wanted. The growth mindset helps them be better at work and at home—a better manager, a better partner. They are able to push themselves to learn and make the organization around them better. That is a powerful thing." He added, "Creating that psychological safety that allows people to push themselves has been the game changer." As Nadella, with his warm and humble demeanor, pointed out to my business school students, the effort to shift to a growth mindset will probably fare better in a context that celebrates learning and growth.

The mindsets Carol studies stem from taken-for-granted beliefs about the brain. Kids with a fixed mindset have internalized the widely held belief that intelligence is fixed. You're either born smart or you're not. To guard against being discovered as *not* smart, these kids shy away from challenging assignments, preferring tasks they know they can do well. But a much-smaller group of kids had internalized a different belief; they saw the brain as a muscle: improved by use. Taking on challenging tasks, they understood, would make them smarter. This growth mindset allowed them to experience failure with curiosity and determination.

Chris Argyris, the late Harvard professor and an academic mentor who profoundly shaped my work, similarly identified Model 1 versus Model 2 "theories-in-use" (roughly equivalent to frames) that shape our behavior. Model 1 thinking implicitly seeks to control a situation, to win, and to appear rational. When we see the world through a Model 1 frame, we routinely make assumptions about others' motives, many of them unflattering. Making things worse, we fail to wonder what we might be missing or what we can learn. Model 2, in contrast, exudes curiosity, is aware there are gaps in our thinking, and is eager to learn. Chris maintained that Model 2 was rare but could be learned with effort. It starts with a willingness to discover your shortcomings, as well as your successes. Relatedly, Maxie Maultsby, a psychiatrist you'll meet later in this chapter, distinguishes between "rational" and "irrational" beliefs.

Each of these thinkers—from wildly different backgrounds—sees the nonlearning frame, geared toward self-protection, as the norm for most adults. The oft discussed *impostor syndrome*, particularly prevalent among high achievers, is a result of this frame. Even though we may hide it behind a veil of positivity or humor, most of us in our childhood shifted from unselfconscious curiosity and learning to defensiveness and self-protection after we internalized the unhelpful idea that we have to be right or successful to be worthy.

But we can overcome it. Just ask Dr. Jonathan Cohen, an anesthesiologist at Moffitt Cancer Center in Florida, who recently tweeted a question: "How does it feel when someone points out my error?" His surprising answer? "Actually, pretty good." And "Just to be clear it didn't always feel that way." When I spoke with him in March 2022, Dr. Cohen explained that he had trained himself to equate someone pointing out his error with "patients getting safer care." He committed to overcoming his automatic dislike of being told he'd made a mistake because that dislike created danger for patients. Like the nurses I'd studied long ago who felt psychologically safe enough to admit mistakes to become a better team, Dr. Cohen taught himself to see error as part of learning that contributed to improving patient care. Ironically, as Cohen's story illustrates, a learning frame is not only healthier, it's also more rational than a performance frame. *It's more in tune with the uncertainty and constant challenges found in any life or job.* We can't shield ourselves from disappointments and failures. But we *can* learn healthy, productive responses to setbacks and accomplishments alike.

How We Think; How We Feel

Sixty-odd years ago a young insurance salesman in Minneapolis named Larry Wilson was miserable. Every time he was rejected by a prospective customer he felt like a terrible failure, an anxious loser unwilling to make the next telephone call. You might say he had a fixed mindset: Why bother to make a call if he was only going to fail again? He was ready to quit his job. But then his boss taught him a simple trick: he could change how he *thought* about those rejections. Because it took a beginning salesperson about twenty calls before making one sale and the average commission was $500, that meant on average a call was worth $25. Now, whenever Larry was told no, he forced himself to cheerfully think, "Thanks for the twenty-five dollars." This simple change not only made him feel better, it also allowed him to do his job better because he could focus on customers instead of on how miserable he felt. Soon, he was averaging ten calls for each commission of $1,000, and whenever he was rejected, he would think, "Thanks for the one hundred dollars." Essentially, he had reframed his thinking about failure. Larry became so successful as a life insurance agent that he became the youngest member at the time (at age twenty-nine) of the industry's Million Dollar Round Table. Then he began designing training programs.

When I met Larry in 1987, he had become a serial entrepreneur, whose latest venture was running team-effectiveness and culture-change programs for companies. I was hired to be director of research. That meant that I took notes about things Larry said in meetings and turned them into serviceable prose for proposals and reports. Larry was a voracious reader of philosophy and psychology and an irrepressible student of the human condition. He also loved to befriend and bring together authors and thinkers who intrigued him most. Which is how the psychiatrist Dr. Maxie Maultsby arrived at the Pecos River Learning Center in New Mexico to talk about how to best translate his rational behavior therapy (RBT) into educational programs for companies.

Drinking endless cups of coffee, I spent many hours conversing with Larry and Maxie on the large balcony overlooking the conference center, the brown adobe buildings contrasting with the deep blue of the Santa Fe sky. Close friends, they were a study in opposite personalities. Larry, with his wide-open smile and exuberant, expressive style, was easily taken up with ideas and possibilities. Maxie was watchful and contemplative, relentlessly rational, wanting to look at a subject from all angles to interrogate its nuances. Together, they were a powerful combination, leaving an indelible mark on my work. Both were passionate about how we humans can live more happily and successfully if we learn how to think about our thinking.

Maultsby's revolutionary idea was that people with healthy brains— by which he meant free from a major biological defect or injury—could help themselves escape emotional suffering without formal clinical therapy. A mentee of psychologist Albert Ellis, who pioneered cognitive behavioral therapy, Maxie gradually developed his own modifications. Simply put, he believed people could learn to control their thoughts and attitudes so as to become happier and healthier. Here's how he put it: Human emotions, hardwired in the thalamus and amygdala, are activated by our *evaluations* of external stimuli—not by the stimuli themselves. These evaluations occur in the cortex and trigger emotions, which in turn lead to behavioral impulses. How we *think* about events is what matters, not the events themselves. Unfortunately, most of the time our thinking is what Maxie called "irrational but believable." That thinking is harmful, he pointed out, because when we think events cause our feelings directly, we're victims.

Maxie was committed to increasing access to better mental health care for everyone. Psychiatry—not to mention authoring a series of self-help books—had not been the obvious career path for an African American boy born in 1932 in Pensacola, Florida. Maultsby's mother had been an elementary school teacher in a segregated school on a turpentine plantation. His father worked on the plantation, boiling gum harvested from trees and distilling it into turpentine. Growing up in his mother's schoolroom, Maxie distinguished himself early as a strong student. At eighteen he was accepted at Talladega College, a historically black liberal arts college in Alabama. Graduating in 1953, he received a scholarship to study medicine at Case Western Reserve University.

After graduating from medical school and opening his own practice, Maultsby spent four years in the U.S. Air Force, where he was inspired to study psychiatry after hearing stories of patients and their families traumatized by war. Still, Maxie said that the biggest obstacle he ever faced in his life was the "oppressive, rigidly enforced rules of segregation and the consequential inferior educational experiences that African American children were forced to endure." Throughout his life he sought to alleviate the suffering of African Americans and saw RBT as particularly suited to this goal because the "short-term efficiency and long-term effectiveness of RBT make it doubly appealing to them, as well as to most economy-minded patients, regardless of their race."

Maxie was an idealist in his single-minded goal of easing human suffering, and in his confidence that people could step up to the challenge. But he was one of the most rational, data-driven people I've ever met. The most important lesson you can take away from Maxie is to master the pause. To challenge your automatic responses in favor of healthier, more productive ones—a habit I'll illustrate with one of Maxie's own stories. When Maxie died in 2016, his legacy included twelve books, dozens of academic articles, and a thriving network of clinics, laboratories, and centers created by doctors and scientists he'd mentored. Yet it's the stories Maxie told of ordinary people learning how to alter their thinking that stuck with me most.

Failing at bridge

Jeffrey was a smart, good-looking, well-liked high school football player who'd experienced a lot of success in his first seventeen years. Jeffrey had worked hard for his academic, social, and athletic accomplishments, but he, along with his teachers and friends, had begun to expect he'd do well in whatever he tried. Over the winter school break, with cold weather limiting their leisure options, three of his friends convinced him to learn how to play bridge, which they loved. A complicated card game played by four people in two competing pairs, bridge is not easy to play well as a novice.

Jeffrey was not an immediate fan. Expecting the game with his friends to be fun, he soon found himself miserable while playing. Each time he'd make a mistake, he got frustrated and angry. To his credit, Jeffrey didn't blame his friends or even the game; rather, he got upset about his own "stupidity." His frustration only grew as they continued to play, preventing him (and his friends) from experiencing the fun that was the goal. After his third session, Jeffrey started to dread bridge and decided to quit.

That could have been the end of the story. But Jeffrey's high school offered a course in Maultsby's rational self-counseling, and Jeffrey had signed up for it. Not because he saw a connection between his bridge experience and the course content, but because the course looked interesting and he wanted to learn more. Soon, Jeffrey started to use the material on himself. Opening his mind to the idea of rational thoughts versus what Maultsby called irrational (and "merely believable") thoughts, Jeffrey realized that his belief that he should be good at bridge right off the bat was irrational. Not based in objective reality. Making mistakes was not evidence of stupidity but rather of inexperience. Making mistakes was a necessary part of learning something new—especially something difficult.

Jeffrey tried bridge again. As a newcomer, he continued to make mistakes, but he no longer beat himself up about them. That made it easier for him to learn from them. When we are flooded with painful negative emotions, Maultsby pointed out, all of us are cognitively less able to diagnose and retain the lessons our failures offer. Now that Jeffrey was approaching his missteps more thoughtfully, with far less negative emotion, he started to improve. Before long, he was about as good at bridge as his friends, and more important, he enjoyed it, and they enjoyed playing with him.

Jeffrey's realization that his thinking was irrational didn't instantly solve his problem. There was no eureka moment after which he became a thoughtful, even-keeled young man who no longer got frustrated and angry. He had to learn the habit of rational self-counseling through repeated practice. He had to become better and better at catching himself in time to stop and redirect the spontaneous negative emotions he experienced when he made mistakes. Over time he was able to catch and correct painful emotions before they took hold. He could even laugh at the irrationality of thinking that a failure in a new endeavor indicated stupidity.

Jeffrey's story is not unlike those of many successful high school students who encounter subsequent hurdles and blame external factors or walk away from new challenging activities, thereby stunting their development. At Harvard, where I teach, many students who are accustomed to being at the top of their class in high school find themselves struggling academically for the first time. More than the coursework, it's their thoughts about their inadequacy that make it difficult for them to learn.

Stop. Challenge. Choose.

Larry Wilson put it simply: Are you *playing to win*? Or *playing not to lose*? Playing to win meant a willingness to take risks in pursuit of challenging goals and satisfying relationships. Playing not to lose, which most of us do most of the time, meant avoiding situations where failure was possible. Playing to win, Larry maintained, was the stuff of great advances and great joy alike but necessarily brought setbacks along the way. Playing not to lose meant playing it safe, settling for activities, jobs, or relationships where you feel in control. The decision, Larry would be quick to explain, was essentially cognitive. You could make up your mind to play to win and thus start on the path to changing your thinking.

Ever skilled at simplification, Larry boiled Maultsby's multistep practice of rational self-counseling down to this: Stop—Challenge—Choose. *Stop* means pause. Breathe. Get yourself ready to *challenge* your spontaneous, usually unhelpful, thinking. Is it rational? Is it promoting your health and helping you achieve your goals? If the answer is no, this is a signal to *choose* what Maxie would call a more rational response—a response that works better in helping you achieve your goals. It's not about right or wrong. It's about what helps you move forward. Table 5.1 offers more detail for each of the three cognitive habits.

How might this work? When Jeffrey no longer wanted to play bridge with his friends, he had to *stop* and ask himself why. The answer: he felt stupid. When he *challenged* his thoughts, he realized he had no reason to be immediately good at bridge. Bridge takes practice. Mistakes are necessary to learning. Only then could he *choose* to continue playing with his friends, learn from his inevitable mistakes, and start to enjoy the game.

This practice also helped Melanie, who had been devastated when her elderly independent father was suddenly immobilized by a stroke. His personality and cognition had not changed, but he was confined to a wheelchair and needed around-the-clock care. For months, Melanie tried to do everything she could to make his life better. She took him to doctors' appointments and hired caregivers. She cooked his favorite meals, visited or called daily, encouraged friends to visit, searched for audiobooks and movies he might enjoy, took care of his bills, prepared his taxes, bought him presents, and more. Still, she could not do enough. Her father was sad. He complained about how limited his life had become. After about six months of this Melanie realized she was burned-out. She had become so wrapped up in the details of her father's life that she'd neglected her own work and family. Her blood pressure rose. Something had to change.

Melanie *stopped* and thought about what she was doing. She stepped back. She took a long walk with a friend and talked about her stress and worry. If she continued at her present pace, not only would her life suffer, but she would not be healthy enough to continue helping her father. With her friend's help, she *challenged* her spontaneous frame of the situation and reframed it to see how much she had done rather than how much more could still be done. She'd made sure that her father was safe and received good care. She had been a good daughter. No matter how much she did, he would not regain his former abilities. His disability was a loss they had to accept. Now she could *choose* to respond to her father's illness in ways that would help him and allow her to live her life. She continued to take him to doctors' appointments but began to visit once or twice a week rather than daily. She cooked occasionally. She asked her siblings for more help and to share the responsibility. Soon her out-of-town sister came for an extended visit, and her brother took over the taxes and bills. Their father was happy to have more contact with all his children. Finally, Melanie could take a vacation. What's more, she'd learned how to balance her own needs with what someone else wanted.

The power of the Stop—Challenge—Choose framework lies in its simplicity. As an aid to reframing, it's also consistent with insights I gained from studying with Chris Argyris, who conducted research with teams of senior managers in companies. To put its wisdom simply, one could say the fundamental human challenge is this:

It's hard to learn if you already know.

Unfortunately, we are hardwired to feel as if we know—as if we see reality itself rather than a version of reality filtered through our biases, backgrounds, or expertise. But we can unlearn the habit of knowing and reinvigorate our curiosity.

TABLE 5.1: **Cognitive Habits for Responding to Failures**

Habit	What It Means	How to Do It	Useful Questions
Stop	Pause to disrupt automatic emotional responses to situational stimuli to make it possible to redirect the spontaneous emotional and behavioral responses.	Take a deep breath to prepare to examine your thinking and consider its impact on your ability to respond in a way that (1) protects your longer-term health and (2) gives you more options.	• What is going on right now? • What is the big picture? • How was I feeling before this happened?
Challenge	Consider the content of your spontaneous thoughts to assess their quality and usefulness for achieving your goals.	Verbalize (to yourself) what's going on in your mind in response to this situation, and ask yourself which thoughts (1) reflect objective reality, (2) support your health and effectiveness, and (3) will be likely to elicit a productive response. Identify alternative interpretations of the situation that are based in objective reality and more likely to help you elicit a productive response—that is, deliberately reframe the situation in a way that helps you move forward and feel better.	• What am I telling myself (or believing) that is causing how I am feeling? • What objective data support or negate my interpretation? • What other interpretation of the situation is possible? • Based on all of the information I have, was my interpretation in my best long-term interests?
Choose	Say or do something that moves you closer to achieving your goals.	Respond in the way your reframed thinking suggests, so that you say and do things that help you move forward.	• What do I truly want? • What is going to best help me achieve my goals?

Choosing learning

Once we're humble enough to admit we don't know, we're ready to approach situations in a new way. Jeffrey had to realize he couldn't succeed right away at everything he tried. Melanie had to accept her losses and limitations. Recall how Ray Dalio, who had been so sure he was right about where the economy was headed until he was catastrophically wrong, shifted his mindset "from thinking, 'I'm right,' to asking myself, '*How do I know* I'm right?'" A powerful question for cultivating self-awareness. His new mindset was open to learning. It made Dalio want to "seek out the smartest people who disagreed with me so I could try to understand their reasoning" and helped him "know when *not* to have an opinion." Much as Melanie had to let go of the version of reality where she could "save" her father, Dalio, before he could successfully build back his company, had to let go of the version of reality fed to him by his own brain to learn also from others.

Chris Argyris called this the uncovering of "the non-learning theories-in-use," which protect our egos but get in the way of our being truly effective (especially in difficult conversations with others). Dalio learned to change his thinking, explaining, "I just want to be right—I don't care if the right answer comes from me." No longer protecting his need to be right, he could then make decisions that were more effective—just as Jonathan Cohen consciously decided to care more about the safety of his patients than about being right. Chris identified our cognitive programming (how we think) as a vital lever we can learn to pull to become more learning oriented and effective, and, I'd add, more joyful. The joy comes from realizing that we can break the link between what happens to us and how we respond. To reframe. As Frankl allegedly put it, "In our response lies our growth and our freedom."

Maxie and Chris had in common a relentlessly rational stance that disguised their shared, sincere, passionate commitment to alleviating suffering and waste by helping people learn and grow. Both of these brilliant, dedicated researchers saw that each of us is capable of a kind of learning and growth not taught in school. Both of them opened my mind to the possibility of failing well. Choosing learning over knowing builds wisdom and equanimity. It opens a doorway glimpsed by too few toward becoming more caring, wise, respectful, willing to challenge (especially oneself), and, ultimately, more fulfilled. In the time I spent with Maxie and with Chris, I began to appreciate how much it pained them that we get in our own way. That we allow ego to drive out learning and connecting.

When I think back to my time in New Mexico, I appreciate how what I learned from Maxie and Larry shaped my thinking and subsequent research. Both men believed that people could learn to alter habitual thinking patterns and that this was a key to their success and happiness. This was the background that led me to graduate school. I was drawn to both of them—wondering quietly whether I had what it took to contribute new knowledge to an already deep and valuable body of research. I also wanted to help make that knowledge useful.

Today my answer is this: choose learning over knowing.

It doesn't matter whether you gravitate to Carol Dweck's growth mindsets, Maxie Maultsby's healthy-thinking habits, Chris Argyris's Model 2 theories-in-use, or Viktor Frankl's powerful memoir. The message is the same. Pause to challenge the automatic thoughts that cause you pain and embarrassment. Next, reframe those thoughts to allow you to choose learning over knowing. To look outward and find energy and joy from seeing what you missed. At the core of the reframing task lie the words we use to express our thoughts, privately and aloud. Am I failing, or am I discovering something new? Do I believe I *should* have done better—and I'm bad for not having done so—or do I accept what happened and learn as much as I can from it? Am I okay with the discomfort that comes with new experiences? Will I give myself permission to be human? Permission to learn?

Permission to Learn

As the comic strip character Pogo purportedly said, we have met the enemy and he is us. Our distorted, unrealistic expectations for avoiding all failures are indeed the culprit. Mastering the science of failing well must therefore start with looking at ourselves. Self-awareness is the first, and most vital, of the three competencies we need to develop. The other two, situation awareness, covered in the next chapter, with system awareness immediately following, can only be developed when we give ourselves permission to keep learning.

CHAPTER 6

Contexts and Consequences

We cannot direct the wind, but we can adjust the sails!

—Dolly Parton

Imagine you're standing in a large room in front of a seven by ten-foot, gray-and-black, grid-patterned rug. You see nine rows of six identical squares. You're told that each square will either beep loudly or remain silent when you step on it, and that your task is to find a path of contiguous *nonbeeping squares* from one end of the rug to the other. You will be given twenty minutes to find the path, with bonus points for doing it faster. The path cannot be detected by looking at the rug. The only way to discover it is to step on squares, one at a time, through trial and failure, to see if they beep.

When I assign students this exercise, called the Electric Maze and designed more than three decades ago by inventor Boyd Watkins, an African American electrical engineer with two degrees from Berkeley, I put them into teams and give them some rules: Only one person can step on the rug at a time; when a team member encounters a beeping square, the team member must step off the rug, and the next person takes a turn. Each time a square emits a beep, the team must start again at the first row. I give the students a few minutes to talk to one another before the exercise starts. Once it starts, they must proceed without talking. They are free to point to the quiet squares or to use their hands to warn of squares already known to beep, in a team effort to help the person on the maze move forward quickly to find the rest of the path.

This is not an intellectually challenging game. Nor does it require expertise. Most students have solved far more difficult problems and faced more challenging situations. It's just a matter of stepping on squares to see if they beep and remembering which ones do. No one on the team has answers for this task, so it can't be solved without experiencing failures (beeps) along the way.

Yet, here's what happens. The first teammate ventures onto the rug and steps, let's say, on a nonbeeping square. Then the person hesitates before stepping on the next square. One foot in midair, the teammate seems to freeze, as if hoping to detect which squares might be safe without having to step on them. Remember, team performance is time based. Hesitating is costly. Standing with one foot in midair is not a smart use of time, but it's understandable. Imagine yourself on the rug, stepping forward onto a beeping square. Your team members groan. Or you step on a quiet square and they cheer! Ironically, the team's reactions exacerbate the hesitation: the next person on the maze becomes even more hesitant, and eventually the team runs out of time. In my experience, most teams fail to find a beep-free path in twenty minutes.

To help participants understand the causes of their failure to solve the puzzle, when I debrief the exercise, I ask, "What were you thinking when you were on the rug, facing a new row of squares, hesitating to step?" The answer is always the same: "I didn't want to make a mistake." If they elaborate, they'll confess to feeling embarrassed by stepping on a beeping square rather than a quiet one.

By now it should be clear that stepping on a new beeping square is not a mistake. It's simply information about the path. It's the right kind of wrong. When something goes wrong in unknown territory (whether a beeping square or a bad first date), it's a failure but not a mistake. Recall that something is only a mistake if you already have knowledge for how to avoid it. What people don't easily put into practice is that the way to perform well in the maze is to collect as quickly as possible information about which squares beep. Logically, teams should applaud their colleagues for discovering both quiet squares *and* beeping squares. Both provide vital new information about the path. Instead, people experience the tiny intelligent failure of a new beep as a mistake and feel embarrassed by it—an embarrassment that's amplified by others' reactions.

It shows lack of appreciation of context.

A new beep is the right kind of wrong. Let's call it a "beep going forward." It's a metaphor for the missteps in our lives in unfamiliar situations. Just as the maze presents a trial-and-failure task that cannot be solved without stepping on beeping squares, when we face novel contexts in our lives, we must be prepared for failures as we navigate the new terrain. If feeling ashamed of or anxious about a new beep in the maze is irrational (albeit human), so, too, is it irrational to feel embarrassed by the "beeps going forward" in our lives.

What if a team on the Electric Maze methodically stepped to find beeps as quickly as possible, eliminating the hesitation? A solution can be found in under seven minutes. A team's inability to accomplish this task in twenty minutes can be seen as a direct result of *misconstruing the context*. This context calls for experimentation, and it helps to team up and support one another through the inevitable failures. Instead, students react emotionally to beeps—as if they had been engaged in a routine task with a playbook for exactly where and when to step. They've spontaneously viewed the maze as a test they were supposed to get right the first time. *They've brought an execution mindset to a learning task.*

University of Michigan psychology professor Fiona Lee and I used the maze in a psychology experiment to show how this mindset worked. We randomly assigned participants to work with a person they believed was a team member but was in fact a lab assistant hired to model either an *execution orientation* (emphasizing the importance of being right and avoiding mistakes) or a *learning orientation* (emphasizing the importance of experimenting and learning). Participants in the learning condition outperformed those in the execution condition. Their partner's instructions were congruent with the task context, and they had an easier time experimenting, which was vital to success. In contrast, when an execution mindset was reinforced, its clash with the novel task made it harder for participants to succeed.

Most of us don't find ourselves standing in front of a literal maze trying to find the right path. But the exercise provides an apt metaphor for our lives. All of us face uncertainty, which brings both risk and opportunities for discovery. All of us can benefit from pausing to consider the context at crucial and not-so-crucial moments in our day-to-day lives. Too many failures in life, and in companies, occur because we don't pay attention to context. Further, too many failures are more emotionally painful than they need to be—when they're simply the beeping squares found in every life.

The goal of the Electric Maze is to elucidate psychological barriers to innovation. We don't like beeps going forward, but innovation won't happen without them. The maze exemplifies new territory, yet participants still feel they're supposed to know the answers. The goal of this chapter is to give you a new way of thinking about context to help you prevent certain kinds of failures while lightening the emotional load intelligent failures bring. Too many preventable failures—in life and in companies—occur because of insufficient attention to context.

Practicing the science of failing well requires awareness of two dimensions of context: (1) how much is known and (2) what's at stake. The first dimension concerns the degree of novelty and uncertainty. The second is about risk—physical, financial, or reputational. Roughly speaking, are the stakes high or low? Stepping on a square that beeps in a classroom exercise would be a good illustration of low stakes. Sending a space shuttle into orbit? High stakes. This is often a subjective assessment; for instance, what might be high stakes financially for me might be low for you. Reflecting on both the uncertainty and the stakes in a situation, subjective or not, is a crucial competency for elite failure practitioners.

The Varying Contexts in Our Lives

Will you fail today?

It depends, to a large degree, on the situations in which you will find yourself. The odds of failing differ dramatically based on the level of uncertainty. How much a failure *matters* differs, too. Is human safety at risk? Could a failure bring serious financial or reputational harm?

This chapter looks at how contextual *un*awareness leads to avoidable failures in some settings and unwarranted anxiety in others. Contextual *awareness*, in contrast, allows you to practice vigilance when necessary and to relax when the stakes are low. It's a Stop—Challenge—Choose opportunity to assess the situation, challenge your automatic beliefs about it, and choose the right mindset. Does the situation call for extreme vigilance or for playful experimentation? Learning to do this analysis habitually not only makes you more effective across a variety of situations, it also reduces the emotional toll so many of us suffer from unnecessary anxiety. When you learn to interrupt your automatic re-actions, you can proceed more thoughtfully—not seeing danger where there isn't any, while practicing vigilance when there is.

Context is partly shaped by the level of uncertainty. On one end of the spectrum are tasks that come with tried-and-true recipes, such as you might use to make chocolate chip cookies, where the results are all but guaranteed. On the other end are tasks without playbooks. Imagine confronting your computer's blank screen hoping to write a new work of fiction. For the cookies, you know exactly what to do and failure is unlikely. In the latter task, an infinite number of possibilities lie ahead, and endless small failures (beeps going forward) await you. Maybe you don't even have a story idea yet. Or maybe that is all you have. It's hard to know where to begin, and the desired result—a published book that will engage readers far and wide—is far from guaranteed. Just like Edison's early attempts to produce a storage battery. Between these two extremes lies a vast landscape of situations.

From consistent to novel

Consistent contexts bring the certainty that novel contexts lack. When procedural knowledge is well developed—as in following the cookie recipe—uncertainty is low and the odds of failure are low. In contrast, in novel contexts, knowledge of how to get the result you want lies somewhere between nonexistent and incomplete, as when you set out to write a book, design a new product, or find a nonbeeping path across an electric maze. Failures are all but guaranteed when uncertainty is high. But those failures don't have to be painful. They provide valuable information, and contextual awareness makes this easier to appreciate.

To understand how contexts vary in your life, think about jobs you've had and the extent to which those jobs came with instructions for getting expected results. Most companies encompass a range of contexts—from routine production (high-volume repetitive work, such as in a fast-food restaurant or automotive assembly line) to research and development (in scientific labs or product design teams). Between these extremes lie the variable contexts, such as you'd see in a hospital, where you have solid knowledge about how to achieve results but must constantly adjust or customize based on small variations in the situation. An emergency room physician, for example, may face multiple unusual patient challenges one day and find the next day relatively routine. In your personal life, you also encounter *consistent*, *variable*, and *novel* contexts. The point isn't to draw solid boundaries between non-overlapping categories, but rather to learn to habitually take stock of uncertainty because of its implications for how to proceed.

Can you do it in your sleep?

Recently, a story in the news about a small child left in a taxicab piqued my interest. A family had taken a taxi home from the airport, and only after the taxi drove off did the parents realize their son was missing. The boy was found in a couple hours—unharmed, and still sleeping in the third row of the minivan, now parked in a lot on the edge of town. I got to thinking about how that mistake might have happened. I could imagine the scene from the parents' perspective: It's late, it's dark, the end of a long trip, and everyone's tired. Other children need care. Luggage. House keys to locate. In the chaos it was easy to assume—as these parents did—that the other had taken charge of their four-year-old.

The story is an example of how readily we tend to downplay variability. Although a ride home from the airport would seem to be predictable and familiar and therefore not require attention, I would argue that the context—multiple bags, multiple children, the late hour—made the family vulnerable to failure. Had they recognized this ride home had moderate variability rather than complete predictability, they might have given it more attention. The cabdriver also neglected to give a seemingly routine task—parking his van at the end of a shift—his full attention. He erred in not checking to make sure the cab was empty. Everyone contributed to a preventable complex failure in a variable context.

Routines are characteristic of a consistent context. Maybe you take the same route to work each day or empty the dishwasher by putting all the clean dishes back in precise locations so you will always know where to find them. Maybe you like to jog around a particular loop in a neighborhood park. You might have a sister or brother or best friend who can always be relied upon to cheer you up if you're down. If you enjoy cooking, you probably have a set of recipes you count on to deliver every time. These activities and relationships make up the consistent contexts that are relatively immune to stressful decisions about what to do and how to do it.

The consistent contexts in your life trigger no anxiety about whether you'll be able to achieve a desired result. In these situations you can say, with confidence, "I've got this." I don't want to suggest that emptying the dishwasher brings joyful exuberance, but rather that it's reassuringly familiar, not to mention satisfying when everything is back where it belongs. The problem is that we too readily treat situations as consistent when they are variable or sometimes even novel. The family coming home from the airport did this when they left a sleeping child in the taxi. Whenever I've entered my classroom at Harvard Business School overconfident because I taught the same case study in a prior year, I'm making this same mistake. I'm facing new students who bring different experiences and expectations; the world around us has been shaped by recent events, and the class discussion will unfold differently from before. For the best possible class, I will need to be alert to nuances at all times. Few of our contexts are truly consistent and predictable, but this doesn't stop us from acting as if they are. When we say, "I can do it in my sleep," what we mean is that we've done it so many times before, we don't need to pay attention.

Familiar yet variable

The *variable contexts* in our lives keep us on our toes. Maybe you're a skilled tennis player, enjoying growing mastery of a game in which each opponent, or each doubles partner, not to mention each match, brings new twists and turns that demand your full attention. Maybe your job presents a variable context—where you apply a particular expertise in a series of different situations throughout the day, as would a physician or a lawyer, or where you team up with different people on different projects at different times. In variable contexts, we use our knowledge or expertise, thoughtfully modifying our actions to respond to what we see happening in the moment. Variable contexts bring more uncertainty than truly consistent contexts, but your ability to navigate the situation is rarely in doubt.

Because of the complexity of the world we live in, the majority of situations we encounter day-to-day are variable and demand at least some of our attention. Even situations that seem consistent may be more variable than you think. Maybe you've made the soufflé countless times at home, but you don't know how it will turn out in someone else's oven when you're visiting for the weekend. Home projects such as hanging pictures on the walls are also variable—you'll need to take measurements carefully to minimize harm to your thumbs or walls.

New territory

Finally, just as at IDEO, where everyone worked on innovation projects, the novel contexts in your life present possibility without a guarantee of results. Achieving success in these contexts necessarily requires trying something new, and it's unlikely to work perfectly the first time. Maybe you want to invent a new dish, blending unfamiliar ingredients. You know enough about cooking to believe the flavors will combine interestingly, but you have to try it to know for sure. Maybe you are about to buy a home for the first time, exploring different neighborhoods, attending open houses, scouring the internet, and learning as much as you can about financing options. Or what about going on a blind date? Taking up scuba diving? Novel contexts, one and all.

Without wandering into novel contexts now and then we are at risk of stagnation, losing out on the chance to try an unfamiliar activity or achieve a new goal. Just as scientists in laboratories do, we must embrace failures in new territory. You cannot avoid them; you might as well welcome the opportunity to learn from them. Perhaps you have had your heart set on a home and lose to a higher bidder. Your dish may disappoint or even be awful. The blind date? Enough said. All these examples are relatively low risks worth taking. That's because the worst that can happen is not all that bad.

What's at Stake?

When practicing situation awareness, the second thing to consider is what's at stake—financially or physically or for your reputation. A good rule of thumb is to cheerfully accept failures with low consequences and to take measures to prevent high-stakes failures. Situations are defined by a combination of uncertainty and potential consequences. When physical, financial, or reputational harm could occur, the stakes are high. Table 6.1 on page 210 shows examples of higher- and lower-stakes situations for all three dimensions.

Unloading the dishwasher, cooking, or trying to navigate across a beeping rug are low-stakes situations, where failure is unlikely to have serious consequences. When you drop a dish while unloading the dishwasher, it's a fairly inconsequential failure in a predictable context. Adopting a "no big deal" response and quickly moving on— maybe pausing to remind yourself to pay attention when your hands are wet—is healthy. In a low-stakes situation in a variable context, where the worst that can happen is, for example, a collapsed soufflé, you want to lightly brush off your mistakes with an "Oh well, things happen" attitude. The phrases "Don't beat yourself up" or "Don't cry over spilled milk" apply.

Julia Child, the pioneering chef who introduced French cooking to a wide American audience, was famous for cheerfully dismissing mistakes in the kitchen of her 1960s television show. After flipping a pancake that fell on the kitchen counter instead of into the pan, she advised, "If this happens, just scoop it back into the pan; remember that you are alone in the kitchen and no one can see you." Seeing her fail so lightheartedly, despite her accomplishment and expertise, not only made the famous chef relatable, but helped viewers believe that they, too, could try out unfamiliar recipes that might otherwise feel too daunting.

Have fun experimenting

Elite failure practitioners such as Child take advantage of low-stakes situations in novel contexts. At best, you will discover something new. At worst? It's simply a beep going forward. A key takeaway from the Electric Maze exercise is *have fun experimenting when the stakes are low*. Gaining experience with failures in a low-stakes environment helps to stave off perfectionism. You can learn to stop to consider whether the stakes are high. Just as we spontaneously underestimate uncertainty, we spontaneously overestimate what's at stake. For most of us, appearing on national television would qualify as high stakes. Not Julia! She (rightly) coded a pancake on the counter, or even a chicken on the floor, as low stakes—a product of human error that was unworthy of embarrassment or shame.

Getting into the habit of recoding the risk level in many of our activities, along with the stakes we incur in carrying them out, is a vital, life-enhancing capability. By cultivating this habit, we lighten the emotional load. We have more than enough situations in our lives where vigilance is essential; when it's not, we can proceed in a more playful and lighthearted way—even when we're doing things that are important to us (cooking, writing an essay, learning a new language). In consistent contexts with low stakes (folding the laundry, going for a run), a casual, business-as-usual approach is fine. Pausing to consider (or, more typically, *re*consider) the stakes allows us to titrate vigilance, mitigating its emotional and cognitive tax.

Titrating vigilance

In contrast, when the stakes are high—especially for human safety—you want to take an approach that ranges from mindful execution to cautious action to careful experimentation, as shown in Figure 6.1, where the gray box encompasses situations in which failures are likely and the stakes are high. The gray box depicts the zone that warrants special care. A bio-manufacturing company must execute with enormous care so that two different vaccine batches are not combined because a mistake could cost people's lives, a company's reputation, and considerable money. Perhaps you are making a presentation at work that will impact a sale or a promotion. That's a variable context and a relatively high-stakes situation because the sale or promotion matters to you. You'll want to exercise care and caution by, for example, practicing your presentation beforehand. Let's say you give this same presentation to an entirely new group. As the context veers closer to a novel context, you can experiment thoughtfully with small changes in your presentation to better reach the new audience.

TABLE 6.1: **Three Dimensions of Consequentiality**

	Higher Stakes	**Lower Stakes**
Physical	Activities with life-or-death consequences, or the potential for grave injury, such as flying an aircraft or conducting surgery	Trying out a new sport where you might suffer sore muscles or small injuries
Financial	Putting a large sum of money into a risky investment	Buying a movie ticket without knowing anything about the film
Reputational	Activities subject to wide public scrutiny for which you may be underprepared or unqualified	Expressing a controversial opinion at a party to someone you don't know well

Obviously you don't want to act recklessly in dangerous situations. But it's also a mistake to weigh yourself down with excessive vigilance in low-stakes situations. This error is made by nearly all Electric Maze participants. Similarly, when you're excessively concerned about how others see you, you may be misconstruing the context as high stakes rather than as a place where you can let down your guard and connect with others authentically.

When vigilance is necessary because the stakes are high, it doesn't have to be painful or taxing. Being excruciatingly present can be energizing. In sailing a racing boat upwind, for example, distractions and concerns fall away when I am forced to live in the moment-to-moment challenges posed by wind, speed, and balance. When I lived in New Mexico and became a weekend rock climber, I had a similar experience. The focus that variable situations demand at times (notably when excellence is required) must not be equated with relentless hard work and misery!

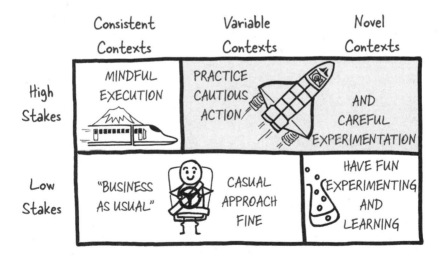

FIGURE 6.1: Navigating Context Type Based on High or Low Stakes

Situation Unawareness and Preventable Failures

A lack of situation awareness can spawn a variety of preventable failures—usually due to a cognitive bias called *naïve realism*. As described by Stanford psychologist Lee Ross, naïve realism gives you an erroneous sense that you see reality itself—not a version of reality filtered through lenses created by your background or expertise. It's a source of overconfidence that can lead to preventable failures. Naïve realism makes us interpret a variable or novel situation as predictable. We've already seen examples of this with the child left in the taxi, or my classroom experiences, but perhaps you've lost a sale you thought was in the bag or believed a date was going well only to never hear from the person again. Overestimating a situation's familiarity and underestimating its uncertainty sets us up for failures that are preventable rather than intelligent.

Situation awareness in failure science means appreciating the level of uncertainty and what it brings. It's about pausing, however briefly, to consider where you are on the continuum from consistent to novel, so as to proceed with an appropriate approach. It's about learning to expect the unexpected, both to avoid preventable failures and to take enough risks to produce your share of intelligent failures. It's also about remaining cognizant of what's at stake.

Underestimating danger

Jay was an engineering and design student working at a metal fabrication studio that made large outdoor sculptures for public parks, private estates, and art galleries. His first weeks on the job, in June 2020, had included instructions about when and how to use safety goggles, helmets, respirator masks, steel-toed boots, and gloves—measures that Jay took seriously and followed diligently. He'd also learned the safe way to handle the large machines that cut steel and aluminum and how to keep a distance from sharp blades, moving gears, and the welding tools' flaming heat. After attaching the pieces of metal to one another, he frequently smoothed out the welds by maneuvering a handheld angle grinder that had been fitted with a sharp-edged and fast-moving wheel.

Yet one afternoon, after he'd been working at the shop for almost a year, Jay bent too far into a tight corner to smooth a rough weld. For a split second his head was too close to the powerfully whirring grinder; he'd lost situation awareness, focusing on the troublesome weld rather than where he stood relative to the powerful tool.

In an instant, the angle grinder jumped back from his hand and gouged his lower lip.

His boss drove him to the emergency room, saying sternly, "Jay, you forgot you were in a dangerous situation."

Jay had mistaken, however momentarily, a variable setting for one that was routine. Accustomed to working with the angle grinder, he'd worked more automatically than consciously. Most of all, he had not paused to recognize *This is a dangerous situation. I could get hurt.* Had he paused to recognize the context—as he had done many times before in tasks with the potential to harm—he might have moved his head or stepped back just enough to prevent being injured.

Although not all preventable failures involve physical harm, this example illustrates what can happen when we forget to pause and assess the context. We lose the chance to choose the approach most appropriate for the context. Most of all, when you recognize that you're in the gray box, where things can and do go wrong, you can proceed with outsize caution and care.

Underestimating variability

What if you were in charge of launching one of your company's existing products in a new market—say, a new country? It would be easy to fall into the trap of approaching this as an execution task. It's a well-understood product, and it's natural to downplay the variability that lies ahead. Let's take a look at how Coca-Cola got caught up in this situation back in 2004 and experienced a complex failure called by business journalists a "fiasco" and a "PR catastrophe."

Dasani water became popular in the United States in the late 1990s when bottled water was increasingly seen as a convenient and healthy alternative to sugary sodas. In the UK, in contrast, the bottled-water market was more established and longer lived than in the United States; however, bottled water was seen differently on each side of the Atlantic. Rather than being viewed as simply a convenient source of drinking water, bottled mineral water was seen in the UK as beneficial and refreshing because it came from an alpine glacier or natural spring. Illustrating this cultural difference, a widely seen BBC television comedy, *Only Fools and Horses*, parodied bottled water in a 1992 episode in which a character sold bottled water straight from a tap—an idea seen as worthy of mockery, which was exacerbated later in the show when the tap water was discovered to be contaminated. The episode, aired during a holiday, was watched by 20 million people, and many times afterward in reruns.

The UK Dasani launch, had it only had to overcome residual negative associations spawned by a TV show, might still have been successful. Few would have rejected Coca-Cola's new water based on the comedy episode. In fact, for the first few weeks, the Dasani product sold well enough.

Coca-Cola had accurately labeled each Dasani bottle "purified water" (chemically treated tap water) to differentiate it from mineral water. In the run-up to the launch, the *Grocer*, an industry magazine, noted, "One senior buyer warned that some consumers may be put off by the water's lack of provenance," but no one really noticed the issue, perhaps due to embedded assumptions about bottled water.

But then, in an unfortunate case of life imitating art, testing revealed that chemicals used in the water-treatment plant in southeast London meant that Dasani water exceeded the legal limit for bromate, a carcinogen. Although the amounts were apparently insufficient to do harm, the negative publicity was impossible to avoid. Coca-Cola was forced to recall half a million bottles of Dasani—an expensive and arguably preventable complex failure. The product was never returned to the UK market, and the company wrote off £7 million spent on the advertising campaign for the launch.

It's easy to point to bad luck as the reason for the launch's ultimate failure. The perfect storm of a remembered TV show, a failure to test the water source carefully in advance, and an overly casual approach to the differences between the two markets combined to kill the product. Had the company appreciated the variability a new market for an old product necessarily brings, the failure might have been avoided. Cautious action to test the waters (pun intended) might have revealed the risks sooner and allowed the company to anticipate and address British skepticism toward a product that had been warmly received in the United States and elsewhere. As journalist Tom Scott concluded, "I don't think the Dasani disaster was inevitable."

Underestimating novelty

Over two years in the making, with over a billion dollars of funding, the new website was expected to handle fifty thousand to sixty thousand users at a time. For the first several hours after its long-anticipated launch, everything appeared to be working properly, but reports soon surfaced that the few users who'd managed to log on found only blank screens, were bumped off the site, or had to wait hours for access. Only six people were able to use the site properly that first day. Only 5 percent of projected users were accommodated during the site's first month. Observers widely panned the technology as "unintuitive, clunky to navigate, and generally impenetrable."

HealthCare.gov, as you may recall, was the online platform created to implement the Affordable Care Act (ACA), a fiercely fought-for law to make health care available to millions of previously uninsured and underinsured Americans. The website was the public portal where anyone could sign in, shop the federal marketplace of health-care plans, and enroll in a chosen plan. But its launch was an abject failure. You may recall the media uproar that accompanied the failure. How could a policy meant to make health care accessible to all fail to ensure the basic ability to enroll?

As details emerged about what had gone wrong, we learned that two major factors were at work. To begin with, those in Washington, DC, consumed with making the ACA a success had focused on passing the legislation—all but equating passing the bill with implementing the policy. Less thought went into figuring out how to design the technology to connect millions of users to thousands of companies offering varied health-care plans, each subject to complex state-specific regulations. Setting up a website is not difficult. You may even be one of the millions of people who have set up a simple website, blog, or e-commerce business through preconfigured software content-management systems and gone live in hours. But, building a two-sided platform to handle tens of thousands of users at a time, all needing customized plans, presents a completely different level of difficulty from individual websites—and, more important, calls for a very different skill set from that required of politicians. Relatedly, President Obama and his team failed to appreciate the degree of novelty that HealthCare.gov presented. Implicitly viewing it as just another website, they failed to mobilize the kind of team and process that such a novel project required. I assign this case study in my class at Harvard to help students appreciate that vision and charisma are not enough. Great managers are those who diagnose the context to organize people and resources accordingly. Otherwise, they set themselves up for embarrassing preventable failures.

The HealthCare.gov failure was more than embarrassing. It reflected badly on the entire endeavor. Although obviously a technology failure—the software did not function—its visibility turned it into what President Obama later called a "well-documented disaster." Most new tech platforms are created behind closed doors. The software developers expect it not to work the first time around and plan for multiple iterations, usually with a small group of selected users, before it's ready to work at scale. They know they're operating in a novel, and potentially high-stakes, context. But here, the people in charge had misconstrued the context as variable, familiar, when it was actually novel, unprecedented. They failed to appreciate the amount of work, and the iterations, that would be needed to succeed. It's as if an early explorer headed off to Antarctica packed for a weekend trip to a familiar location—bringing a hat and gloves in case the weather turned cold. Confronting the extreme, unpredictable weather and dire need for special equipment and guidance, the expedition soon would be doomed. Analogously, creating and launching a massive two-sided internet platform was not a "just do it" type of job, but rather a serious innovation project. One journalist reported that federal officials had "failed to recognize the enormity of the undertaking, were disorganized and fragmented, were hampered by late and shifting ACA policies, used poor contracting practices, and ignored problems until it was too late." Worse, warnings that the technology was not working were ignored. Problems were not reported up the hierarchy. No one believed it was safe to tell their bosses the site was in trouble.

Fortunately, a team of tech superstars from Silicon Valley were recruited almost immediately to fix the site. With the experience to diagnose the situation and the know how to manage accordingly, the team worked to rebuild both the culture and the technology. Many of the original software engineers were included. But this time everyone experimented relentlessly and systematically to figure out what would work and what would not. Mikey Dickerson, from Google, led the team of programmers to overhaul the website's code. He held stand-up meetings twice a day where the team would discuss problems, admit errors, and ask questions in a psychologically safe, no-blame culture. He posted a short list of meeting rules on the wall: "Rule 1: The war room and the meetings are for solving problems. There are plenty of other venues where people devote their creative energy to shifting blame." At one meeting, Dickerson applauded an engineer who admitted that his coding mistake had resulted in a site outage.

The HealthCare.gov launch was a complex failure in a novel context and was *not* the right kind of wrong. Danger signals were missed. Hypothesis-driven experiments were not run. Learning from small failures along the way did not occur—dooming the project to a far larger-scale, more visible, more destructive-in-reputation failure than was necessary. Intelligent failures, which have novel territory in common with the HealthCare.gov launch, are small, controlled disappointments—rather than painful fiascoes.

Mapping the Failure Landscape

The relationship between context type and failure type has probably already jumped out at you. For example, new contexts and intelligent failures go hand in hand. A 70 percent failure rate (nearly all of the failures intelligent) is not atypical for scientists at the top of their field. In novel contexts, you must experiment to make progress, and intelligent failures come with the territory. Each is a useful discovery. Although authors can't easily quantify their failure rates, by the time I finish writing this book, more words will have been deleted than retained. In novel territory, this can't be avoided. But imagine if most commercial airline flights never made it to their destination, or most of the meals served at McDonald's didn't taste right. Consumers would be incensed. With even a 1 percent failure rate in these high-volume, relatively consistent contexts, the companies would soon be out of business. As uncertainty increases, the chances of failure increase, and the type of failure tends to differ accordingly.

Predictable and basic

In predictable contexts, we often generate basic failures because of the temptation to "do it in your sleep." Mistakes creep in despite access to foolproof knowledge about what to do to get the result you want. Maybe you forget to set the timer and burn the cookies. Although it's easy to beat yourself up for small screwups, it's unhelpful. The healthy response is to take note of the mistake, learn from it, and then look forward rather than backward. This is true even for mistakes that lead to severe consequences, such as when texting while driving leads to a car accident. Learning from setbacks, small and large, is part of the science of failing well.

Variable and complex

Complex failures are especially common in variable contexts. You will lose many of your tennis matches. If the sun had stayed behind the cloud, your knee hadn't been bothering you, and your opponent hadn't unexpectedly returned that serve, the outcome would have been different. Losing the match was a complex failure, but not a tragic one.

To thrive in the variable contexts in our lives we must be vigilant *and* resilient. I'm sure you can think of complex failures in your life, and you're particularly likely to find them in trips by air. When I was interviewing for graduate school back in 1990, I traveled to Boston from New Mexico, where I was working for Larry Wilson. Nervous about the interview, I arrived at the Albuquerque airport, a ninety-minute drive from my home, parked my car, and flew to Dallas in the first, uneventful leg of my journey. But then dramatic thunderstorms and resulting flight delays and cancellations triggered a massive breakdown in air traffic management at the Dallas–Fort Worth airport. Every gate in the terminal had an aircraft that could not leave because its crew had exceeded the safe-working-hour limits, and new crews were unavailable because of this blockage of every gate. The airport filled up with stranded passengers, airport restaurants ran out of food, and all hotel rooms in the area were booked. I was smack-dab in the middle of a complex failure in a variable context. I had to spend the night stretched out on the floor in the terminal, waiting for morning, when the airlines sorted out the chaos. This failure was not caused by something I did or did not do (other than not building in a buffer day to ensure I arrived in Boston on time). Fortunately, my interviewers did not hold this complex failure against me and spoil my chances of joining the doctoral program when I arrived in town a day late.

Novel and intelligent

When we venture into new territory—moving to another city, starting relationships, learning a language, creating a recipe—failures are inevitable. The academic scientists who discover new chemical reactions or the latest galactic body expect a high failure rate along the way to the occasional spectacular success. Even in the corporate setting, over 90 percent of newly developed drugs fail in the experimental stage and never make it to market. Most of us don't face failure rates that high in our day-to-day lives. But we do need to learn to appreciate the value of experimenting in our lives so as to embrace the lessons from intelligent failures in novel contexts.

My husband is a good cook. He's also a scientist who frequently travels to other universities to present his work. He's rarely more enthusiastic than when he's returned home from a trip that included being taken to a top restaurant by his hosts and wonders whether he might be able to re-create some exquisite dish he enjoyed. Several years ago, he set out to replicate the octopus he'd enjoyed at a celebrated New York restaurant. Maybe you already know how difficult it is to cook octopus—but it definitely qualified as new culinary terrain for him. Alas, the results were abysmal. I recall that he started with a recipe and branched out to vary the ingredients and cooking method in ways that must have made sense to him. To say the dish was chewy and rubbery would be accurate but understated. It was inedible. (I wish I could say my reaction to the failure was as cheerful and supportive as it should have been, but I digress.) Was it nonetheless worth trying? Yes, of course. Did he ever try again? Again yes. Although it has never become my favorite, today his octopus is tasty.

Our lives are full of simple, complex, and (if we're trying hard enough) intelligent failures. A relationship between context and failure type is easy to see: novel contexts are home to intelligent failures, consistent contexts spawn basic failures, and variable contexts are conducive to complex failures.

True but incomplete.

Mapping the rest of the landscape

As I'm sure you've already realized, you can generate an intelligent failure in a consistent context. But you can also experience a basic failure in a novel context. Let's call these *off-diagonal failures*. Every other combination is possible, too, as you will see. Marrying the three failure types with the three context types gives us nine failure-context combinations, as shown in Figure 6.2. Along the diagonal are the three iconic failure types in their home turf. Now let's take a look at six other failure stories to get a sense of the rest of the failure landscape.

Someone managing a factory production line may periodically run a small experiment to test an improvement idea, only to find that it doesn't work. That's an intelligent failure in a consistent context. Or a well-run production process might be shut down by a hurricane's disrupting a faraway parts supplier, while a sudden flu takes out a quarter of the workforce who might otherwise be able to replace the missing parts. At home, your favorite batch of cookies might be ruined by a power outage. Both constitute complex failures in consistent contexts.

The Air Florida pilots in the Washington, DC, snowstorm who mistakenly approved "anti-ice off" during the preflight checklist demonstrated the ease with which a basic failure can occur in a variable context. When researcher H. Clayton Foushee put teams of pilots in the deliberately variable context of a flight simulator and challenged them to land safely after surprise malfunctions, intelligent failures helped advance the safety of passenger air travel. If you decide to experiment with a new backhand grip playing tennis and it leaves you worse off after trying for a while to make it work, that, too, qualifies as an intelligent failure in a variable context.

Lastly, it should be clear that novel contexts—those places where intelligent failures advance the ideas and products that change our world—are not devoid of either complex or basic failures. Remember how Jen Heemstra used the pipette incorrectly, ruining an experiment. All sorts of complex failures can happen in novel contexts, despite the most thoughtful planning and hypothesizing. Just ask the scientists whose research programs hit a dead end when a global pandemic shut down supply chains and sent team members home.

Developing context awareness is as crucial for preventing unwanted failures as for encouraging us to have more fun experimenting when we can safely do so. By adapting your approach, you can thrive in any context. Consistent contexts give us an opportunity to relish reliability and continuously improve our skill in the tried-and-true. In variable contexts, we can enjoy being energized by heightened vigilance. Celebrating good catches—having reframed the close call from bad to good—helps to reinforce our awareness that things *will* go wrong, but our ability to notice and correct errors before real harm occurs is what matters most. Novel contexts, especially when the stakes are low, provide opportunities to experiment thoughtfully and relish the lessons

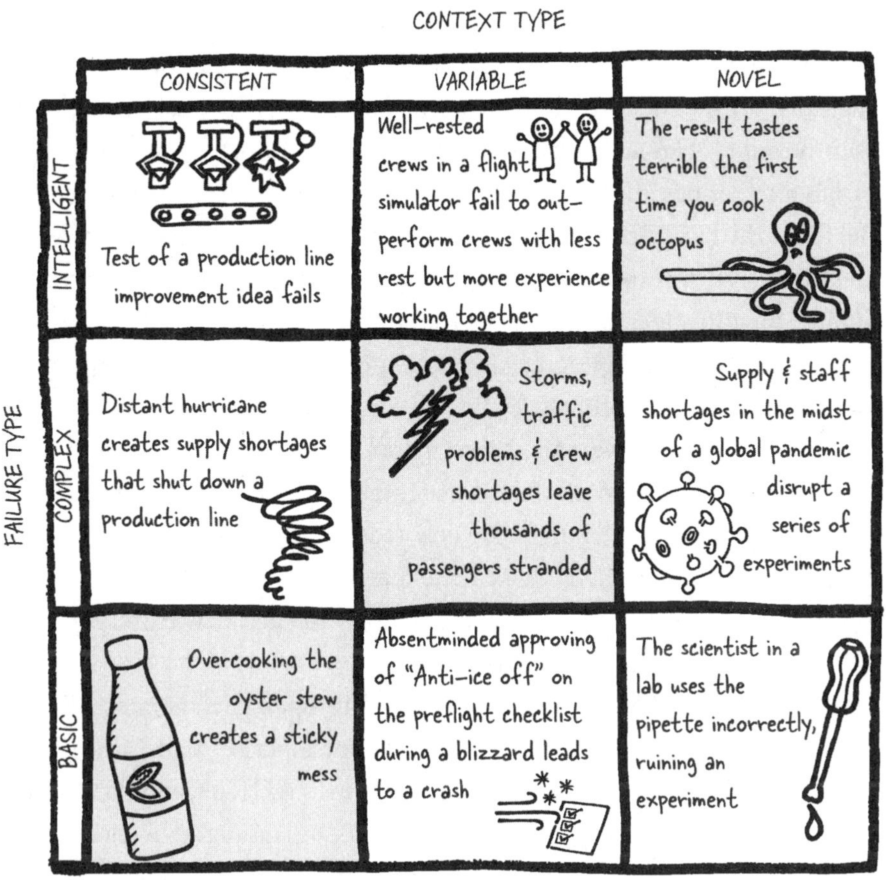

CONTEXT TYPE

	CONSISTENT	VARIABLE	NOVEL
INTELLIGENT	Test of a production line improvement idea fails	Well-rested crews in a flight simulator fail to out-perform crews with less rest but more experience working together	The result tastes terrible the first time you cook octopus
COMPLEX	Distant hurricane creates supply shortages that shut down a production line	Storms, traffic problems & crew shortages leave thousands of passengers stranded	Supply & staff shortages in the midst of a global pandemic disrupt a series of experiments
BASIC	Overcooking the oyster stew creates a sticky mess	Absentminded approving of "Anti-ice off" on the preflight checklist during a blizzard leads to a crash	The scientist in a lab uses the pipette incorrectly, ruining an experiment

(Left axis label: FAILURE TYPE)

FIGURE 6.2: The Failure Landscape

intelligent failures bring. To learn how to smile when we hit a beep going forward.

Expect the Unexpected

Ben Berman has been involved in aviation safety for decades. A former captain at United Airlines whose impressive career includes accident investigations at the National Transportation Safety Board and research on how human vulnerabilities such as distractions, interruptions, and cognitive errors affect flight-crew performance at NASA, Berman exudes humility. He's also wise enough to call attention to the context variability that lies ahead in any air journey. To do that in the commercial flights he led, Captain Berman would routinely tell the cockpit crew members with whom he was newly paired, "I've never done a perfect flight." What this tells us is that Berman understands that even the best and most experienced pilot may face unexpected challenges and cannot be counted on to respond perfectly.

In my research, I've called this a *framing statement*. Framing is something experienced leaders do naturally because they recognize that people need help to diagnose and recode the context to be most effective. Berman recalled, when I spoke with him in early May 2022, how he thought about those early moments with each new team:

> I wanted to break the ice, and I wanted to open the channel. I would start by saying, "Well, I've never done a perfect flight, and I'm going to prove it to you again." And they would laugh, and then I'd say, "So, I need you; I want you to speak up and tell me when I'm doing something wrong, because it will happen. And I'll do the same for you." And they always nodded and smiled.

Berman believes that there is no such thing as a routine flight, and he wants every member of the crew to be unafraid to speak up quickly with a question or a concern:

> [One goal] was to invite their inquiry, to open the channel of communication. And the other was to recognize the truth that I *was* going to make a mistake. I *have* never done a perfect flight. I've come close sometimes, but I still get mad at myself when I'm flying and I forget to press a button, and the copilot reminds me. I get

mad at myself because I'm looking for perfection. I certainly don't get mad at the copilot for telling me!

What struck me most acutely in Ben's comments was his vital understanding of the context in which he worked: the moderate uncertainty of a variable context, along with high stakes. Perfectionism and ego are sources of danger in such a context. He explained, "There's enough dynamism, enough distractions, enough fatigue, enough complacency. All the things that lead to error. It *will* happen. I am going to make mistakes, and I need the whole crew to participate. That's why I was saying that to them."

Experts in almost any field take context into account habitually. The rest of us have to remind ourselves to do it. To practice situation awareness is to appreciate where you are right now, so you can adopt the right mindset for the context and the stakes. Perhaps you can think of a time at work when you tormented yourself with anxiety about whether you would succeed in a role or a project. I know I can. It happened many times while I was writing this book! Situation awareness allows you to take stock of where you are and proceed appropriately, sometimes to reduce unhelpful anxiety and other times to lower risk. It's about developing the habit to pause and check—both for in-the-moment reactions and when planning some project or event—by asking yourself two essential questions: Where am I on the context spectrum? And what's at stake?

While sizing up the uncertainty and the stakes, you might ask yourself, "Is this something I've done before? Are there experts or guidelines I can use to increase the chances of success?" For example, the start of any new book project brings uncertainty: how to structure the book and whether anyone will want to read it are entirely up in the air. But during the writing, the stakes are low. Anything I write that comes out wrong or doesn't convey my idea clearly can be edited repeatedly until it's better. Edits cost nothing and no one else has to see the work until I'm ready. I could diagnose the context as consistent with the lower-right corner of Figure 6.1 on page 211, where it's okay to "have fun experimenting and learning."

More generally, situation awareness helps us feel better about experimenting when it's safe to do so and helps us be cautious when warranted to prevent unwanted failures.

CHAPTER 7

Appreciating Systems

A bad system will beat a good person every time.

—W. Edwards Deming

Spencer Silver was trying to develop an adhesive strong enough for use in aircraft construction. The year: 1968. The place: 3M's central research laboratory near Minneapolis. Experimenting one day, Silver used more than the recommended amount of a chemical reactant and was astonished to find that he'd created a thin, weak substance that could be removed from surfaces as easily as it stuck to them. But the strange misfit substance wouldn't be strong enough to glue a broken toy together, let alone to withstand the extreme conditions of a metal aircraft in flight. He had clearly failed in his assigned research task. Most likely the adhesive would be doomed to sit on the lab shelf as a curiosity.

You probably already know that Silver's laboratory "failure" would become the opening chapter in a multibillion-dollar business success story called Post-it notes. But you may not appreciate the degree to which 3M had built a system that dramatically increased the chances of successful innovation.

The journey that eventually turned a failed aircraft adhesive into a wildly popular product—and how easily it could have been missed altogether without a special combination of persistence and collaborative happenstance—sheds useful light on the nature of systems. In addition to organizational systems such as 3M, all of us operate in systems in our everyday lives—family systems, ecosystems, and school systems, to name a few. This makes system awareness—especially understanding how systems can produce unwanted failures—a crucial skill in the science of failing well.

A system's results are less shaped by its individual parts than by how the parts relate to one another. This simple but powerful idea can help you analyze and design various systems in your life to get better results. Later in this chapter I'll return to how 3M designed a system to generate the right kind of wrong and thereby spawn countless innovations. But first, let's take a closer look at what it means to think in terms of systems.

Systems and Synergy

Derived from the Greek for "putting together," the word *system* refers to a set of elements (or parts) that come together to form a meaningful whole—that is, a recognizable entity, whether a family, a company, a car, or a baseball team. Systems exhibit *synergy*: the whole is more than the sum of the parts. Put slightly differently, the behavior of the whole can't be predicted by the behavior of the parts examined separately. Only by considering the *relationships between* parts can you explain a system's behavior. There are man-made systems and nature-made systems. In every case, how elements interrelate is what matters most.

Consider the striking difference between graphite, the soft gray substance in pencils, and a diamond, that sparkling gemstone so prevalent in engagement rings. Although we know them as profoundly different substances, both consist exclusively of carbon atoms. The dif-

228

ference lies in the geometric relationships between the carbon atoms. In diamonds, the atoms arrange into a triangulated matrix structure that creates a stable, strong material. In graphite, the carbon atoms are organized hexagonally in planes that can shift, giving graphite its softness. Buckminsterfullerene, a third naturally occurring carbon system, wasn't discovered until 1985. In *buckyballs*, as scientists playfully dubbed the new form, sixty carbon atoms link together, each with two close neighbors, to form a geometric sphere resembling a soccer ball. The discovery earned scientists Robert Curl, Harold Kroto, and Richard Smalley a Nobel Prize in 1996 and gave rise to a handful of innovative materials used in medicine, electronics, and even in paint. Again, buckyballs' properties are explained by the relationships between the parts—not by the parts themselves.

These and other obscure insights from my early career as Buckminster Fuller's chief engineer left me with a deep appreciation for systems. Fuller was quick to point out that most people's education hadn't prepared them to see systems. He believed that ever-increasing specialization threatened our ability to appreciate how systems work. Moreover, in school we learn to break problems down into parts, which enables focus and progress in many fields of knowledge but blinds us to larger patterns and relationships. Traditional management systems similarly break work down into parts, inhibiting collaboration and innovation in favor of reliability and efficiency.

As we saw in chapter 4, systems with interactive complexity and tight coupling are vulnerable to breakdowns. By taking the time to consider how a system works, many complex failures can be avoided. This starts with understanding how a system's elements interrelate and what vulnerabilities those relationships create. Whenever we say an accident was "waiting to happen," we're intuiting that a system was vulnerable to failure. Complex failures, as noted in chapter 4, have multiple causes; yet too often we look for the single cause or culprit. Getting into the habit of looking for relationships between elements in a system allows us to anticipate and prevent all kinds of failures and breakdowns and, just as important, allows us to learn more from the failures that do occur. Many of them will turn out to have been predictable had you stepped back to consider the system.

Your twelve-year-old son wants to join the travel baseball team in addition to the town team he's already on. Sounds like fun, not to mention a chance to develop his skills and play more often a sport he loves. It's an easy yes, right? Not so fast. First, let's pause to consider how the decision will affect other parts of your son's life, his siblings' lives, and your family's other activities. The extra hours devoted to baseball practice must come from somewhere, perhaps leaving less time for homework, which could in the longer run affect study habits or academic achievement. The games are scheduled in the evenings several days a week, requiring parent driving and limiting family dinners. Joining the team also costs money, perhaps making funds unavailable for something else. What about the activities your other children want to join? A simple yes today brings multiple consequences for others and for the future. A decision in one part of a family system at one moment often affects other parts and later times. The point is not to say no indiscriminately to any alteration in your family's activities. Rather, it's to diagnose the most important interrelationships so as to say yes, or no, thoughtfully. What you want is to benefit from the simple act of asking, (1) "Who and what else is affected by this?" and (2) "What might happen later, as a consequence of doing this now?"

Once you start seeing systems—seeing connections between parts—you can begin to see ways to alter the most important systems in your life or organization to reduce unwanted failures and to promote greater innovation, efficiency, safety, or other valued outcomes. Recall the lax gun safety on the set of *Rust*; tragedy could have been prevented with a better-designed system complete with repeated checks to keep real bullets out of fictional battles.

System awareness also helps you feel less bad about some of the things that go wrong in your work or personal life. When you start to see systems more clearly, you understand better that you are not *wholly* responsible for most of the failures that occur. You can feel responsible for your *contributions* to them—and determine to do better next time—but suffer less from the delusion that you're entirely to blame.

System design is not just for preventing failures. Equally important is the opportunity to design systems thoughtfully to achieve particular goals. For instance, later in this chapter we'll look at how 3M designed a system to *foster* innovation, rather than simply announcing innovation as a goal and hoping for more of it. This chapter will not do justice to entire fields such as systems thinking, system dynamics, ecological systems, family systems, or organizational systems. Instead, I hope to provide just enough technical explanation to illuminate the role of system awareness in the science of failing well. The ability to step back and take a broader view—to see how something you care about may be part of a larger system—can be learned with practice. But first, let's take a look at a classic exercise used in business schools around the world to introduce people to the surprising dynamics of systems, so they can become better systems thinkers.

Experiencing Systems

Exclamations of frustration erupt around the classroom. Twenty teams, each with four Harvard Business School students lined up together at a long table, are participating in a classic classroom exercise called the Beer Game. Some are laughing from the sheer absurdity of their unexpected failures. No actual beer is being consumed, but the game, developed by MIT professor Jay Forrester back in the 1960s, endures as a popular session in management education. I first taught the exercise to managers at Apple Computer back in the late 1980s and brought it to Harvard Business School's first-year students a decade later. Originally played with pen, paper, printed tablecloths, and poker chips, the simulation's purpose is to teach you to see systems—to help you stretch your vision beyond your natural focus on parts so as to appreciate how relationships between parts may create unintended results.

Each team includes four student roles, each symbolizing a player in a beer supply chain: a factory, a distributor, a wholesaler, and a retailer. Retailers order beer from wholesalers, who order from distributors, who order from the factory. Students playing retailers sit next to a stack of cards that they turn over each "week" (that is, each round in the simulation) to reveal how much beer the "customer" wants to buy. All students record their inventory and orders in a spreadsheet each round of the "fifty-week" simulation, along with the associated financial costs, as a way of tracking their performance. The four players on a team do not communicate with one another (except through ordering and delivery), but they can see each other's inventory. The final team score is the sum of their tallies. The only decisions students must make during the simulation are how much beer to order each round.

No other tasks involve decisions. Students playing wholesalers, distributors, and factories look at incoming orders (from their downstream customer) and fill the orders by sending the requested cases of beer into the supply chain. It takes three weeks to receive inventory after an order is requested. If there's not enough inventory, the suppliers ship what they have and record the gap (called a stock-out) in the inventory record. It costs fifty cents a week for each case of beer stored in inventory, and it costs twice as much, a dollar per case per week, to have a stock-out. This cost structure simulates the negative impact to a business of being unable to provide a product to a customer who's ready to pay for it on the spot, often driving that customer to do business elsewhere. Most companies would rather bear the cost of storing a little extra inventory than to lose a sale. So, the incentive structure built into the game makes sense. Once you receive new deliveries from your supplier, you can belatedly ship backlog cases to your customer.

So where does the frustration come from?

A few rounds into the game, everyone is facing extreme oscillations in their downstream customer's ordering patterns, leaving them first with too little inventory, then later with too much, and then with too little again. A lovely "sine wave" of orders and inventory. Early in the simulation, orders seem to be rising steeply. Maybe it's a national holiday, students think, and beer drinking has surged for the weekend. Caught off guard by lost sales, they decide to order more the next week, and the next—until the beer finally arrives! Unfortunately, soon enough, they have way more inventory than they can sell. Students groan under the weight of the mounting costs on their spreadsheets.

Called the bullwhip effect by operations management scholars, a huge distortion in demand results from the design of the system. The further you get from the retailer, the worse the distortion. Factories have the biggest swings of all because they're three links in the supply chain away from the retailer, whose oscillations are relatively small—yet still bigger than necessary. As the simulation wears on, the students keep groaning (and laughing) about how much money they've lost.

Where do these expensive inventory failures come from? The short answer is that they come from the system. Each person makes what they see as rational decisions, week after week, to minimize costs. So far so good. But when combined, these individual, locally rational decisions give rise to wasteful cost overruns in the game's supply chain. In real life, these oscillations wreak havoc on people's lives, often provoking layoffs and even company bankruptcies.

The Beer Game, invented by Forrester and made popular by Peter Senge, who described the exercise in his seminal 1990 book, *The Fifth Discipline*, constitutes a pretty simple system. It presents a supply chain with only four entities, connected by simple buying-and-selling relationships. Real-life supply chains might include several distributors for each factory, dozens of wholesalers, and hundreds or even thousands of retailers—creating far more complex systems capable of producing even greater distortions, as the global coronavirus pandemic demonstrated. Moreover, each player in the game makes only one decision each "week": how much to order. Despite this simplicity, or perhaps because of it, it's possible to see how their individually rational decisions combine in fascinating ways to produce undesired dynamics.

Three specific features in the Beer Game combine to create a system failure. First, the simple cost structure favors inventory over stock-outs, encouraging students to order buffer stock—that is, to order slightly more than the customer asked for the previous week. Second, the delay between making an order and its being received from the supplier tempts players, waiting impatiently for that needed inventory, to place a slightly higher order the next week. Third, a onetime increase in orders from the retailers' customers in the fourth week of the simulation introduces a small shock that triggers anxiety about stock-outs—further encouraging overordering.

But the true cause of the system failure is that people try to optimize their own part of the system and do not step back to consider how their actions impact others. Although students know that their performance will be calculated as a team score, they come to the game with a strong assumption: *if everyone optimizes their own performance, the team will do well.* Alas, this is faulty logic. Everyone's actions affect others in the system: when someone orders *more* than a role has in stock, that role incurs a costly stock-out. Only the rare student steps back and considers the cost impact of an overly large order on the supplier who is, after all, a team member, even though it's easy to calculate these costs. When I order more from you than you have in stock, I am creating an expensive problem in your business (and because you are part of my team, your costs impact our team performance). But stepping back from a narrow focus on our own situation to see how our actions may impact the broader system, which will in turn impact us, is not something most of us are naturally inclined to do.

Whenever I teach the Beer Game, I ask students to explain the failure during the debrief. Why do they think they ended up with such enormous cost overruns? They answer quickly that the crazy customer, buying beer from the retailer, was ordering too much beer, then went on a dry spell, and finally came back to ordering again.

The students place the blame squarely on that deck of cards containing retail customer orders. I then reveal that the retail customer orders were basically flat; after one small uptick at week four, that boring customer ordered the same amount of beer week after week after week. Students are stunned. At the peak, some of the factories in the simulation had produced more than ten times what the retail customer ordered. It was the students' own decisions that created the costly failure.

At this point, I have their attention.

Simulations such as the Beer Game are powerful because they give us a chance to be surprised by the unexpected failures that result from our assumptions. They're microcosms that make otherwise invisible patterns visible. Only *once* in my years of teaching have I seen a team spontaneously minimize costs by practicing systems thinking. When asked why her team had performed so well, a student said, "I could see that my team members couldn't deliver the quantity I wanted, and that backlog would have cost us money." Not rocket science! But rare nonetheless. When our assumptions don't reflect the relationships and dynamics of a system, we're at risk of experiencing preventable failures.

Supply chains are particularly vulnerable to system failures, as we experienced during the COVID-19 pandemic when factory shutdowns and shipping delays in one part of the world affected what people could buy in another. Had more companies made decisions based on the capacity of other players in the system, the disruption might have been far less. The Beer Game brings to life in a classroom the costs of maximizing performance in one part of a system while failing to consider how that part connects to the goals of other parts. Once students see that their own mental models—not the assumed wild ordering patterns of customers—caused their poor performance, they sit up and take notice. They start to wonder, Where else might I be contributing to the very failures I blame on other people or situations outside my control?

Systems Thinking

Temporal discounting, discussed in chapter 3, refers to our tendency to downplay the magnitude and importance of events that happen in the future. Add to that our tendency to forget to pause and consider the possible unintended consequences of our decisions and actions in general, and it's easy to recognize the source of problems ranging from your unwanted weight gain to climate change. Systems thinking is not a panacea, and simply learning about it won't magically solve problems created by its absence. But with repeated practice, your thinking habits can be changed to build system awareness into your life.

Practicing systems thinking starts with consciously expanding your lens from its natural preference for *here and now* to include *elsewhere and later*.

Two simple questions can help:

1. Who and what else will be affected by this decision or action?
2. What additional consequences might this decision or action cause in the future?

Most of us know to be wary of the quick fix—the Band-Aid that plasters over but doesn't solve an underlying problem—but we still take these tempting shortcuts often—ignoring, or failing to make the connection to, the part where the problem recurs or even worsens. We're vulnerable to falling into the trap of what Senge calls the "fix that fails." This classic *system dynamic* describes a short-term solution that ends up exacerbating the problem it was intended to fix.

Our mental models are partially to blame. A mental model is a cognitive map that captures your intuitive notions about how something in the external world functions. Its power comes from being taken for granted: you don't consciously pay attention to your mental models, but they underlie your understanding of how things work and thus shape your responses in largely invisible ways. Most important, mental models encode beliefs about cause and effect. This is neither good nor bad—just descriptive of how your brain works. Mental models are invaluable in helping us make sense of the complex and chaotic world around us so we can navigate it without being paralyzed—unable to make simple decisions—in the face of complexity. But our default mental models don't usually include system effects, until we learn to pause and challenge some of our automatic thinking.

We tend to think about cause and effect as operating in one direction and in a time-bounded, local manner: X causes Y. Saying yes to my son's request to join the travel baseball team makes him happy. End of story. We miss noticing how an intended result (Y) becomes a cause of something else (Z). Treating job stress with alcohol, for example, soothes anxiety in the moment but may, if overused, create an alcohol dependence that over time worsens a person's job and life, further increasing both the dependence and the stress.

Consider the fixes that have failed in your experience—whether at work or in some other aspect of your life. To fix a work overload, you push a meeting scheduled this week to next. When next week rolls around, your workload has not gotten any better, and the delayed meeting now concerns a bigger problem than before. What should you do instead? Here's a good start: make a serious assessment of system capacity (your capacity) for projects, prioritizing those that matter most, and saying no to the others. Otherwise, you simply kick the can down the road. Fixes fail because a symptom demands a response, often urgently, triggering a solution that alleviates the symptom in the short run, but produces consequences that make the problem worse over time.

Take the proverbial toddler having a tantrum and demanding candy while you're at the grocery store. The easiest fix, especially for a frazzled parent, is to simply give the child the candy. But that only works for a short time—until the sugar rush abates and the bad mood returns. Worse, it sets a precedent for rewarding bad behavior, increasing the chances for future demands. The quick fix ignores both the near-term feedback loop (today's sugar rush) and the longer-term effects (behavioral problems that set in).

Anticipate downstream consequences

Right before the holidays in December 2021, fifty-seven container ships were idled in the ocean near the largest port in the United States, Los Angeles, unable to unload their cargoes, serve the demands of holiday shoppers, and get back to their designated routes. The delays went on for weeks, and solutions remained stubbornly elusive in the months that followed. And who can forget the giant ship stuck in the Suez Canal earlier in 2021?

The shipping industry suffered more than its share of complex failures during the global pandemic. Were these just exogenous shocks from pandemic-induced shortages that threw an otherwise healthy system into breakdown? Systems thinking suggests additional considerations.

To capitalize on efficiencies of scale and reduce costs per unit shipped, container ships had over several decades been made bigger and bigger. Many of them became so big that by 1991 only a few ports were large and deep enough to accommodate them. Can you see the bottleneck on the horizon? Unless everything is perfectly timed, many ships will be unable to access a port. Even small perturbations in staffing or ordinary operations were magnified by the shrinking number of ports able to accept the growing number of giant ships. The margin for error had shrunk during the pandemic.

As *Wired* reporter Michael Waters wrote, "Container ships have gotten so big so quickly that many ports can't really accommodate these giant boats, creating a backlog that directly explains why your holiday gifts are arriving late. Plus, small and midsized ports risk getting sized out entirely."

How do you fix the breakdown? Linear thinking, uninformed by systems thinking, immediately suggests what will happen next. As Waters reported, "To create enough space to welcome this ballooning number of megaships, some ports have responded with extensive ocean-dredging projects. But it isn't cheap. Jacksonville is spending $484 million to deepen its channel. Houston's dredging project will cost closer to $1 billion." Mind-numbingly expensive, such projects work in the short term but mostly kick the can down the road. This happens because of the failure to ask the simple question, What might be the result of this decision in the future?

Even skilled professionals trying hard to do the right thing fall prey to favoring the here and now over the elsewhere and later.

Resist the quick fix

Boston University professor Anita Tucker and I studied nurses carrying out the dozens of tasks that occupied them throughout long hospital shifts. Taking detailed notes, complete with time stamps, to document the work of these dedicated caregivers at nine hospitals, Anita observed that nurses confronted "process failures" surprisingly often—almost one an hour. A process failure was anything that disrupted a nurse's ability to complete a task, such as an unexpected supply shortage in bed linens or medications. The nurses were acutely aware of these frustrating daily hurdles. Their jobs were hard enough! On average nurses were working an extra (unpaid) forty-five minutes simply to tie up loose ends before leaving the hospital.

We discovered that nurses' responses to process failures fell into two categories. What we called "first-order problem-solving" was a work-around to complete the task without addressing causes of the problem. For example, a nurse working the night shift who ran out of clean linens to change her patients' beds simply walked to another unit that had linens and took from their supply. Problem solved. The work-around required minimal time and effort. She'd taken the initiative and been resourceful in caring for her patients. Never mind that the other unit was now in short supply. You can see in this example the simple failure to ask, Who else might be affected by this action?

In contrast, for 7 percent of the process failures, nurses engaged in what we dubbed "second-order problem-solving." This could mean simply informing a supervisor or someone in charge of linens about the shortage. Second-order problem-solving got the immediate task done *and* did something to prevent the problem from recurring. Second-order problem-solving for a toddler throwing tantrums for candy might entail a few gentle but firm words to calm the child or distracting with a toy, while refraining from rewarding the bad behavior. It also might mean pausing to consider whether a nap was overdue (a possible cause of the tantrum) and resolving to do future errands after rather than before nap time.

We can easily understand why busy nurses rarely engaged in second-order problem-solving. But this left them vulnerable to continued frustration because the work-arounds didn't reduce the frequency of future process failures. The average time a nurse spent on work-arounds (a few minutes here, a few minutes there) added up to about half an hour per shift—a substantial waste of skilled professionals' time. Like all quick fixes, the nurses' work-arounds created an *illusion of effectiveness*. Confront a problem, implement a work-around, get on with your day. End of story.

Except that it's not.

When we analyzed the hospital nursing care as a system, we realized that work-arounds, despite being effective in the short term, actually made the system worse over time. You read that correctly. Reliance on work-arounds does not just fail to improve the system, it makes it worse. To show how this works, in Figure 7.1 the text and arrows capture what we might call the *simple-fix dynamic*. The more process failures there are blocking task execution (factor 1), the more first-order problem-solving (factor 2) happens. Here I use the convention for

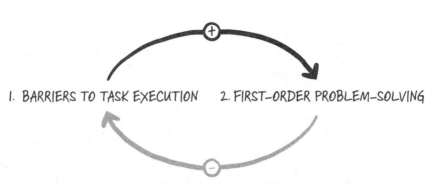

FIGURE 7.1: A Simple-Fix Balancing Loop Linking Barriers and Problem-Solving

diagnosing systems that I learned from Peter Senge: the plus sign on the arrow between two elements in a system dynamics diagram indicates that an increase (or decrease) in one factor drives an increase (or decrease) in the other factor. Another way to put it is that the two factors move in the same direction. Conversely a minus sign on the connecting arrow (shown in gray) indicates that an increase in one factor will lead to a decrease in the other. Thus, as depicted, first-order problem-solving reduces the barriers. This two-element, two-relationship system is called by system dynamicists such as Senge a balancing loop. At first glance it looks like a system that's working.

Now let's step back and get a broader view of the system.

Redraw the boundaries

You redraw the boundaries of your decision or action when you go beyond here and now. Members of successful teams in the Beer Game must redraw boundaries to include the team's total costs, rather than focusing on minimizing their individual costs. A small question about a travel baseball team is seen as part of a larger set of related issues.

Instead of drawing the boundary around your son and the team, you deliberately include other family members and future months, or even years, in the system you're diagnosing. You don't have to (nor could you) include the entire universe. Where relevance ends is undeniably a judgment call.

For the nurses worn down by obstacles and work-arounds, what if we include factors just outside the little system in Figure 7.1? We soon discover additional dynamics playing out over time. Eight additional relevant factors are included in the redrawn, expanded hospital system in Figure 7.2, creating a reasonably complete set of the most relevant factors and dynamics. For example, many of the nurses we spoke to

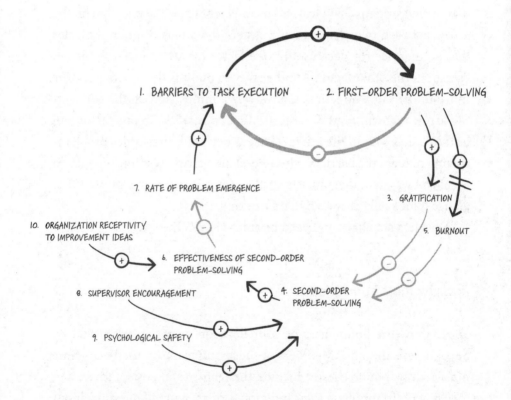

FIGURE 7.2: Expanding the Boundaries of the Simple System

described a "hero feeling" from using work-arounds that ensured that patients got the care they deserved. Whether walking down the hall to locate the extra linens or going to the pharmacy to obtain a missing drug, the nurses derived gratification (factor 3) from overcoming the many little hurdles their jobs threw in their path. But this hero feeling lessened their motivation to engage in second-order problem-solving, as depicted by the negative arrow linking gratification to second-order problem-solving (factor 4).

Worse, over time (two slashes on an arrow between elements in a system diagram indicates a delayed effect) the effort and time nurses put into work-arounds contributed to burnout (factor 5). This further diminished their capacity for second-order problem-solving, in turn reducing the effectiveness of such efforts (factor 6) and allowing process failures to continue unabated (factor 7). By engaging in systems thinking we see that an apparent equilibrium between two activities is *illusory*. It looks stable in the short term, but over time (and in other parts of the system) things are getting worse.

Given this problematic system dynamic, what's a nurse (or nurse manager) to do?

Find the levers

For the toddler throwing a tantrum for candy, the levers are those that help you practice positive redirection and limit-setting, including a regular nap schedule, to help a toddler develop healthy, happy behaviors. These levers exist in the larger system of parenting, not in the moment of the breakdown. Doing this thus starts with redrawing the boundaries of the system—to go beyond simply reacting to problems in the moment and instead step back and anticipate the downstream consequences of decisions that make sense in the here and now. Similarly, how should one handle the pervasive problem of stress so many people feel? Perhaps your first decision might be to use alcohol to relax, but by expanding the boundary you might find that exercise is another lever to alleviate stress and enhance long-term health. You expand the boundary of a system to bring in a new element (exercise) to arrest the eroding dynamic (alcohol dependence) created by a fix that fails.

On the left in Figure 7.2 lie three factors that can alter the erosion dynamic to invigorate the second-order problem-solving that nudges the system toward improvement. Supervisors encouraging and rewarding nurses for their extra effort (factor 8) to prevent a problem's reoccurrence is one lever for increasing second-order problem-solving to reduce the flow of process failures. Second, building a psychologically safe workplace (factor 9) allows people to speak up about problems and ideas for solving them. Third, organizational receptivity to improvement ideas (factor 10) makes people more likely to offer them.

The levers for improving the system were outside what initially looked like the relevant system: the barriers and the typical nurse responses. By consciously redrawing the boundary of the system, you identify other factors affecting the results you care about. You're looking for factors that produce unwanted results as well as those that might help change them.

Clearly, it's hard to resist the allure of the work-around. It's even harder to get the genie of giant container ships back in the bottle. But holding ourselves accountable for an ounce of anticipation (my larger ship may be cheaper for me today, but it will limit the number of ports I can serve, which will increase the chance of bottlenecks and delays and so on, ultimately costing money and leading to disappointed customers) forces us to think about how to design systems more thoughtfully. The burgeoning green shipping movement, for example, which aims to reduce greenhouse gas emissions from the industry by incorporating carbon-free maritime routes, includes ports and giant ships as part of the system redesign. And designing systems starts with clarity about what you're trying to achieve.

Designing Systems

I suspect that you, like me, have spent time in at least one organization where the incentives encouraged counterproductive behavior. For example, a few years ago I worked with a pharmaceutical company trying to improve teamwork among employees. Executives were fully aware that their knowledge-intensive business could only thrive when diverse experts teamed up to innovate. The leaders were sincere in their desire to make collaboration easier. But the company's performance review system required managers to rank their employees from best to worst—a collaboration killer that hadn't been revised in years.

This kind of disconnect happens often. Management practices are designed by experts in one part of a complex organizational system, reflecting logic that makes sense to them. Meanwhile, unintended consequences in another part of the system circle back to thwart the best-laid plans. Let's say a retail company, in an effort to attract mid-week shoppers, decides to move a special promotion from a typically busy Friday to Wednesday. Sounds like a good idea at headquarters, right? But the store manager must then shift schedules "from Friday to Wednesday, forcing employees to rearrange their lives, which in turn drives absenteeism and turnover."

I wish I could say that my years of study and research have turned me into a consistent systems thinker whose family gleaned the benefits. Unfortunately, far too often I instead fall into the here-and-now trap. One of those times was when I chose that easy yes when my son asked to join the travel baseball team. The incentive in place, I suppose, was (as is so often the case) to make my child happy. But let's fast-forward into the coming months of family life: night after night spent mostly watching the older son sit on a bench for hours while the younger one ran around the bleachers; all of us bemoaned the loss of family dinners, the long drives to games, and the lack of time for homework. The boys liked baseball a lot. But baseball had taken over our lives, occupying an outsize role in the family system. This small system breakdown fortunately lasted only a single baseball season.

Systems thinking lends itself to better system design. It's possible to design organizational systems—or family schedules—so that many elements reinforce a key priority, say, quality or safety or perhaps innovation. Let's take a look at some best-in-class systems in each of the categories.

A system for innovation

How do you increase the chances that a failed adhesive turns into a brilliant product? With a system designed to bring curious risk-takers together. Encourage and celebrate boundary spanning. Provide resources and slack time. Normalize intelligent failure and celebrate pivots. Declare that you want a significant portion of your company's revenues (or school's curricula or family's activities) to come from new and different products, courses, or experiences. Successful innovation does not come from the lone genius. Importantly, each of these familiar elements of innovation is reinforced by each of the others. The whole is more than the sum of the parts.

A few years after Silver's failure to invent an airplane superadhesive, Arthur Fry, another 3M research scientist, was out playing golf at Tartan Park, the company-owned course. Yes, you read that right. 3M had a golf course for its employees. It was one of the elements of a system that encouraged people to connect with one another, to take a brain-clearing walk to get unstuck or to simply get some fresh air. Always curious about what other people were working on, and eager to help develop new products, Fry kept track of what was going on across the organization, which kept him coming back to Tartan Park. He liked walking around outside and running into people. Arriving at the second hole one day, he made some casual inquiries.

"Well, we've got a guy named Spence," began Fry's colleague on the golf course. The colleague then described Silver's odd sticky substance. The matter might have ended there except for another element of 3M's innovation system: the Technical Forum. This was a lecture series that encouraged people to share ideas and discoveries made inside the company. Fry made it a point to attend a talk by Silver at the forum and heard him describe some experiments that had failed with coating a bulletin board with the adhesive. Although by then assigned to other projects, Silver remained convinced that his discovery of "acrylate co-polymer microspheres" had potential; he'd even taken out a patent on it. His frequent promotion of the material with colleagues left him with the moniker Mr. Persistent.

Both Silver and Fry were elite failure practitioners who relished the chance to explore in ways that were both serious and playful. They were good scientists, but we cannot underestimate the importance of a system that was designed to produce innovations. What else did that system entail?

In one of the most provocative elements of 3M's system—provocative, at least, in an era in which companies valorized efficiency—engineers were allowed to spend 15 percent of their paid time pursuing crazy ideas that might turn out to be failures. Later adopted by Silicon Valley companies such as Google and IDEO, the policy reflected an understanding that paying scientists to experiment would produce a lot of failures along with the occasional lucrative success. The economics work—so long as you're patient. That is, so long as you expand the boundary of the system to include the future profitability of the company, not just the present.

At the time that Fry met Silver, 3M's most successful products were tapes: Scotch tape, reflective tape, magnetic tape to record television programs, double-coated tape, and the company's latest hit: Scotch Magic tape.

Perhaps that's why in 1974, on a Sunday morning in a Presbyterian church in St. Paul, Minnesota, when Fry was frantically thumbing for the correct page in his hymnal, he remembered Silver's misfit adhesive.

Wednesday evenings, during choir rehearsal, he often put little pieces of paper into the book to mark the music the choir would sing during the service. Sundays, when he opened the hymnal, to Fry's annoyance the pieces would often flutter out. This Sunday, something clicked. Fry found himself wishing for a better bookmark, one that could stick to the pages of his hymnal without pulling it apart. Maybe Silver's adhesive would solve the problem. Fry started to think about sticky notes in pads. At work the next day, Fry procured a sample of the microspheres and began to experiment. His colleagues were not sold on the idea, and he decided to set up shop in his home basement, where he spent a few months building a machine to produce the sticky notepads.

Years later, in his late seventies, he would emphatically assert that what happened at 3M over the next six years to develop today's ubiquitous Post-it notes "wasn't an accident." It was instead the result of a series of intelligent failures, supported by a system designed to encourage persistence to produce innovation. Let's take a look at a few of the hurdles that had to be overcome. First, Fry had technical hurdles to get the microspheres to a consistency that could be applied to a narrow band along the lower edge of one side of a strip of paper, so as to share prototypes with his colleagues and supervisors. Yet even that success was dubious; realistically, how many people would want to buy a bookmark, no matter how nifty its application?

What Fry calls the "eureka, head-flapping moment" happened when he sent a report to a supervisor with a note on the front written on part of the bookmark and the supervisor wrote back on the same piece of paper. A sticky *note* that could be repositioned had so many more uses for so many more people than a sticky bookmark!

Apparently convinced by Fry's proof of concept, 3M executives then agreed to produce a small run of sticky notepads. That hopeful step, however, soon turned into more of a setback: subsequent market testing of the new product in a few cities produced little enthusiasm from consumers. But Fry saw this first failed attempt to sell what was then called Press 'n Peel as inconclusive. He decided on a new experiment—

marketing to a different demographic, the people who worked at 3M. From his office, Fry distributed pads one at a time to friends and colleagues. He instructed people to return when they wanted another pad. Importantly, he kept a careful log of how many pads each person used. The data he collected was promising: up to twenty pads per individual per year. After more usability test runs within the company—pallets of the pads that were set out in the halls quickly emptied!—3M was finally convinced to launch an intensive marketing campaign in 1980. The rest, as they say, is history.

A system for quality

In designing a system to reduce basic failures and promote continuous improvement, no company rivals Toyota. It's not incidental that Toyota calls its approach, which has evolved over decades of experimentation, the Toyota Production *System*, or TPS. Manufacturing experts agree that this system creates far more value than the mere sum of its parts.

Let's start with the Andon Cord, which factory workers are invited to pull when they suspect a potential error on any vehicle. This is the best-known element in TPS, and for good reason: its symbolism (we want to hear from you, and we especially love to hear about problems so we can make things better) captures the overarching ethos of the system. The desire to halt any error in its tracks, before it disrupts other steps in the process, also reveals an intuitive appreciation of system effects. A single small error can easily compound into a major failure downstream if left uncorrected. The roots of the Andon Cord trace back to Sakichi Toyoda's nineteenth-century loom designed to come to a safe stop whenever a thread broke.

Another crucial element of TPS is its focus on eliminating waste (*muda*) wherever possible. Excess inventory is a form of waste (just recall the Beer Game!), so *just-in-time* (JIT) production (build only what is needed, when it is needed, by your customer) is a crucial element of the system. JIT also complements the Andon Cord. The two elements work together to ensure that defects are discovered and resolved rather than piling up in work-in-process inventory. Both elements build learning into the system, to enable continuous improvement (or *kaizen*).

Countless articles and books have been written on Toyota, and this chapter will not attempt to do justice to the intricacies of this remarkable production system and why it works. But my former student Steven Spear and colleague Kent Bowen at Harvard summed up the system in a way that for me connects its disparate parts and explains its power:

> . . . The key is to understand that the Toyota Production System creates *a community of scientists*. Whenever Toyota defines a specification, it is establishing sets of hypotheses that can then be tested. In other words, it is following the scientific method. To make any changes, Toyota uses a rigorous problem-solving process that requires a detailed assessment of the current state of affairs and a plan for improvement that is, in effect, an experimental test of the proposed changes. With anything less than such scientific rigor, change at Toyota would amount to little more than random trial and error—a blindfolded walk through life.

Create "a community of scientists"? In a factory? Absolutely. TPS and the systems designed for innovation at 3M and IDEO have in common that they create communities of scientists. Helping you think like a scientist—curious, humble, willing to test a hypothesis rather than assume it's right—is what ties them together. A key difference between Toyota and 3M is the scope of leeway for experiments. Toyota's community of scientists works to perfect a system of production designed to remove unwanted variation and ensure perfect quality; the scope of experiments is limited for the most part to those that improve existing processes. At 3M, in contrast, scientists are invited to go wild, think outside the box, and imagine useful products that don't yet even begin to exist. But in both systems, psychological safety plays a vital role.

Consider the story told by James Wiseman to a *Fast Company* reporter. Wiseman had brought considerable experience as a manager in other manufacturers when he joined Toyota in Georgetown, Kentucky, in 1989 to manage its statewide public affairs program. His prior work experience made him surprised by what he found at Toyota. Fujio Cho, who would later become chairman of Toyota worldwide, was Georgetown's plant manager. One Friday, in a senior staff meeting, Wiseman had an experience that forever changed his understanding of how Toyota worked.

Wiseman had spoken up during the meeting and, as he put it, had been "reporting some of my little successes." He went on, "I gave a report of an activity we'd be doing . . . and I spoke very positively about it, I bragged a little." So far, nothing special to see here. Bragging (or at least presenting one's work in as positive a light as possible) in the presence of the boss is completely normal workplace behavior. We've all done it!

But here the story takes an unusual turn. Wiseman continues, "After two or three minutes, I sat down. And Mr. Cho kind of looked at me. I could see he was puzzled. He said, 'Jim-san. We all *know* you are a good manager, otherwise we would not have hired you. But please talk to us about your problems so we can work on them together.'"

Wiseman called this "a lightning bolt" moment. He suddenly glimpsed that "even with a project that had been a general success, [people at Toyota] would ask, 'What didn't go well so we can make it better?'" Note the growth mindset implicit in his words, reminiscent of Carol Dweck's seminal research.

What Wiseman noticed that day can be seen as a vital element of TPS: a deeply ingrained belief that problem-solving is a team sport. Failures are opportunities for improvement. Competent professionals are *expected* to successfully execute most of their tasks, so successes are not seen as worthy of colleagues' valuable time. Hence the "puzzled" look on Mr. Cho's face. Puzzlement occurred because an expected be-havior (share your problems so we can work on them together) didn't happen, while an *unexpected* one (bragging) did.

What I love most about this story is that Wiseman's boasting would not have raised an eyebrow in 99 percent of work environments I've studied. We are socialized to share accomplishments and good news in front of the boss. Nothing puzzling about it! The most impressive result of TPS in my view is that the system normalizes failure—bad news, re-quests for help, and problems alike. It creates a community of scientists. Not incidentally, the essence of failing well is thinking like a scientist.

Once you understand the basic elements of a system for quality and improvement, it's easy to apply aspects to your everyday life. For example, complex failures are rife when shepherding small children out the door on time on a school day, with unwillingness to get out of bed, undue dallying about what to wear, misplaced homework papers, and voluble protests about the day ahead. Such complications make for stressful mornings and interfere with punctuality. But the problems can be eliminated by small changes that build a better morning system. One day you might try setting the morning alarm ten minutes earlier. Laying out clothes the night before can reduce time spent deciding what to wear in the morning. You don't need to venture way outside the bounds—say, skipping school altogether—but you have consid-erable opportunity to test small improvements that might make the system work better. The key is to focus on the relationships among the moving parts in your morning system, including how your child feels about school, how long it takes to eat breakfast, whether homework was completed, and so on. Knowing this, to avoid a delay in the morning, you might, for example, "pull the Andon Cord" the night before on a potential homework glitch or pack a snack to supplement an inade-quate breakfast.

If 3M presents a good system for innovation, and Toyota presents a system for ensuring quality in a predictable context, how would we design a system to prevent both basic and complex failures in a variable context? A good place to look for answers is a modern tertiary-care hospital, which epitomizes a variable context.

A system for safety

Large modern hospitals encompass a nearly incalculable number of interconnected processes that intersect with myriad health-care professionals and patients every day. This complexity and variability combine to create the potential for a dizzying array of complex failures. When ten-year-old Matthew was mistakenly given a potentially fatal morphine dose, at least seven causes, including being wheeled to a floor with nurses less experienced in postoperative care and a difficult-to-read medication label, contributed to the complex failure you saw in chapter 4. Fortunately, the overdose was reversed in time to prevent a worse outcome. Yet the inherent risk in that context makes it foolish to rely on luck or heroism. Instead, it helps to design a system for safety—or, put another way, a system for learning. The primary focus of the learning is to avoid the wrong kinds of failures while continuing to improve patient care. The nurses that Anita and I studied had not all been working in such a system.

Just over two decades ago, pioneers in patient safety started trying to figure out what such a system would look like. I studied the work of one of these pioneers: Julianne "Julie" Morath, a passionate advocate for patient safety who led an initiative that built a system for learning. When I first met Morath, in January of 2001, she was chief operating officer (COO) at Children's Hospital and Clinics in Minneapolis, Minnesota. Calm, warm, and articulate, she worked tirelessly to educate and engage everyone at the hospital to join her in the pursuit of "100 percent patient safety." Morath has since become a celebrated national leader in the patient safety movement whose many achievements include authoring the influential report *To Do No Harm*, helping create the Lucian Leape Institute of the National Patient Safety Foundation at the

Institute for Healthcare Improvement, and completing a term as elected member of the Board of Commissioners of the Joint Commission.

When she arrived at Children's in 1999, Morath soon discovered that she'd inherited a hospital culture that approached medical errors according to "the old ABC model of medicine: Accuse, Blame, Criticize." To alter that culture and the behaviors it produced, she introduced several new elements to hospital operations, each of which can seem simple and inadequate on its own, but which come together to create a surprisingly effective system for learning. For instance, she held forums to present research about the prevalence of medical error in modern hospitals—at the time estimated to cause ninety-eight thousand preventable deaths in U.S. hospitals annually.

Use Systems Thinking to Change How We Think about Error

One of the points Morath would make in the sessions held to change how people thought about error was this: health care is, by its nature, "a complex error-prone system." With this, she was teaching people that, like it or not, they were working in a system where things *would* go wrong. The only question: Would they speak up about these process failures fast enough to help fix them before patients were harmed? Morath was helping people to understand, with echoes of Charles Perrow, that some systems are inherently dangerous. The central implication of this point? *Do not assume someone is to blame.* When people view medical accidents as evidence that someone screwed up, they will have a hard time speaking up for fear of being blamed or shamed. The "systems view" of medical accidents that Morath was introducing to the hospital more accurately represents reality. Most accidents, Morath would often explain, holding up a Swiss cheese sponge, resulted from a series of small process failures lining up, rather than from one person's error.

Unsurprisingly, at first the dedicated health-care professionals at Children's pushed back. They simply did not believe that their hospital had a safety problem. Perhaps many of them had privately experienced a safety incident but felt alone in their shame. No one had talked about these failures openly before.

Rely on inquiry

So Morath faced a challenge: How to help people to see and accept their hospital's failures? Rather than doubling down on her logic—*You work in a complex error-prone system, don't you see? Things will go wrong!*—she instead invited clinicians to reflect on their experiences that week with their patients, then prompted, "Was everything as safe as you would have liked it to have been?" Her aspirational question opened the floodgates. Most people had been in what Morath called "a health-care situation where something did not go well," and once they reflected on the many problems they had noticed, they became eager to talk about what had happened and how they might improve.

Morath set up a Patient Safety Steering Committee (PSSC) to help lead the initiative. A key element of the system she built, the PSSC was a cross-functional, multilevel team to ensure that perspectives from all over the hospital would be heard. Another new element was a policy intended to make it easier for people to speak up about error, called *blameless reporting*. Recall from chapter 3 that similar policies are found in many companies and families serious about safety. With the new policy came new tools and procedures to enable employees at every rung of the hierarchy to communicate confidentially without fear of punishment. As in aviation, this not only gave people a voice, but allowed the hospital to gather data about system weaknesses and places where things were likely to go wrong. The use of a narrative format allowed for multicausal rather than single-cause accident reporting.

New language

Another element of the patient safety system was what Morath called Words to Work By—a roster of suggested terms designed to help shift mindsets from blaming to learning. Morath substituted neutral-sounding words such as *study* for the more threatening word *investigation*, which put people on the defensive. The introduction of Focused Event Studies—small groups that convened to identify all of the causes of an accident shortly after it had occurred—was another new element. Output from these sessions often helped improve processes to prevent similar errors—in short, a vehicle for second-order problem-solving! Dig deeper into what made these sessions work and you will find a set of explicit norms and ground rules to promote candor and ensure confidentiality. Moderators trained in psychological safety paid careful attention to nonverbal cues that might indicate someone was uncomfortable or hesitant to share a dissenting view. Focused Event Studies also included documentation of the findings so that whatever had been learned could be anonymized and shared throughout the organization.

Synergy

It should be clear that a simple list of these elements would not immediately convey the power created by how they work together. Words to Work By reinforces the willingness to report errors that was fostered by the blameless reporting. Education in error prevalence combines with the systems view of medical accidents to remove shame and blame, and so on. The whole is more than the sum of its parts. But you know that a learning system you've designed is working when it starts to generate new, supportive elements on its own. And that's what happened at Children's.

Frontline nurses came up with and implemented two more elements of the patient safety system: Safety Action Teams and Good Catch Logs. Safety Action Teams were self-organized groups of nurses who met to identify and reduce potential hazards in their clinical areas. Second-order problem-solving indeed. The Good Catch Logs were a way of celebrating near misses: by documenting good catches, nurses identified additional opportunities for process improvement.

As with the system at 3M that supported people's intelligent failures in ways that encouraged product innovation, and the system at Toyota that made quality improvement second nature, Children's Minnesota built a robust learning system that turned everyone into an active participant in patient safety. Morath's approach reminds us that system design is more than simply coming into an organization and flipping a single switch. It's flipping multiple switches and understanding how they work as a system.

Today, when I teach the case study on Morath that Mike Roberto and Anita Tucker and I wrote back in 2001, I'm amazed by how students—executives and MBA students alike—struggle at first to see how the system works as a whole. They tend to list the parts and diagnose them, one by one, as bad or good, missing the forest for the trees. But, as in the Beer Game, when the light bulbs do go off—when students glimpse that the whole is more than the parts—it's exciting and powerful.

Understanding Systems to Better Navigate Failure

Appreciating the dynamics of systems is the last of the three competencies for practicing the science of failing well. After self-awareness and situation awareness is system awareness. Mastering system awareness starts with training yourself to look for wholes rather than zooming in, as we naturally do, on the parts. It's about expanding your focus, even if briefly, to redraw the boundaries and see a larger whole and the relationships that shape it.

Much of our education and work experience has taught us to diagnose and become experts in parts, shortchanging the value of looking at the relationships that tie them together. We can learn to see and appreciate systems and use this knowledge to reduce preventable failures.

Don't forget that appreciating systems helps us see that we are not wholly responsible for all the failures in our vicinity. This is not to let us off the hook for our contributions to failures, but rather to help us see that we are parts of larger systems, with complex relationships, some of which are beyond our ability to predict or control. This insight has played a vital role in the modern patient safety movement, notably in helping people speak up quickly about things that go wrong, or when they're unsure about something. Systems thinking empowers us to design systems better able to achieve their stated goals, such as quality, safety, or innovation.

Neither systems thinking nor system design are simple, straightforward skills. Systems offer endless complexity. The boundaries of a system can always be drawn differently. What part of a system you consider of interest is a judgment call, and drawing boundaries is inherently creative. For instance, I could have redrawn the boundaries when my son asked to join the travel baseball team to encompass not just him and his request in the moment but also the whole family and our next few months. Or, I could have gone even further, to consider the impact this decision might have on other boys in the town, or even (absurdly) on his entire life. A judgment call indeed. The point isn't to capture the correct system boundaries but to undertake the systemic thinking that helps you make a decision more mindfully. That can seem distressing (there is no right answer!) but also empowering (you get to choose!). The choices you make can expand your opportunities for experimenting and learning.

CHAPTER 8

Thriving as a Fallible Human Being

For me, losing a tennis match isn't failure. It's research.

—Billie Jean King

When Barbe-Nicole Ponsardin Clicquot was suddenly widowed at the age of twenty-seven, she was expected to retreat to a quiet life of motherhood and domesticity. Perhaps she would remarry. Born in Reims, France, in 1777, an era when women did not own property and were not even allowed to make household financial decisions, Barbe-Nicole now found herself in a new situation as a result of her tragedy. Widowhood, it turns out, granted a woman most of the financial freedoms of a man. A widow—*une veuve*—could honor her late husband's memory by continuing, say, a shared dream of a wine business in the chalky soil of the Champagne region. A widow could manage a business, try out new ideas, fail, and maybe even succeed.

Born into a wealthy family, Barbe-Nicole was not considered pretty, flirtatious, or charming—nor did she favor fancy dresses or social events. Had Instagram existed, pictures of the nearby wineries would likely have garnered more likes than those of her less than perfect appearance. At age twenty-one, in a union arranged by her parents, she had been married to François Clicquot, the scion of another wealthy mercantile family in Reims.

They were a good pair and spent the next six years learning about and trying to enter the risky wine business. The Champagne region in northeast France was then known mostly for its still white wines, but bubbles were coming into vogue across Europe, especially in Russia. François's family were wine distributors who owned a few vines to complement their main enterprises in banking and the textile trade. To grow the business, François traveled for months at a time to such places as Germany and Switzerland; he was a newcomer trying to drum up accounts and break into markets. Champagne proved to be a hard sell. Customers were limited to a relatively small number of aristocrats who could afford its luxury, and the competition from established wineries was stiff. Those first trips were disappointing.

The weather was also fickle. When François and Barbe-Nicole finally procured a decent number of orders, the vines withered in the fields in a series of overly dry, hot summers. Growing and harvesting grapes, as well as the crafting, bottling, and shipping of wine, were ripe for failure at every step. Yet that did not stop the Clicquots. They were determined. You could say they had grit. They began visiting local vineyards and small family estates, tromping into stone cellars, measuring, tasting, and learning. They found and hired a trusted salesman, Louis Bohne, who set off on a yearlong journey to Russia with hopes of boldly conquering a new market, only to find that they'd badly miscalculated. That summer the fields were too wet and muddy, leading to another failed harvest. Six years of business with little to show.

Then, in October 1805, François died after twelve days of an infectious fever. Barbe-Nicole soon made the surprising decision to run the nascent wine business herself. Never mind that the business was close to collapse and François's death made its chances of success more remote than ever. But Barbe-Nicole intuitively practiced situation awareness: she faced high uncertainty and thus failure was likely, but the stakes were manageable. The Clicquot family had resources with which to speculate. If only Barbe-Nicole could convince her father-in-law to risk some of them. Banking and wool-trading operations had filled both families' coffers for generations, but Barbe-Nicole remained determined to pursue champagne. She must have seemed fiercely intelligent and capable because when she asked her father-in-law, Philippe, for a loan against her inheritance—an amount equivalent to a million dollars today—he said yes despite the considerable business risk.

Under one condition.

Philippe Clicquot insisted that she apprentice for four years to wine-maker Alexandre Jérôme Fourneaux to further learn the intricacies of the craft and trade. Entering novel territory, rife with uncertainty, Barbe-Nicole had to work hard, prepare, and learn all she could from available knowledge and experience. By now Napoléon Bonaparte was well into waging what would become twelve years of war throughout Europe, creating an extremely unattractive business environment. Shipping and trade restrictions were levied; ports were blockaded unpredictably. As a ship crossed the ocean, bottles of the delicate wines in its hold frequently exploded. One year, a third of Clicquot's stock—over fifty thousand bottles—was ruined by heat during an extended stop-over in Amsterdam. Moreover, the protracted hardships of war meant that the relatively small customer base that might be able to afford luxury wines was not often in the mood to celebrate.

Fourneaux did not continue the partnership with Barbe-Nicole once the four years were up. (He and his son would build their own wine business, which was sold in 1931 to Pierre Taittinger, who relaunched it under his family name.) Despite such relentless failure, the widow Clicquot's determination held strong. By all accounts she was a hands-on, detail-oriented, first-in-and-last-out, type A entrepreneur with little time or inclination for personal musings. At the end of her life, in the 1860s, when she had become the Grande Dame of Champagne, Barbe-Nicole wrote to a great-grandchild, "The world is in perpetual motion, and we must invent the things of tomorrow. One must go before others, be determined and exacting, and let your intelligence direct your life. Act with audacity." Act with audacity! In other words, *play to win*.

To be sure, that first decade of near bankruptcy saw some successes, along with repeated, painful failures. The favorable weather of 1811 led to a bountiful harvest, made all the more fabulous because it coincided with a comet's passing overhead. Winemakers, including Clicquot, branded the corks with stars to commemorate the auspicious year. Three years later, in the winter of 1814 when Russian troops occupied Reims, Barbe-Nicole was able to sell them wine from her stocked cellars. Although she'd been unable to reach the Russian market during wartime, now she had eager customers on her doorstep, appreciative connoisseurs who would become ambassadors for Veuve Clicquot when they returned home. That April, when Napoléon finally abandoned the throne, Russian officers celebrated in Reims with her sparkling champagne.

Now that war was over, people started lifting champagne glasses in celebration all over Europe. Soon the shipping and trade blockades would be lifted. In what became a stunning first-mover coup, Barbe-Nicole secretly chartered a boat to smuggle over ten thousand bottles of her best champagne—the 1811 comet vintage—to Königsberg and then to St. Petersburg, beating out her competitors. Wine merchants were said to fight on the dock to buy her champagne and to storm Louis Bohne's hotel room, clamoring to buy at any price. A second shipment soon followed. Czar Alexander made the Veuve his favorite. Within weeks, Barbe-Nicole and her Veuve Clicquot champagne had become famous.

Making champagne was then difficult, costly, and time-consuming. After her stunning coup in Russia, with orders rolling in, her problem was to speed production. The second fermentation—adding sugar and yeast to produce bubbles—lasted for several months. Clarifying cloudy wines meant storing bottles on their sides so that the yeast would be exposed to most of the juice. As the yeast died, leaving lees (residue following fermentation), the bottles had to be tilted so that the lees sank to the neck of the bottles to be disgorged. Once disgorged, the bottles were topped off (back then, usually with brandy), recorked, and stored.

With so much wine to store and age, Barbe-Nicole ingeniously designed special racks, called *pupitres*, that held the bottles at an angle and could be turned so the lees would gather in the neck of the bottle. This seemingly simple innovation was revolutionary, resulting in the clear sparkling wines for which she would become famous. Its efficiency was crucial in allowing high-volume production of stable wines, and the widow Clicquot and her wines jumped to the front of the postwar marketing line.

By the summer of 1815, Veuve Clicquot was a roaring success. Its proprietor had made a fortune and launched an empire. Despite countless moments when she might have retreated into relative ease, Barbe-Nicole Ponsardin Clicquot had persevered and built one of the most successful and enduring companies in the wine industry. Her technical innovations allowed the clear sparkling wine that today we know as champagne. The sole woman among a small group of entrepreneurs in the first decades of the nineteenth century, she played a pivotal role in transforming the champagne industry from a rural, artisanal craft to an international business. She both ran the business and crafted the wines.

Today we celebrate Veuve Clicquot's *success* as a pioneering wine-maker and entrepreneur, but her fuller life story reveals *failure* to be an essential part of that journey. As an elite failure practitioner, Barbe-Nicole was well ahead of her time. Her resilience in the face of repeated failure implies the serenity to accept that she didn't control the weather or the political climate that so affected her business results. Willing to take thoughtful risks while learning how to improve the champagne quality and expand the business, she seems not to have beaten herself up over the many things that did go wrong in the making, selling, and shipping of fine wines. Perhaps she intuited the concept of intelligent failure—new terrain, pursuing an opportunity, and only risking failures never too large to overcome—and this explains her ability to persist resolutely for years before her business began to thrive. The connection between champagne and celebration also serves as a reminder that all of us can celebrate failure as part of a full and meaningful life.

Embracing Fallibility

How do you thrive as a fallible human being? I first heard Maxie Maultsby, the brilliant psychiatrist, use this term thirty years ago. He'd even abbreviate it—FHB. I smile when I think of Maxie's earnest desire to help all of us FHBs thrive by learning to think differently. Thriving, he might add, starts with *accepting* our fallibility.

A certain freedom comes from learning to live comfortably with who you are. Fallibility is a part of who we are. Self-acceptance can be seen as brave. It takes courage to be honest with oneself, and it's a first step in being honest with others. Because failure is a fact of life, failing is not a matter of *if* but when and how.

But thriving as a fallible human being also means learning to *fail well*: preventing basic failures as often as possible, anticipating complex ones so as to prevent or mitigate them, and cultivating the appetite for more frequent intelligent failures. Learning to recognize and learn from each of the three failure types and strengthen each of the three awareness zones is a lifelong process.

We can learn to live joyfully with our fallibility. Though it may seem counterintuitive, failure can be a gift. One of its gifts is the clarity a failure can bring about which of our abilities need work; another gift is insight about our true passions. Failing a multivariable calculus exam in college was caused by my inadequate studying. But it forced me to ask myself hard questions about the work that I truly loved—and that which I was likely doing to please or impress others. That was a gift, even if it didn't feel like one at the time.

The unequal license to fail

Failure can also be seen as a privilege. As journalist and University of Colorado professor Adam Bradley points out in a *New York Times* article, "One of the greatest underrecognized privileges of whiteness might be the license it gives some to fail without fear." He explains that being a member of a minority culture often means your failures, especially if they become public, are seen as representative of an entire group. Your individual failure reflects badly on everyone else like you. John Jennings, professor of media and culture studies at the University of California, Riverside, told Bradley, "I want to get to the point where Joe Schmo Black guy is just safe, can be ordinary—even mediocre." In other words, Joe Schmo Black guy has the freedom to fail. That inventor and acoustician James West, whose intelligent failures resulted in more than 250 patents, including one for the electret microphone, was African American makes his success that much more noteworthy. He succeeded in his field despite the entrenched racism that had him being mistaken for a janitor while employed as a scientist at Bell Labs. Imagine the pressure he must have felt to avoid reducing the chances for others like him to follow in his footsteps at Bell Labs and other elite institutions.

Women, especially women in academic science, also lack the luxury of failing unobtrusively. We are at risk of feeling pressure to succeed at all times lest we spoil other women's opportunities. Jen Heemstra endorses "a culture in science and academia where people can be open about their failures without consequences." A realist, she adds, "I'll say that our responsibility to share our failures is proportional to the amount of power we have in the academic system." As a tenured professor with her own lab at Emory University, Heemstra is now quite open about her failures. But she wasn't always that way. Her most painful failure—not being voted for tenure the first time around (at a previous university)—turned out to be a gift. The failure was an interruption, forcing reflection. As Jen explained to information-technology researcher Veronika Cheplygina, who also studies failure:

> It [failing a tenure vote] was definitely the most painful failure of my life, as I felt like I had let down my family and my research group members—basically all of the people I care most about. For anyone who hasn't experienced that, it is a truly horrible feeling. But it can also be a beautifully humbling experience as well. Seeing how all of those people stood by me in the midst of the struggle ended up seismically shifting my worldview and priorities. It gave me a new view of what academia could be and a fire to make that into a reality. It also made me fearless. This specific failure that I had long been afraid of ended up happening to me. It was the exact thing that I had deeply dreaded, and I found myself suddenly thrust into it and with no choice but to cope and keep moving forward. As I continued to work hard and succeed in spite of that and eventually came out of the situation, I realized that I'm stronger than I ever thought I was and that people's opinions of me don't have to define me.

Note that Jen didn't try to slough off or ignore what she calls "a truly horrible feeling." She acknowledged and named her feeling and let herself feel bad for a time. This is in line with findings from a 2017 study led by professor Noelle Nelson that focusing on your emotions, rather than thinking about the failure (which tends to generate self-justification), helps people learn and improve. Eventually, Jen developed a keen interest in failure that led to research into understanding how undergraduates experience failure in STEM courses and how this affects their decision to continue science careers. She and others have designed an undergraduate research curriculum to engage students in hands-on laboratory learning and give them experience with the right kind of wrong that is so central to discovery.

As a young woman in academia, anticipating the pain that Jen experienced years before she experienced it, I used to force myself to confront that I would likely be turned down for tenure. I would remind myself that other opportunities existed for researchers and teachers—in university and company settings alike. When I lost *this* job, I would coach myself, I'd find another. Preparing myself for the failure helped me feel more lighthearted about it, which helped me focus on doing the work that I loved without being tormented by the looming failure.

Embracing failure is a mainstay in queer (LGBTQIA) theory and politics. In his seminal book *The Queer Art of Failure*, transgender media theorist Jack Halberstam argues that the measure and meaning of success is not defined by the individual but rather comes from communities, and that the norms of "success" lead toward a "mindless conformity." In contrast, embracing failure allows a "free space of reinvention" from which to critique assumptions imposed by the world. Halberstam is part of a group of queer thinkers who see the experience of failure to meet society's expectations as foundational to queer culture. Mainstays of what it means to live a "successful" life, such as biological prosperity, financial security, health, and longevity, had long been denied to queer people by discriminatory adoption laws, biases in hiring, acts of violence and prejudice, and even the HIV/AIDS epidemic. In failing to live up to heteronormative expectations, queer people must find their own ways to "succeed," and a core and now celebrated part of this success is the recognition of having first failed.

For instance, drag performance, as an art form, celebrates the experience of queer people—welcoming rather than downplaying a lack of conformity to society's expectations. Through its exaggerated contrast, the show makes society's default expectations more visible. It makes us aware of heteronormative culture as a lens through which we view the world—nudging us out of our default sense, as naïve realists, that we objectively see reality. In the competition reality-television show *RuPaul's Drag Race*, a group of mostly male-identified contestants adopt characters who are pastiches of femininity in hyperbolic performances of models and pageant contestants. The show celebrates liberation from expectations on a prime-time stage. And it's wildly popular. The premiere of its thirteenth season on January 1, 2021, was, at the time, the show's most watched episode, garnering 1.3 million viewers via simulcast, a number comparable to the 1.32 million viewers who tuned in to an average NBA game during the 2020–21 season.

Sometimes accepting fallibility means accepting *society's* fallibility so as to respond with equanimity to an injustice. Acclaimed astrophysicist Jocelyn Bell Burnell, who played such an instrumental role in the discovery of pulsars while working as a research assistant for Antony Hewish, was not given credit when he was awarded the Nobel Prize in 1974. Several years afterward, Jocelyn Bell Burnell reasoned that since a supervisor assumes final responsibility for a project's failure, the same should hold for a project's success. "I am not myself upset about it—after all, I am in good company, am I not!" she said. Credit goes to Jocelyn Bell Burnell for her maturity and strong sense of self. Knowing that your contribution matters without needing the validation of external acclaim is surely a sign of wisdom. The high road rarely leads to regret.

Over the past few years as inequities in society have moved to center stage in national conversations around the world—finally achieving the attention they deserve—I frequently felt inadequate in my lack of expertise in the science of diversity, equity, and inclusion. Those who'd followed my work in psychological safety rightly saw an important connection to these issues. Yet I had not directly studied that link. Cultivating psychological safety is not the same thing as cultivating belonging, and many have conflated the two in recent years. Here's how I see it. Psychological safety, which means believing it's safe to speak up, is enormously important for feeling a sense of belonging. But belonging is more personal, while psychological safety is more collective (it is conceptualized in research studies as an emergent property of a group) and, I think, it is co-created by individuals and the groups to which they wish to belong.

The more I study the research on the psychology, sociology, and economics of inequality, the more massive the undertaking of correcting these societal failures feels. At the very least, I argue that as a society we should aspire to creating a world where everyone has an equal license to fail intelligently. That is not the case today. But I believe that we're ever so slightly closer to that aspiration than we were even just a few years ago. Recognizing our heteronormative lens is an important first step. Nonetheless, I regret not focusing on these challenges earlier.

What we regret

What's the relationship between failure and regret? At first glance, one might think people would dwell on and regret their biggest failures. But the research suggests otherwise. To better understand regret, bestselling author Daniel Pink collected regrets from more than sixteen thousand people in 105 countries.

Pink categorized the regrets into four categories, one of which he calls "boldness regrets." These were especially plentiful. People regretted not having been bold enough to take a chance with a business or a long-held dream. They regretted not having been brave enough to ask out a person they were interested in. By limiting the upside and protecting against the downside (playing not to lose), many harbored painful regrets about their lives. Interestingly, Pink found that people did *not* regret having taken a chance and failing. He maintains that by studying regret we learn what constitutes a good life. Just as everyone fails, everyone has regrets. Regrets and failures are part of being human, and only by learning to treat ourselves with compassion and kindness rather than contempt and blame can we find a sense of balance and fulfillment. Just as we can lessen some of the burden of our mistakes by disclosing them, so can disclosing our regrets defang their bite and allow for sense-making. People like others more, not less, when they disclose vulnerabilities. This is partly because we respect their courage.

Resisting perfectionism

Perfectionism, or holding yourself to excessively high standards and self-criticism, is the subject of considerable research. Thomas Curran, a professor at the London School of Economics and Political Science, is an expert on the topic. In his surveys of college students, Curran has discovered a substantial increase over the past twenty-seven years in the percentage of young people who feel they need to be perfect. He distinguishes between the pressure we put on ourselves to be perfect and the expectations we feel from others and society at large. Both types of pressures, he has found, can lead to depression and other mental illnesses.

Another problem is that those suffering from perfectionism have a hard time trying something new because they can't tolerate that they might fail. In an ever-changing world this reluctance puts them at risk of falling behind. Perfectionists are also particularly vulnerable to burnout. "The way that perfectionists are built," says Curran, "makes us very sensitive and vulnerable to those setbacks and failures, which occur all the time, because it's a threat to that idealized version of who we want to be and who we think we should be."

It's hard to thrive as a fallible human being when you fall prey to the trap of perfectionism. Eric Best, a diving coach who works with Olympic medalists, coached organizational psychologist Adam Grant back in the 1990s when Grant was in high school. A self-admitted perfectionist, Grant recalls with humor and insight his struggles with imperfect dives in an engaging conversation on his *WorkLife* podcast with Best in 2022. To help his divers (and the rest of us) enjoy a healthier relationship to our work or hobbies, Best suggests aiming for excellence rather than perfection. He emphasizes realistic goals—those that are a reasonable stretch from where you are now, rather than seeking to achieve a "perfect ten" standard. Learn to measure yourself on progress rather than on distance from an ideal state. Consciously pick just a few things you want to improve rather than getting bogged down by everything you did wrong.

When parents understand the psychological dangers of the perfection trap and the crucial role failure plays in learning and development, they more easily welcome both failures and successes from children. No child learns to ride a bike without falling over. By making it safe to fail, parents and teachers encourage children to embrace a growth mindset that supports learning. Parents who detect perfectionism in their children can help them reframe failures from shameful or even just disappointing to necessary elements of learning something new. Saying "Falling is just part of learning to ride a bike" is preferable to "Too bad your clothes got dirty when you fell off the bike." Recall that Jeffrey reframed his bridge mistakes as normal and necessary given the challenge of the new game. By focusing on the satisfaction of improving, any of us can help ourselves—and the others we care about—to push back against the irrational idea that mastering something difficult should be easy.

Fail more often

The most important reason to embrace our fallibility is that it frees us up to take more risks. We can choose, more often, to *play to win*. As Ray Dalio tweeted on October 20, 2022, "Everyone fails. Anyone you see succeeding is only succeeding at the things you're paying attention to—I guarantee they are also failing at lots of other things. The people I respect most are those who fail well. I respect them even more than those who succeed."

As a senior in high school, my older son announced he'd accepted a summer job selling solar panels door-to-door. I instantly worried because I knew he'd be in for a lot of rejection. I just couldn't see how Jack—my thoughtful, introverted son, a graceful athlete and straight-A student—would cope with so much rejection. In worrying, I wasn't thinking only of the usual brush-offs faced by all salespeople. Solar energy, a hot-button issue linked to climate change, could make for more than a cool "No. I'm not interested." As a parent, it's natural, albeit unhelpful, to want to shield your kids from failure. But I was wrong. Jack had a great summer. Many customers said yes, and he was excited to be transforming some of New England's roofs. Yes, most said no, but Jack had learned from Larry Wilson years earlier to silently say to himself, "Thanks for the twenty-five dollars." Sure, a few people were downright hostile, but Jack quickly learned not to take it personally. The summer built up his failure muscles and sparked an ongoing interest in renewable energy.

Another way to fail more often is to pick up a new hobby. When my friend Laura decided to take up ice hockey in her early forties, I was equal parts perplexed and impressed. Laura and I grew up together in New York City when few "girls" even thought about playing ice hockey, and neither of us had been particularly gifted athletes in high school. We were more likely to get together to do homework or revisit key moments from a recent high school dance. Now, many years later, I wondered why Laura, still a close friend, with two children at home and plenty of actual hard-won skills, would choose to spend precious free time hauling around heavy gear, falling on the ice, and, most of all, tolerating an activity she was not yet good at. I admired her willingness to do something badly in a semipublic arena. My admiration was well-placed. She has continued to play ice hockey with the same dedicated team for years. Playing in her adult ice hockey league has become Laura's passion. Today Laura calls herself a "hockey fanatic."

Our fear of being bad at it can make it difficult to try a new sport, language, or other endeavor—remember Jeffrey almost quit bridge for good. For one thing, we fall prey to perfectionism, with its unrealistic expectations for success. For another, most of us don't want to look bad or incompetent in front of other people, and when we try something new, we may find ourselves surrounded by people doing the same activity well.

Hobbies present a great arena in which to practice failure. Hobbies are about fun and the stimulation of learning something new rather than about achievement or making a living—a low-stakes context. Also, it is less embarrassing to fail at a new hobby than in your career. Remind yourself that it's okay to be bad at something on the way to getting better at it. Whether learning a new language or a new skill, trying something new in any context builds muscle for risk-taking when the stakes are higher.

Celebrate the pivot

When I first met Jake Breeden, then vice president, head of global learning solutions, at pharmaceutical giant Takeda, we talked about his observation that celebrating failure in most companies remained a tough sell—despite the widely used rhetoric. "As mature as we would like to think ourselves, when something is framed as failure, we tend to shut down," he said. Celebrating failure, he decided, was psychologically unrealistic because "failure implies an ending. A bad ending!" When I interviewed Jake in December 2021, he was excited about a solution he'd found, one driven by empathy for how people really experience failure. In the companies where he'd worked, most projects, especially the ones with failures, led to *more* projects. "We're always pivoting," he explained. This makes celebrating pivots easier than celebrating failure. Celebrating the pivot was all about focusing on the next step—on the opportunity to make progress toward the goal. Celebrating the pivot is forward rather than backward facing—making it immune to regret and full of possibility.

In any new context, it's crucial to pause to consider where to experiment next. What is it that most needs to be learned to get us where we want to go? We can think of the pivot as a way to tell a different story. Instead of "We made a plan and then we failed, and here's the moral of the story," it's a narrative about change. "We made a plan, things didn't go as planned, so we pivoted." Jake's reframe here is more than about language. It focuses on where the story goes next. It brings suspense rather than shame.

Unsurprisingly, Jake found that people pushed back at first, saying, "Isn't this just a matter of semantics?" To which he agrees. "But words change meaning," he points out. "And 'just semantics' understates the importance of using the right words. All of a sudden just by changing the language, we got more failure talk!" Here's where situation awareness meets self-awareness. We need the right language to help us meet failure successfully.

Jake described what happened when Takeda's president of research and development brought him in to work with a drug development team after a disappointing result: a potential safety issue signaled in a clinical trial led to the suspension of one of the company's most promising new drugs, despite all the hopes and dreams and dollars invested in it. The company's stock price even took a hit.

In a session with the head of the clinical area along with other people from the project, Jake took care to frame the story not as a celebration of failure but as a timely catch before anyone was hurt:

> Here's what we're going to celebrate. We're going to celebrate the fact that our signals are so finely tuned that we can stop this before it hurt anybody seriously. We're going to celebrate the fact that we've got so many other things in the pipeline, that all our eggs aren't in one basket. We're going to celebrate the fact that we're sharing this in this open way, and we're going to celebrate that we remain committed [to this therapeutic area].

Whether you pivot a project onto a better path, or pivot yourself into a new role or a better relationship, pivots are integral to navigating the uncertainty that comes with novel contexts. Celebrating pivots is an easy way for managers in a company or parents in a family or partners in a relationship to reinforce acceptance of the fallibility of any person, project, or plan.

Mastering the Science of Failing Well

If accepting fallibility is a first step, what else helps us thrive as fallible beings in an imperfect world? Failing well is not an exact science. The manual is still being written and will forever be revised. To begin, when you consciously stretch to try new things, your experiments necessarily bring the risk of failure. This is how you get more comfortable with it. When you take more risks, you will experience more, not less, failure. But two good things happen. One, you realize that you don't die of embarrassment. Two, you build muscle so that each next failure stings less. The more you experience failure, the more you realize you can still be okay. More than okay: you can thrive.

To do this, it helps to incorporate a few basic failure practices—persistence, reflection, accountability, and apologizing—into your life. Although not intended to be a complete or perfect list, each of these practices can help you build a healthy relationship to failure.

Persistence

One evening when Sara Blakely was twenty-seven and selling fax machines door-to-door, she cut off the feet of a pair of pantyhose to wear to a party underneath cream-colored pants. Although they rolled up, the stockings otherwise made her look and feel great. She decided to modify the design, and soon it was warmly received by family and friends. Sara then got the idea to manufacture and sell her footless, body-shaping hose to other women.

That's when she began to meet with failure.

Manufacturers and patent lawyers laughed at her idea, showed her to the door, or both. After all, she had no experience in fashion, business, or manufacturing. Many people might have given up. But Sara persevered. She thought of her parents, who had always made sure their school-age children accepted and even embraced failure as a necessary part of a full life. At the family dinner table, her father had routinely asked Sara and her brother what they'd failed at that day—and congratulated them for trying. Their father was training them to understand that it's okay to be a fallible human being.

Sara resolved to try harder. Along with a healthy, cheerful attitude toward failure, she possessed the perseverance and passion to pursue long-term goals, much like Barbe-Nicole. Both demonstrate what University of Pennsylvania psychology professor Angela Duckworth calls grit. Sara researched and wrote her own patent application and drove from Atlanta to knock on the doors of hosiery mills in North Carolina. None saw the wisdom in her idea until finally one mill owner decided to take a chance.

Experimenting with different syllables and sounds, Sara eventually came up with a name for her company: Spanx. For the first customer orders, she designed her own packaging and used her bathroom as a fulfillment center. Much later Spanx expanded to sell swimwear and leggings, and in 2012 *Forbes* crowned Blakely the youngest self-made billionaire. The following year she pledged to give half of her wealth to charity, most of it to support women in their endeavors.

The role of perseverance in Sara Blakely's success is undeniable, and Duckworth's research on grit finds that perseverance and passion for a long-term goal strongly predict achievement across many settings. Uncorrelated with IQ, grit is thus an important complement to talent. Sustained effort over time is crucial for success. Interest in grit in education and child development has skyrocketed as a result of this important work, and it would be hard to deny grit's role in achievement. A book on failure, however, must address the fine line between persistence and stubbornness. I have known researchers who clung to a losing idea far longer than the data suggested was wise, wasting valuable time in their careers and sometimes leaving the field altogether. Failing well, I believe, means knowing when to do more than a slight pivot. It means knowing when to give up—on a business idea, a research project, or a relationship—to free up your future for a brand-new course of action.

How do you know when to persist and when to give up? A rule of thumb to justify persistence is to find a credible argument that the not yet realized value you seek to create is indeed worthy of continued investment of time and resources. To make sure your stubbornness is not misguided or that you are not clinging to an unrealistic dream, you must be willing to test your argument with others in your target audience. Make sure to go to people willing to tell you the truth! Blakely believed in and wanted the product she was developing for herself, a sentiment reinforced when she saw how much her friends and family loved her new design. The enthusiastic response from her initial target audience cemented her confidence that Spanx would sell if she could only get over the hurdle of finding a manufacturer.

Drawing this fine line is at least partly a function of taking the time for honest reflection.

Reflection

Most serious musicians keep practice journals. Typically arranged chronologically, like a diary, practice journals are basically notebooks to jot down what was done during each session, how it felt, what to work on next, and, yes, mistakes. Preparing a piece of music for performance means many, many mistakes during rehearsals and learning from those mistakes to not only hit the right notes, but also to improve in more nuanced challenges such as phrasing or tempo.

Percussionist Rob Knopper has spent so much time reflecting on his mistakes and failures that he's become an expert who coaches other musicians on how to handle and make productive use of their mistakes. Failed auditions are his specialty. Now a percussionist with the Metropolitan Opera Orchestra, he readily admits, "I failed my way through years of unsuccessful auditions and rejected applications" before he got his job. Among other things, he advises aspiring musicians to keep a practice journal for each individual piece, which includes a systematic record of obstacles encountered and solutions found that can be consulted as necessary in the future. Knopper also shares candid, detailed descriptions of performances at crucial moments in his career that were marred by shaky hands, wrong notes, or less-than-satisfactory musicianship. Painful, cringe-inducing experiences. What he's learned: "Bad performances give you two of the most important things you could have to make improvement: an indication on what needs to be improved and the motivation to do it."

In life, as in music practice, we have a rich source of failures we can learn from. Instead of looking away from them in denial, it's better that we dig in and learn from them. Mining near misses can be especially gratifying. Pilots who record and reflect on, for example, losing and then regaining control of an aircraft can spur an investigation into whether there's a problem that needs to be fixed. Rapid response health-care teams trained to determine whether a patient's symptoms signal imminent cardiac arrest can use the results of their reflection to implement steps to improve patient care. To reduce the preventable basic and complex failures in our lives, it's essential to invest time in deliberate, honest reflection.

Let's say that over several hours you misplace the car keys, are late to a meeting, and almost slip on an icy walkway. Maybe this series of near misses is mere coincidence. But it could also be a sign that you are stressed, tired, or preoccupied. If you take a moment to reflect, you can probably figure out if you need to take a break or slow down to avoid, for example, a serious fall on the ice. What about a child who begins acting out and is doing poorly in school? Psychologists tell us those are signs the child is distressed—and it's best to reflect on possible root causes so as to intervene or make positive changes. This, too, is a near miss. Finally, with reflection, when we do it right, we start to become far more aware of the smaller and larger ways in which our behavior has contributed to the various failures in our midst.

Accountability

Taking accountability for our failures requires a small act of bravery. But an important part of thriving as a fallible human being is noticing and taking responsibility for your contribution to a failure without feeling emotionally devastated by it, or wallowing in self-blame or shame. Taking accountability means saying such things as "We'd agreed that I would call the plumber about the leaky sink, and because I put it off, there's now a problem with the floor" or "The instructions I gave to the team were confusing and contributed to the misunderstanding" or "I didn't listen when you told me how important it was to attend your soccer game and missed it because I let myself get too busy at work."

A beautiful strength lies in the willingness to say "I did do it" rather than blaming others, which is our default position (not because we're bad people, but because of the fundamental attribution error hardwired into our brains). Consider a senior executive—let's call him Jim—in a global company who recalled a deep sense of relief after owning up to his role in a major business failure. Months earlier, despite grave reservations, Jim had said nothing as his colleagues enthusiastically discussed the potential takeover of another company. In a postmortem discussion of the complex preventable failure that ensued, Jim confessed to his colleagues that he had let them down earlier by not speaking up with his concerns. Openly apologetic and emotional, Jim took full responsibility for his failure, admitting that he had not wanted to be "the skunk at the picnic." Taking a sincere interest in the contribution you make to a failure is part of becoming wiser and healthier as a fallible human being.

Of course, it would have been better if Jim had spoken up, or if you'd called the plumber, clarified team instructions, or made time for your child's sports game. Once you acknowledge your accountability, however, you can look for creative paths out of the setback and ways to design systems that help reduce future errors. Maybe someone else in your household would be more attentive to home maintenance problems? Or should you make sure you have the plumber's number in your contact list so as to make the task easier? Now that you see the trouble your team is in, you can revise the instructions to get back on track or ask for feedback from team members on how to avoid such misunderstandings. You can make an effort to arrange your schedule to accommodate at least some of your child's sports events.

It's easy to see how accountability and apology go hand in hand.

Saying you're sorry

With fallibility comes failure, and with failure comes an opportunity to apologize. A good apology wields almost magical powers in repairing the relationship damage failures cause. According to recent research on forgiveness, "thorough apologies" increase positivity, empathy, gratitude, and, yes, forgiveness, while reducing negative emotions and even lowering heart rates. But if apologies are so effective, why do we so often avoid them? And are all apologies equally effective?

Let's start with the personal apology—between you and another person.

Understand that when you do something wrong—with or without intent—a rupture occurs in that intangible thing that exists between you and another person. The role of an apology is to repair that rupture. A good apology signals that you put the relationship ahead of your ego. Indeed, effective apologies send a clear message that you care about the other person. Effective apologies do more than repair a relationship; they can deepen and improve it. By the same token, a bad apology makes things worse.

Good apologies, alas, are not the norm. Nor are they easy. That's because accepting that you've harmed another person automatically poses a threat to your self-image as a good person. It threatens your self-esteem. To take responsibility for harm is to confront that threat directly, something most of us shy away from. This reluctance is especially pronounced if you hold a fixed mindset about personality in general and believe deep down that causing harm means you're a bad person rather than a good person who made a mistake. As Carol Dweck has shown, people who believe abilities are malleable don't retreat into defensiveness. Instead, they resolve to learn. A second barrier to apologizing is not caring about the relationship with the person you harmed. A third barrier is the belief that an apology won't help. Perhaps we're also hampered by a tacit norm that equates silence with self-protection. Silence feels natural even when our failures are far from criminal.

GETTING IT RIGHT

The quality of our apology matters. Considerable research arrives at a common set of attributes of an effective apology: clearly express remorse, accept responsibility, and offer to make amends or changes going forward.

While offering excuses ("It's not my fault because my alarm didn't go off") backfires, explaining your actions can sometimes work ("I am so sorry I didn't call—my mother had a fall and I was so frantic to get her to the hospital I simply forgot"). A successful apology communicates that you value the relationship and are willing to make amends for your shortcomings ("I'm really looking forward to talking with you. When is convenient to reschedule our call?"). Ultimately, an apology means accepting and admitting that you have failed.

An ineffective apology can fall short in one or more ways, but our fear of accepting responsibility for failure is often the deeper explanation. Accepting responsibility can feel like admitting an intent to harm, akin to admitting that you're a bad person. Consider how easy it is to apologize when you accidentally bump into someone in a crowded store. Because the lack of intentionality in that small basic failure is undeniable, it removes that fear. Think of something more substantial in your life that called for you to apologize. If you decided to apologize, did you resist common but ineffective apologies such as "I'm sorry you feel that way" or "I'm sorry that you misunderstood what I said" or "I didn't expect you to be so sensitive"? By way of contrast, some common phrases for an effective apology include "I am truly sorry for what I did" and "It was wrong, because . . ." and "I take full responsibility, and moving forward I promise to . . ." In formulating an apology, focus on your impact, not on your intention, to mitigate the fear of owning up to your role. As I write these words, I am conscious of my own short-comings: How often do I offer an effective apology to those who matter most in my life? To be a student of failure is to be a student of one's own failures, first and foremost.

I began my research career (and this book) with the surprising discovery that good teams don't necessarily *make* more errors, but they do report more errors. Medical-error expert Lucian Leape, with whom I worked on that study, talks about the importance of apologies for preserving trust in the doctor-patient relationship and for healing. He says there's a lot of confusion over the use of the word *sorry*—most notably, he points out, it's not always an admission of liability. Lucian taught me that an apology is essential in medicine because taking responsibility for harm helps both the patient and the caregiver. Showing remorse, he would say, is a way of making amends and showing the patient that "we're all in this together." Lucian's work highlights another benefit of genuine apologies: helping to build a climate in which employees feel psychologically safe enough to speak up about errors and ideas alike.

LEADERS IN THE PUBLIC EYE

A public apology between leaders and larger audiences works according to the same basic principles as the one-to-one personal apology. Consider some well-publicized examples. In 2018, when a Starbucks employee called the police on two men of color who sat at a table and did not order anything immediately, the company quickly grasped that the relationship it had been carefully crafting was in danger. For years, Starbucks's value proposition was to be customers' "third place," after work and home. In your third place, people don't call the police on you for no reason. Starbucks decided to shut down eight thousand stores for a half day to conduct employee sensitivity training. Contrast that approach with that of Equifax, whose executives waited almost six weeks to come clean after a breach of the most sensitive data collected from nearly half of all Americans in 2017. Rather than offering to make genuine and valued amends, the company asked consumers to hand over their Social Security numbers *again* to *possibly* ascertain whether data had been compromised. Not acknowledging that trust had already been broken, they also offered to sell identity-theft protection. Equifax came off as complacent, uncaring, and unworthy of confidence. As did Yahoo! CEO Marissa Mayer, back in 2013, when after a major email outage affecting a million Yahoo! users she apologized *in a tweet*: "This has been a very frustrating week for our users and we are very sorry."

An effective public apology—much like a private one—must demonstrate care for the relationship by expressing remorse, taking responsibility, and making amends. After the HealthCare.gov launch fiasco, when the website crashed as thousands tried to sign up for insurance, Health and Human Services secretary Kathleen Sebelius apologized for the "miserably frustrating experience" people were having. Sebelius took full responsibility, showing empathy and determination: "I apologize. I'm accountable to you," she said during testimony before a House Energy and Commerce Committee hearing. "I am committed to earning your confidence back." President Barack Obama acknowledged his own contribution to the failure on NBC News, noting that people "are finding themselves in this situation based on assurances they got from me."

After Neiman Marcus suffered a data breach over the 2013 holiday season that exposed customer credit card data to potential theft or abuse, CEO Karen Katz stepped up quickly. She published a letter apologizing to customers and offered a free year of credit monitoring service to any customer who had shopped at Neiman Marcus with a payment card over the past year. "We want you always to feel confident shopping at Neiman Marcus," she wrote, "and your trust in us is our absolute priority." Her apology directly addressed the concerns people likely had about their data—and offered amends (free credit monitoring).

In 2018, comedy writer and producer Dan Harmon made a public apology in his podcast *Harmontown*. Harmon, the creator of indie-hit comedy *Community* and critically acclaimed animated sitcom *Rick and Morty*, had repeatedly engaged in sexual and professional misconduct ten years earlier toward a writer working for him, Megan Ganz. In January 2018, on a different podcast, Ganz had alluded to that earlier experience. A week later, Harmon apologized publicly, stating that he had received a lot of advice, including legal advice, to not speak up at all. He explained that his apology—and his making it in public rather than just to Ganz in private—was about accepting the ramifications and consequences of his failure. Detailing the events of his misconduct directly, clearly, and at points with transparent, wrenching detail, Harmon never deflected the blame from himself to the situation, even as he sought to provide context for it. He ended by explaining his prior silence:

> So, I just want to say, in addition to obviously being sorry, but that's really not the important thing, I want to say I did it by not thinking about it, and I got away with it by not thinking about it. And if she hadn't mentioned something . . . I would have continued to not have to think about it, although I did walk around with my stomach in knots about it, but I wouldn't have had to talk about it.

In his talk he acknowledged knowing that what he did was wrong, which had led him not to repeat his behavior. He admitted having expressed his attraction to Ganz in a "filthy, creepy" manner. He appeared to understand his failure and to have learned from it. What did he do right? He thought carefully about what he was going to say, exhibited compassion toward Ganz, and told his story without making excuses or seeking to avoid the ramifications of his actions. In a small way, a genuine apology helps create a healthy failure culture for others.

A Healthy Failure Culture

Since my initial discovery of the dramatic effect of interpersonal climate on hospital-error reporting, I've spent years trying to understand the kinds of environments where people can work and learn without excessive fear. Where they appreciate the need for continued learning, for risk-taking, and for speaking up quickly about what goes wrong. In these kinds of environments, we enjoy being challenged. When failures occur, we learn from them with an open mind and a light heart and keep moving forward. Freed from self-protection, we can play to win. This book is about helping you—as an individual—practice the science of failing well, but it's a lot easier in a healthy failure culture. A few practices can help you build such a culture in the communities that matter to you.

Call attention to context

A simple but powerful step that follows thoughtful consideration of the stakes you face, along with the level of uncertainty, is to call other people's attention to what you see. When Captain Ben Berman tells a flight crew, "I've never flown a perfect flight, and it's not going to happen today," he is calling attention to context. When Children's Hospital COO Julie Morath tells staff, "Health care is a complex error-prone system," she is calling attention to context.

Astro Teller, director of X laboratories, Alphabet's moonshot factory, is acutely aware of context. He points to the almost absurd level of challenge the lab takes on: "We've deliberately chosen to work on hard problems whose answers are five to ten years over the horizon."

His words convey: "don't expect to succeed today—or even this year! Go wild."

Teller elaborates, in his widely read blog, "The massive problems facing us this century need the widest array of minds, the wildest imaginations, and enormous commitments of time, resources, and attention. . . . My number one job is helping Xers reset and free themselves from these invisible but pernicious constraints so they can free up their potential." It seems to be working. Teller jokes that people come to work and cheerfully say, "Hey, how are we going to kill our project today?" Killing a project sooner frees up precious resources. Failing often is a way to strength-test ideas. For example, the lab's work on self-driving cars was motivated by the huge problem of human error causing car accidents. Would more passengers be safer if cars were driven without humans?

The Self-Driving Car Project began in 2009 by adding autonomous-driving software and hardware features to existing automobiles. But tests by drivers quickly revealed a design failure: people did not remain alert enough to take back control of the car when necessary. So the teams pivoted to a new and even more ambitious goal—designing a fully self-driving car. In February 2020, Teller wrote, "Sometimes it takes dozens of iterations; one team at X right now is working on improving how people hear, and they explored 35 different ideas before they found the one we're going to pour fuel on." In highly innovative companies, not only are intelligent failures welcome, but sharing them widely is baked into the culture.

Encourage failure sharing

Imagine that you have a desirable number of Twitter followers or have beaten out the competition in a contest you care about or gained greater success relative to your peers. You now may be the target of what psychologists call malicious envy, defined as "a destructive interpersonal emotion aimed at harming the envied individual." My colleagues at Harvard devised a series of experiments to show that revealing your failures decreased others' malicious envy. Intuitively, this makes sense. We admire instead of envy people as enormously successful as Simone Biles, Ray Dalio, or Sara Blakely not in spite of their failures but to a large degree because of them. It's difficult to like (and not be bored by) people who only boast about their accomplishments, especially when these boasts are delivered with dashes of arrogance. Sharing failures makes us more relatable and likable—and human.

Giny Boer, CEO of European fashion retailer C&A, told me it was important to her "to establish a culture in which our coworkers are truly in the center and empowered to grow. The foundation for this is a safe environment, where everyone feels valued . . . and where it is also okay to make a mistake." This is why she established Failure Fridays, where, as she put it, "colleagues share what did not go well and—most importantly—what they learned from it. When our colleagues share these stories, they [also] help others to learn."

In addition to cultivating closer relationships, sharing mistakes widely promotes innovation. If scientists in a lab work on a new vaccine candidate that fails, they should tell everybody! When an intelligent failure is buried or goes undiscussed, others may repeat the same experiment. The result? Inefficiency. When someone else in your organization repeats a failure that wasn't shared, it's the worst kind of waste. That is why innovation powerhouses such as IDEO encourage employees to share failures widely. That doesn't, however, mean it's easy for us fallible human beings to do.

As a case in point: Melanie Stefan, a young scientist, published a short article in *Nature* pointing out that her professional failures were much more numerous than her successes and suggesting that people keep a running tally—what she called a "CV of Failures"—to inspire colleagues who might be feeling dejected by the sting of rejection. One person who took up the gauntlet and made his failures public was a professor of economics, Johannes Haushofer, then at Princeton. The document, still posted on his website, lists rejections from degree programs, academic journals, jobs, awards, and so on. Perhaps Haushofer's wry humor helped his CV of Failures go viral, such that the last item on his list reads, "This darn CV of Failures has received way more attention than my entire body of academic work."

Jon Harper is an educator from Maryland who hosts a podcast called *My BAD.* In each episode (he's produced more than one hundred) he interviews a teacher who shares with listeners a mistake the teacher made in the classroom. The purpose of the podcast, Harper has said, is for teachers to realize they are not alone. But in confessing missteps made with students and colleagues, interviewees also talk about what they've learned. For example, elementary school principal Benjamin Kitslaar returned to school after a paternity leave six weeks after the academic year had begun. Teachers—only recently returned to classrooms after teaching remotely during the pandemic—faced many new challenges. Kitslaar, full of ideas about all that needed to be done, believed he was encouraging his staff. But after receiving an email from one of his staff saying that Kitslaar didn't understand the stress the teachers were already experiencing implementing new measures and that he needed to slow down in his demands, he realized he'd made a mistake. Kitslaar said he appreciated the email. This "wake-up call" helped him "get a better pulse on the staff." He did slow down and has since learned how important it is to keep communication lines open with his staff. Kitslaar's shift was only possible because of his capacity for self-awareness.

The Failure Institute hosts their trademarked Fuckup Nights to help people become more authentic in work and life. Participants stand onstage and share their failure stories with an audience and are celebrated with the pomp usually reserved for pop stars. The five founders, all friends, conceived the idea in Mexico City in 2012 after they spent a life-changing evening honestly sharing their biggest failures. They began holding monthly events and—as testimony to failure's being a precursor to success—have since grown into a global enterprise that spans three hundred cites and ninety countries. Their success can be seen as a virtuous cycle—where participants take the risk of speaking about a failure, receive applause, feel rewarded, and discover together what a psychologically safe environment feels like. Can they take it back to their work and home lives?

Reward the right kind of wrong

A cheerful humor accompanies instituting failure awards in your company or family. Recall the failure parties at Eli Lilly, which encouraged people to speak up sooner rather than later about failed projects. Redeploying scientists to new projects rather than squandering time belaboring a failure can save hundreds of thousands of dollars. But rewarding failure can seem fraught. Many managers and parents worry about creating a permissive, anything-goes atmosphere, where people might believe failure is just as good as success. But that confuses rewarding disclosure and transparency with rewarding sloppiness, stupid mistakes, or the failure to try. Most people are motivated to succeed, and to be recognized for their competence. They are less motivated to reveal and analyze failure, and it takes a little encouragement—often in the form of playful rituals—to make it happen.

Failure parties and awards to spur risk-taking are no longer unusual. Grey Advertising, for instance, has a Heroic Failure Award, launched by then chief creative officer, and later president, Tor Myhren after he worried that his team had become too conservative. Myhren's own experience with failure—a commercial he directed for Cadillac in 2006 was panned as the worst Super Bowl ad—inspired the idea. After that visible failure, Myhren changed firms to join Grey and took the lead on a 2007 E*Trade Super Bowl ad featuring a talking baby. Wildly successful, the talking baby became a fixture of E*Trade's advertisements for years to come. At Grey, the Heroic Failure Award's first winner was Amanda Zolten, who hid a box of a potential client's kitty litter product, freshly "soiled," under a conference table before the pitch meeting began. When the litter was revealed, several of the executives walked out, but Myhren was impressed and announced, without knowing if the clients would agree to work with Grey, that Zolten would be receiving the new award. Tata Group similarly launched their Dare to Try Award to celebrate audacious attempts to innovate that failed. Winners include an engineering team at Tata that developed an innovative new transmission that was too expensive to be implemented, and another team that created safe and effective plastic car doors that met with consumer mistrust. NASA, in the aftermath of the tragic *Columbia* shuttle failure, instituted the Lean Forward, Fail Smart Award, to shift its culture to encourage speaking up quickly with ideas and concerns.

A healthy failure culture rewards intelligent failure. Without it, there can be no innovation. Without innovation, no organization can survive over the long term. But vaguely negative consequences for *not trying* can make a healthy failure culture even more powerful. When I visited X at Google's beautiful offices in the fall of 2019, Astro Teller told the assembled group of employees something I had long hoped to hear a company executive say—but until then never had. In response to a question, Teller noted that neither he nor anyone else could promise that layoffs would never happen. But if layoffs *were* needed, the first to go would be people who had never failed. Context is critical to interpreting that statement. If you're leading a moonshot factory, you simply cannot afford to have people on the team who are unwilling to take risks. People who take smart risks will, inevitably, sometimes fail. That's what good performance looks like! A hospital leader or a flight captain might say it differently: those who experienced an error or a mishap and failed to report it will be the first to go. In a healthy failure culture, people share a belief that learning and failing go hand in hand, and that makes it just a little easier to speak up quickly.

In your family, this might take the form of rewarding teenagers for persevering through challenges, despite setbacks, and letting them know you're impressed when they acknowledge where they fell short. This is entirely consistent with Angela Duckworth's research on grit—defined by perseverance and passion for long-term goals. Grit includes a willingness to accept responsibility for your impact on things that go wrong, not just on things that go right (an element of character).

Managers around the world have asked me, "How do I know if my team has a healthy failure culture?" I answer—after checking that the team's work involves uncertainty, novelty, or interdependence—with a question: "What percent of what you hear in a given week is good news versus bad, progress versus problems, agreement versus dissent, 'All's well' or 'I need help'?" Typically, I show the model you see in Table 8.1.

TABLE 8.1: **Diagnosing a Healthy Failure Culture**

How much of what you usually hear is:

This?	Versus This?
Good news	Bad news
Progress	Problems
Agreement	Dissent
All's well	I need help

I note that if they're mostly experiencing the left-hand side of this table, they will be happier. It will feel better. But, alas, it's probably not a good sign. Given the uncertainty and challenge of the work they do, it's unlikely that people don't have bad news, problems, dissenting views, or a need for help. It's more likely that you're simply not hearing about it.

Most of them get it immediately. Their eyes get wide—as they realize that what *feels* good is probably *not* good from the perspective of a healthy failure culture that has psychological safety for speaking up with problems, concerns, and questions.

The Wisdom to Know the Difference

Barbe-Nicole Clicquot had to master the science of failing well without the benefit of modern rhetoric and research. Did she intuit the difference between basic, complex, and intelligent failures? Is that why her failure portfolio was so impressive? Her ability to take risks, play to her strengths, withstand setbacks, and keep moving forward demonstrates implicit mastery of the science of failing well. Self-aware, she understood her strengths (brains, determination, passion about winemaking) and her shortcomings (plain, uninterested in society's pastimes) and bet on her strengths. A situation-aware entrepreneur, she managed risk brilliantly. She understood and shaped the larger system she loved—the technology, the region, the industry—through bold actions, ingenuity, and immense patience that helped build a global market for champagne. A systems thinker, she accommodated the built-in delays that spanned harvesting, producing, and distributing her wines, to grow the market in a disciplined, deliberate way.

The science of failing well, like any other science, is not always fun. It brings good days and bad. It's practiced by fallible human beings working alone and together. But one thing is certain. It *will* bring discovery. Discoveries about what works and what doesn't work in achieving the goals that matter to you, along with discoveries about yourself. Elite failure practitioners around the world and throughout history—athletes, inventors, entrepreneurs, scientists—have taught me a great deal about the unique combination of curiosity, rationality, honesty, determination, and passion that failing well requires. Their example nudges and inspires me to try to keep improving my own skills and habits, and I hope it will do the same for you.

To bring a flawed book to its necessarily flawed ending, I find myself coming back to the vexing issue of discernment. In the most widely adopted version of theologian Reinhold Niebuhr's Serenity Prayer, the "wisdom to know the difference" between what one can and cannot

292

change provides the key to serenity. In the science of failing well, discernment is also vital for achieving serenity and the self-acceptance it brings.

Glossed over in presenting a framework of failure types is the considerable challenge of drawing lines—say, between intelligent and not-so-intelligent failures. Just how new must new territory be? How confident must you be that there's an opportunity? How well considered your hypothesis? How big is too big? Similarly, the clear line between a basic single-cause failure in known territory and a complex failure blurs as soon as we step back to glimpse a larger system. That simple mistake? It was probably caused by a sleep deficit, caused by a sick child, caused by a day-care exposure, and on (and on) it goes. But the goal of a framework is simply to help us think differently, so we can take thoughtful action. Not to provide or insist on rigid classifications.

Discernment is also needed for diagnosing situations and systems. How high are the stakes? How should uncertainty be assessed? What relationships matter most for predicting the system's behavior? Where do you draw the boundaries to identify the system that you want to diagnose or alter? All of these challenges come down to judgment and experience. The more practice you get with the science of failing well, the more you will become comfortable and fluent in using its concepts. This book does not end with an exam on the right kind of wrong that you can pass or fail. It ends with an invitation to practice and thereby help develop the science of failing well.

Most important, discernment matters in developing the self-awareness to confront our failures, the smaller and the larger, the personal and the professional. Acknowledging our shortcomings requires and builds wisdom. Wisdom allows us to know when we've done as well as we can, and confronting ourselves will always be the hardest part of failing well.

Also, the most liberating.

Acknowledgments

Writing this book was an adventure that brought insight and anxiety in equal measure. As with all book projects, at (many) moments I doubted the wisdom of embarking on this one. But for my fellow adventurers, I would not have arrived at this final moment of anxiety where I now sit at my laptop acutely aware of how inadequate these words will be in expressing my appreciation to each of them.

Thank you, first, to my agent, Margo Fleming, who approached me a few years ago to suggest I write a book on failure. I fought her off for as long as I could—saying, at various times over several months, "I wrote an article in *Harvard Business Review* about failure; isn't that enough?" or "Are you sure we need another book on failure?" Margo insisted that the book she wanted to read on this fraught (yet increasingly timely) topic had yet to be written, and somehow I was the one who had to write it. By pushing me to write "just" a proposal, Margo artfully reeled me in and wore me down. After a while, I began to believe that she was right. This book needed to be written, and I needed to sit down and do it. Once I got started, Margo was there, cheering me on, applying its ideas in her life, connecting me to publishers, and remaining quietly confident that I'd get it done.

But it takes a team to get a book like this done. Of the many people who contributed to that outcome, I am especially grateful to have been able to work with thought partner and writer Karen Propp on this project. To convert my ideas into a finished book, it was essential for me to think aloud to map concepts and stories into chapter outlines, and Karen played a crucial role in that process. She also helped me find and develop stories to animate the ideas and frameworks. Several other colleagues and research associates, including Dan Falk, Jordan Gans, Ian Grey, Patrick Healey, Susan Salter, and Paige Tsai conducted valuable background research. As this journey was nearing an end, I discovered the extraordinary talents of Heather Kreidler—fact-checker, reference chaser, detail lover, and perceptive reader—who made sure this book stands on solid ground, while also managing the tedious but invaluable ensuring of references, formatting, permissions, and more with remarkable enthusiasm and grace. Lastly, the care and craft of copyeditor Steve Boldt is deeply appreciated, along with that of Jaye Glenn, who implemented corrections in page proofs with intelligence and a sharp eye—even finding errors I'd missed.

Stephanie Hitchcock, my amazing editor at Atria, offered feedback and encouragement at just the right moments throughout this journey. She drilled down on details that didn't make sense and stepped back and saw what was missing in entire sections. Sometimes I didn't immediately know what to do with her suggestions—such as the occasional push to take you, my reader, by my side, to invite you in to take a look at an idea *with* me. But I'd eventually arrive at a eureka moment of understanding, smiling as I put her genius to work. Stephanie stood up for you, my readers, from start to finish. She made sure that I spoke to you in your lives, not just in your jobs and companies.

Special thanks go to Amelia Crabtree, an artist and physician in Australia, for ably translating some of my frameworks into cheerful figures that enliven the dry conceptualizing of an academic. I'm grateful to Nancy Boghossian for finding Amelia and for so much more that kept me going throughout this project. Brendan Timmers, a designer in the Netherlands, produced the elegant system dynamics figures in chapter 7, making a complicated set of interacting causal relationships easy to trace and understand.

As a systems thinker, I feel it's only right to trace the early motivation for this work to the brilliant Steve Prokesch at *Harvard Business Review*, who first trusted that I had something meaningful to say for that magazine's special issue on failure back in 2011. Steve's relentless pushing for clarity and logic made me a better writer then, as well as today.

For the research that underlies this book and its ideas, I owe an enormous debt to the thoughtful individuals—nurses, doctors, engineers, and CEOs alike—in the many organizations that opened their doors to this academic researcher. I am grateful for their willingness to be interviewed and studied. I also thank the Division of Research at Harvard Business School for generous financial support that funded my research.

Finally, I am grateful to my family. Most of all to my husband, George Daley, whose love and confidence—not to mention his exquisite cooking—sustained me and made it possible for me to devote so much time to getting this book done. He has been there for every success and failure for the past three decades, never losing faith in me or in my work. As a scientist, George has spent countless hours failing well—and succeeding brilliantly. Humble enough to claim my ideas have helped him succeed, George gave me confidence that they may help others as well. But this book is dedicated to our two sons, Jack and Nick, who inspire me every day with their curiosity and commitment to making a better world.

Notes

Prologue

3 **research paper from this first study:** Amy C. Edmondson, "Learning from Mistakes Is Easier Said Than Done: Group and Organizational Influences on the Detection and Correction of Human Error," *Journal of Applied Behavioral Science* 32, no. 1 (March 1, 1996): 5–28, doi: 10.1177/0021886396321001.

Introduction

8 **test the effects of fatigue on error rates:** H. C. Foushee, "The Role of Communications, Socio-psychological, and Personality Factors in the Maintenance of Crew Coordination," *Aviation, Space, and Environmental Medicine* 53, no. 11 (November 1982): 1062–66.

9 **a revolution in passenger air travel:** Robert L. Helmreich, Ashleigh C. Merritt, and John A. Wilhelm, "The Evolution of Crew Resource Management Training in Commercial Aviation," *International Journal of Aviation Psychology* 9, no. 1 (January 1999): 19–32; Barbara G. Kanki, José M. Anca, and Thomas Raymond Chidester, eds., *Crew Resource Management*, 3rd ed. (London: Academic Press, 2019).

9 **interplay of pilots, copilots, and navigators:** For an overview of Hackman's work on teams, see J. Richard Hackman, *Groups That Work (and Those That Don't): Creating Conditions for Effective Teamwork*, 1st ed., Jossey-Bass Management Series (San Francisco: Jossey-Bass, 1990).

10 **ready-made "team diagnostic survey":** Ruth Wageman, J. Richard Hackman, and Erin Lehman, "Team Diagnostic Survey," *Journal of Applied Behavioral Science* 41, no. 4 (2005): 373–98, doi: 10.1177/0021886305281984.

11 **These failures are "intelligent":** Sim B. Sitkin, "Learning through Failure: The Strategy of Small Losses," *Research in Organizational Behavior* 14 (1992): 231–66.

11 **Despite happy talk about celebrating failures:** For examples of the "all failure is good" culture, and some pushbacks, see Shane Snow, "Silicon Valley's Obsession with Failure Is Totally Misguided," *Business Insider*, October 14, 2014, https://www.businessinsider.com/startup-failure-does-not-lead-to-success -2014-10; Adrian Daub, "The Undertakers of Silicon Valley: How Failure Became Big Business," *Guardian*, August 21, 2018, sec. Technology, https://www .theguardian.com/technology/2018/aug/21/the-undertakers-of-silicon-valley -how-failure-became-big-business; Alex Holder, "How Failure Became a Cultural Fetish," *ELLE*, February 22, 2021, https://www.elle.com/uk/life-and-culture /elle-voices/a35546483/failure-cultural-fetish/.

14 **hired a research assistant:** Today Andy is a full professor at Brandeis University with expertise in psychology and international business.

15 **used the term *psychological safety*:** Amy C. Edmondson, "Psychological Safety and Learning Behavior in Work Teams," *Administrative Science Quarterly* 44, no. 2 (June 1, 1999): 350–83.

15 **teams and organizations with higher psychological safety:** For an overview of this research, see chapter 2 of my book *The Fearless Organization: Creating Psychological Safety in the Workplace for Learning, Innovation, and Growth* (Hoboken, NJ: John Wiley and Sons, 2018). For academic reviews on the role of psychological safety in promoting learning and performance across a range of contexts, see Amy C. Edmondson and Zhike Lei, "Psychological Safety: The History, Renaissance, and Future of an Interpersonal Construct," *Annual Review of Organizational Psychology and Organizational Behavior* 1, no. 1 (2014): 23–43; Amy C. Edmondson et al., "Understanding Psychological Safety in Healthcare and Education Organizations: A Comparative Perspective," *Research in Human Development* 13, no. 1 (January 2, 2016): 65–83; M. Lance Frazier et al., "Psychological Safety: A Meta-Analytic Review and Extension," *Personnel Psychology* 70, no. 1 (Spring 2017): 113–65; Alexander Newman, Ross Donohue, and Nathan Eva, "Psychological Safety: A Systematic Review of the Literature," *Human Resource Management Review* 27, no. 3 (September 1, 2017): 521–35; Róisín O'Donovan and Eilish Mcauliffe, "A Systematic Review of Factors That Enable Psychological Safety in Healthcare Teams," *International Journal for Quality in Health Care* 32, no. 4 (May 2020): 240–50.

19 **Checklists are just one of the tools:** See, for example, Atul Gawande, *The Checklist Manifesto: How to Get Things Right*, 1st ed. (New York: Metropolitan Books and Henry Holt, 2010).

Notes

Chapter 1: Chasing the Right Kind of Wrong

23 **Clarence Dennis was operating:** To learn more about this story and the groundbreaking early days of cardiac surgery, see G. Wayne Miller, *King of Hearts: The True Story of the Maverick Who Pioneered Open-Heart Surgery* (New York: Crown, 2000); James S. Forrester, *The Heart Healers: The Misfits, Mavericks, and Rebels Who Created the Greatest Medical Breakthrough of Our Lives* (New York: St. Martin's Press, 2015).

25 **"Error exposes truth":** Forrester, *Heart Healers*, 63.

26 **2 million of these lifesaving medical procedures:** Peter Zilla et al., "Global Unmet Needs in Cardiac Surgery," *Global Heart* 13, no. 4 (December 2018): 293–303, doi: 10.1016/j.gheart.2018.08.002.

27 **process negative and positive information:** For an overview of some of this research, see Roy F. Baumeister et al., "Bad Is Stronger than Good," *Review of General Psychology* 5, no. 4 (2001): 323–70, doi: 10.1037/1089-2680.5.4.323.

27 **saddled with a "negativity bias":** Paul Rozin and Edward B. Royzman, "Negativity Bias, Negativity Dominance, and Contagion," *Personality and Social Psychology Review* 5, no. 4 (November 2001): 296–320, doi: 10.1207/S15327957PSPR0504_2.

27 **stronger than good:** John Tierney and Roy F. Baumeister, *The Power of Bad: How the Negativity Effect Rules Us and How We Can Rule It* (New York: Penguin, 2019).

27 **"loss aversion":** Amos Tversky and Daniel Kahneman, "Loss Aversion in Riskless Choice: A Reference-Dependent Model," *Quarterly Journal of Economics* 106, no. 4 (1991): 1039–61.

27 **participants were given a coffee mug:** Daniel Kahneman, Jack L. Knetsch, and Richard H. Thaler, "Experimental Tests of the Endowment Effect and the Coase Theorem," *Journal of Political Economy* 98, no. 6 (December 1990): 1325–48.

28 **major failures at over fifty companies:** Sydney Finkelstein, *Why Smart Executives Fail and What You Can Learn from Their Mistakes* (New York: Portfolio, 2003). Discussed in Mark D. Cannon and Amy C. Edmondson, "Failing to Learn and Learning to Fail (Intelligently): How Great Organizations Put Failure to Work to Innovate and Improve," *Long Range Planning* 38, no. 3 (June 2005): 299–316.

28 **"the buck stops here":** "'The Buck Stops Here' Desk Sign," Harry S. Truman Library & Museum, National Archives and Records Administration, https://www.trumanlibrary.gov/education/trivia/buck-stops-here-sign.

30 **"miss one hundred percent of the shots you don't take":** Wayne Gretzky in response to Bob McKenzie, editor of *Hockey News*, in 1983. Another good example of failures on the way to gaining mastery is the Nike commercial "Failure," performed by Michael Jordan (Wieden+Kennedy, 1997).

30 **failure means you are "in the game":** Maya Salam, "Abby Wambach's Leader-ship Lessons: Be the Wolf," *New York Times*, April 9, 2019, sec. Sports, https://www.nytimes.com/2019/04/09/sports/soccer/abby-wambach-soccer-wolfpack.html.

30 **make failure their "fuel":** Abby Wambach, "Abby Wambach, Remarks as De-livered" (commencement address, Barnard College, NY, 2018), https://barnard.edu/commencement/archives/2018/abby-wambach-remarks.

30 *less* **likely to feel the sting of failure:** Victoria Husted Medvec, Scott F. Madey, and Thomas Gilovich, "When Less Is More: Counterfactual Thinking and Satis-faction among Olympic Medalists," *Journal of Personality and Social Psychology* 69, no. 4 (1995): 603–10, doi: 10.1037/0022-3514.69.4.603.

30 **"counterfactual thinking":** Neal J. Roese, "Counterfactual Thinking," *Psycho-logical Bulletin* 121, no. 1 (1997): 133–48, doi: 10.1037/0033-2909.121.1.133.

30 **reframe gave them joy instead of regret:** See, for example, James P. Robson Jr. and Meredith Troutman-Jordan, "A Concept Analysis of Cognitive Reframing," *Journal of Theory Construction & Testing* 18, no. 2 (2014): 55–59. Appraisal the-ory is also relevant here: Klaus R. Scherer, "Appraisal Theory," in *Handbook of Cognition and Emotion*, ed. Tim Dalgleish and Mick J. Power (New York: John Wiley and Sons, 1999), 637–63.

31 **Clinical psychology research shows:** Judith Johnson et al., "Resilience to Emotional Distress in Response to Failure, Error or Mistakes: A Systematic Review," *Clinical Psychology Review* 52 (March 2017): 19–42, doi: 10.1016/j.cpr.2016.11.007.

31 **resilient people make more positive attributions:** Ibid.

31 **launched a revolution in "positive psychology":** Martin E. P. Seligman and Mihaly Csikszentmihalyi, "Positive Psychology: An Introduction," in *Flow and the Foundations of Positive Psychology* by Mihaly Csikszentmihalyi (Dordrecht, Netherlands: Springer, 2014).

33 **activating a fight-or-flight response:** Joseph E. LeDoux, "The Emotional Brain, Fear, and the Amygdala," *Cellular and Molecular Neurobiology* 23, no. 4–5 (2003): 727–38, doi: 10.1023/A:1025048802629; Joseph E. LeDoux, "The Amyg-dala Is Not the Brain's Fear Center," *I Got a Mind to Tell You* (blog), *Psychology Today*, August 10, 2015, https://www.psychologytoday.com/us/blog/i-got-mind-tell-you/201508/the-amygdala-is-not-the-brains-fear-center.

34 **different organizational contexts set the stage:** See chapter 2 in Amy C. Ed-mondson, *Teaming: How Organizations Learn, Innovate, and Compete in the Knowledge Economy* (San Francisco: Jossey-Bass, 2012).

36 **"No plan survives contact with the enemy":** Helmut von Moltke, "Über Strate-gie," in *Moltkes militärische Werke*, ed. Großer Generalstab (Berlin: E. S. Mittler, 1892–1912), vol. 4, pt. 2, 287–93. See also Graham Kenny, "Strategic Plans Are Less Important Than Strategic Planning," *Harvard Business Review*, June 21,

2016, https://hbr.org/2016/06/strategic-plans-are-less-important-than-strategic
-planning.

37 **brain circuits for social pain and physical pain:** Naomi I. Eisenberger, "The
Pain of Social Disconnection: Examining the Shared Neural Underpinnings of
Physical and Social Pain," *Nature Reviews Neuroscience* 13 (June 2012): 421–34,
https://www.nature.com/articles/nrn3231; Matthew D. Lieberman and Naomi I.
Eisenberger, "The Pains and Pleasures of Social Life: A Social Cognitive Neuroscience Approach," *NeuroLeadership Journal* 1 (September 11, 2008), https://
www.scn.ucla.edu/pdf/Pains&Pleasures(2008).pdf.

37 **Fear activates the amygdala:** Pankaj Sah and R. Frederick Westbrook, "The
Circuit of Fear," *Nature* 454, no. 7204 (July 2008): 589–90, doi: 10.1038/454589a;
LeDoux, "Emotional Brain, Fear, and the Amygdala." LeDoux has said in more
recent years that the amygdala-fear linkage is far more complex than originally
thought. For example, Joseph E. LeDoux and Richard Brown, "A Higher-Order
Theory of Emotional Consciousness," *Proceedings of the National Academy of
Sciences* 114, no. 10 (2017): E2016–25, doi: 10.1073/pnas.1619316114; LeDoux,
"Amygdala Is Not."

37 **designed to be protective:** LeDoux, "Amygdala Is Not."

37 **fear inhibits learning:** For a brief primer on the role of emotions, including
fear, in learning, see Ulrike Rimmele, "A Primer on Emotions and Learning,"
OECD, accessed November 13, 2021, https://www.oecd.org/education/ceri/
aprimeronemotionsandlearning.htm.

38 **Studies find today's teens:** Jean M. Twenge, *iGen: Why Today's Super-Connected
Kids Are Growing Up Less Rebellious, More Tolerant, Less Happy—and Com-
pletely Unprepared for Adulthood: And What That Means for the Rest of Us*
(New York: Atria Books, 2017).

38 **the antidote to the interpersonal fear:** For an overview of much of this evidence, see Amy C. Edmondson, *The Fearless Organization: Creating Psychological Safety in the Workplace for Learning, Innovation, and Growth*, 1st ed.
(Hoboken, NJ: John Wiley and Sons, 2019).

38 **in most studies of psychological safety:** For some examples, see Ingrid M.
Nembhard and Amy C. Edmondson, "Making It Safe: The Effects of Leader
Inclusiveness and Professional Status on Psychological Safety and Improvement
Efforts in Health Care Teams," *Journal of Organizational Behavior* 27, no. 7
(2016): 941–66; Amy C. Edmondson, "Learning from Failure in Health Care:
Frequent Opportunities, Pervasive Barriers," *Quality and Safety in Health Care*
13, suppl. 2 (December 1, 2004): ii3–9; Amy C. Edmondson, "Speaking Up in
the Operating Room: How Team Leaders Promote Learning in Interdisciplin-
ary Action Teams," *Journal of Management Studies* 40, no. 6 (2003): 1419–52;
Amy C. Edmondson, "Framing for Learning: Lessons in Successful Technology
Implementation," *California Management Review* 45, no. 2 (2003): 34–54; Fiona

Lee et al., "The Mixed Effects of Inconsistency on Experimentation in Organizations," *Organization Science* 15, no. 3 (May–June 2004): 310–26; Michael Roberto, Richard M. J. Bohmer, and Amy C. Edmondson, "Facing Ambiguous Threats," *Harvard Business Review* 84, no. 11 (November 2006): 106–13.

41 **spectrum of reasons for failure:** Amy C. Edmondson, "Strategies for Learning from Failure," *Harvard Business Review* 89, no. 4 (April 2011).

42 **one of the most challenging moves in gymnastics:** "The Hardest Gymnastics Skills in Women's Artistic Gymnastics (2022 Update)," *Uplifter Inc.*, October 9, 2019, https://www.uplifterinc.com/hardest-gymnastics-skills.

43 **"produced only corpses":** Miller, *King of Hearts*, 5.

43 **Lillehei had been determined to push ahead:** Ibid.

44 **tried hypothermia as a means:** Ibid.

45 **Lillehei's first triumph:** Forrester, *Heart Healers*, 70.

45 **the mortality rate for cardiac surgery:** Ibid., 87.

45 **risk of dying from the surgery:** McMaster University, "Better Assessment of Risk from Heart Surgery Results in Better Patient Outcomes: Levels of Troponin Associated with an Increased Risk of Death," *ScienceDaily*, March 2, 2022, www.sciencedaily.com/releases/2022/03/220302185945.htm. See also "Surprising Spike in Postoperative Cardiac Surgery Deaths May Be an Unintended Consequence of 30-Day Survival Measurements," Johns Hopkins Medicine, April 10, 2014, https://www.hopkinsmedicine.org/news/media/releases/surprising _spike_in_postoperative_cardiac_surgery_deaths_may_be_an_unintended _consequence_of_30_day_survival_measurements.

45 **a modern innovation in cardiac surgery:** Amy C. Edmondson, Richard M. Bohmer, and Gary P. Pisano, "Disrupted Routines: Team Learning and New Technology Implementation in Hospitals," *Administrative Science Quarterly* 46, no. 4 (2001): 685–716, doi: 10.2307/3094828.

Chapter 2: Eureka!

50 **influenced her to major in chemistry:** Released in 1997, *Gattaca* (its letters G, A, T, and C represent the four nucleobases of DNA) takes place in a future when society is classified into those with superior genetics, called Valids, and humans conceived naturally, called In-Valids, who are assigned only menial jobs. In the plot an In-Valid eventually secures and succeeds at an elite position on a space mission to one of Saturn's moons despite his supposed intellectual inferiority. Andrew Niccol, screenwriter, *Gattaca*, drama, sci-fi, thriller (Columbia Pictures, Jersey Films, 1997).

51 **used a chemical reagent called glyoxal:** Steve D. Knutson and Jennifer M. Heemstra, "EndoVIPER-seq for Improved Detection of A-to-I Editing Sites in

Cellular RNA," *Current Protocols in Chemical Biology* 12, no. 2 (2020): e82, doi: 10.1002/cpch.82.

51 **applications for controlled or time-released therapeutic drugs:** Steve D. Knutson et al., "Thermoreversible Control of Nucleic Acid Structure and Function with Glyoxal Caging," *Journal of the American Chemical Society* 142, no. 41 (2020): 17766–81.

52 **central role embracing failure plays in science research:** Jen Heemstra (@jenheemstra), "The Only People Who Never Make Mistakes and Never Experience Failure Are Those Who Never Try," Twitter, January 13, 2021, 8:04 a.m., https://twitter.com/jenheemstra/status/1349341481472036865.

53 **Much ink has already been spilled about Edison:** For example, see Margaret Frith and John O'Brien, *Who Was Thomas Alva Edison?* (New York: Penguin Workshop, 2005); Edmund Morris, *Edison* (New York: Random House, 2019); Randall E. Stross, *The Wizard of Menlo Park: How Thomas Alva Edison Invented the Modern World* (New York: Crown, 2007).

54 **he had thousands of "results":** Frank Lewis Dyer, *Thomas Edison: His Life and Inventions*, vol. 2 (Harper and Brothers, 1910), chap. 24, 369.

54 **From an early age, Jocelyn Bell Burnell:** Ben Proudfoot, "She Changed Astronomy Forever. He Won the Nobel Prize for It," *New York Times*, July 27, 2021, sec. Opinion, https://www.nytimes.com/2021/07/27/opinion/pulsars-jocelyn -bell-burnell-astronomy.html.

55 **"I wanted to understand what it was":** See Ben Proudfoot, "Almost Famous: The Silent Pulse of the Universe" (video), featuring Jocelyn Bell Burnell, July 27, 2021, at 5:42, https://www.nytimes.com/2021/07/27/opinion/pulsars-jocelyn -bell-burnell-astronomy.html.

55 **"started a whole new research project":** Ibid., at 6:54.

55 **Nobel Prize–winning discovery:** Martin Ryle and Antony Hewish, "Antony Hewish, the Nobel Prize in Physics in 1974," Nobel Prize Outreach AB, https:// www.nobelprize.org/prizes/physics/1974/hewish/biographical/.

58 **"create, trial, and test":** "Design Technology," Brighton College, accessed October 22, 2021, https://www.brightoncollege.org.uk/college/arts-life/design -technology/.

58 **unintentional self-injury while opening an avocado:** Jill Seladi-Schulman, "What Is Avocado Hand?," Healthline, November 16, 2018, https://www .healthline.com/health/avocado-hand.

58 **raised money for manufacturing the Avogo:** "Avogo—Cut and De-stone Your Avocado at Home or on the Go," Kickstarter, accessed October 22, 2021, https://www.kickstarter.com/projects/183646099/avogo-cut-and-de-stone -your-avocado-at-home-or-on.

59 **company paid the price:** Tom Eisenmann, "Why Start-Ups Fail," *Harvard Business Review*, May–June 2021, https://hbr.org/2021/05/why-start-ups-fail.

59 **"the 'fail fast' mantra":** Ibid. See also Tom Eisenmann, *Why Startups Fail: A New Roadmap to Entrepreneurial Success* (New York: Currency, 2021).

60 **product-development history:** "The 10 Worst Product Fails of All Time," *Time*, https://time.com/13549/the-10-worst-product-fails-of-all-time/. Other details on the failure of Crystal Pepsi are discussed by Reuben Salsa, "Pepsi's Greatest Failure: The Crystal Bubble That Burst," May 27, 2020, https://bettermarketing .pub/pepsis-greatest-failure-the-crystal-bubble-that-burst-9cffd4f462ec.

60 **"shouldn't be seeing something like that":** Proudfoot, "Almost Famous," at 5:42.

60 **"explored a variety of products that already exist":** "Avogo," Kickstarter.

61 **Atal's curiosity ultimately led to the development:** Bishnu Atal's comments during "A Conversation with James West" (video), Acoustical Society of America, March 4, 2021, at 1:12:23, https://www.youtube.com/watch?v =yWExMa38o88.

62 **failure bonuses to employees:** Astro Teller, "The Unexpected Benefit of Celebrating Failure," TED2016, https://www.ted.com/talks/astro_teller_the_unexpected _benefit_of_celebrating_failure.

62 **introduced "failure parties":** Thomas M. Burton, "By Learning from Failures, Lilly Keeps Drug Pipeline Full," *Wall Street Journal*, April 21, 2004, https://www .wsj.com/articles/SB108249266648388235.

63 **embarrassing and expensive fiasco:** For more detail on the story see Edmondson, *Teaming*, chap. 7.

64 **a "quantitative futurist":** Blake Morgan, "50 Leading Female Futurists," *Forbes*, March 5, 2020, https://www.forbes.com/sites/blakemorgan/2020/03/05/50 -leading-female-futurists/.

65 **creating a profile to attract a life partner:** Amy Webb, "How I Hacked Online Dating," TEDSalon NY, 2013, https://www.ted.com/talks/amy_webb_how_i _hacked_online_dating.

68 **a "growth mindset":** Carol S. Dweck, *Mindset: The New Psychology of Success* (New York: Ballantine, 2006).

68 **invention that underwent a stop-and-go journey:** Rachel Ross, "Who Invented the Traffic Light?," Live Science, December 16, 2016, https://www.livescience .com/57231-who-invented-the-traffic-light.html.

69 **the first electric traffic signal:** Ibid.

69 **improve upon previous iterations:** Biography.com editors, "Garrett Morgan," Biography, accessed November 4, 2021, https://www.biography.com/inventor /garrett-morgan.

69 **Morgan witnessed a spectacular accident:** "Garrett Morgan Patents Three-Position Traffic Signal," History, accessed October 24, 2021, https://www .history.com/this-day-in-history/garrett-morgan-patents-three-position-traffic -signal.

69 **find a use for the fallen apples:** "Engineering for Reuse: Chris Stark," Engineering Design Workshop: Engineering Stories, Boston Museum of Science, accessed October 22, 2021, https://virtualexhibits.mos.org/edw-engineering-stories.

70 **James West's:** Information about James West was taken from "James West: Biography" and "James West: Digital Archive," HistoryMakers, accessed October 23, 2021, https://www.thehistorymakers.org/biography/james-west; "Meet Past President of ASA, Dr. Jim West," *Acoustics Today* (blog), September 17, 2020, https://acousticstoday.org/meet-past-president-of-asa-dr-jim-west/.

70 **Brotherhood of Sleeping Car Porters:** James West, "James West Talks about His Father's Career," interviewed by Larry Crowe, HistoryMakers A2013.039, February 13, 2013, HistoryMakers Digital Archive, sess. 1, tape 1, story 7.

71 **fired from that job for her activism:** "Meet Past President," *Acoustics Today.*

71 **two Purple Hearts:** James West, "James West Talks about His Experience in the U.S. Army," interviewed by Larry Crowe, HistoryMakers A2013.039, February 13, 2013, HistoryMakers Digital Archive, sess. 1, tape 4, story 3.

71 **grandfather's pocket watch, all 107 pieces:** James West, "James West Describes His Earliest Childhood Memories," interviewed by Larry Crowe, HistoryMakers A2013.039, February 13, 2013, HistoryMakers Digital Archive, sess. 1, tape 1, story 9.

71 **favorite failure stories is about the old radio:** James West, "James West Remembers Being Electrocuted at Eight Years Old," interviewed by Larry Crowe, HistoryMakers A2013.039, February 13, 2013, HistoryMakers Digital Archive, sess. 1, tape 2, story 5.

72 **"how can I better understand the physical principles":** Ibid., at 5:23.

72 **the interaural time delay:** James West, "James West Talks about His Experience Interning at Bell Laboratories, Part 1," interviewed by Larry Crowe, HistoryMakers A2013.039, February 13, 2013, HistoryMakers Digital Archive, sess. 1, tape 4, story 5.

72 **"What can you do to help this group":** Ibid.

72 **different type of headphones:** W. Kuhl, G. R. Schodder, and F.-K. Schröder, "Condenser Transmitters and Microphones with Solid Dielectric for Airborne Ultrasonics," *Acta Acustica United with Acustica* 4, no. 5 (1954): 519–32.

73 **the larger headphones worked as he'd predicted:** West, "James West Talks about His Experience Interning at Bell Laboratories, Part 1."

73 **"I had to figure out":** Ibid.

74 **breakthrough came when West and Sessler:** James West, "James West Talks about His Experience Interning at Bell Laboratories, Part 2," interviewed by Larry Crowe, HistoryMakers A2013.039, February 13, 2013, HistoryMakers Digital Archive, sess. 1, tape 4, story 6.

74 **first manufactured by Sony in 1968:** James West, "James West Talks about the Electret Microphone, Part 2," interviewed by Larry Crowe, HistoryMakers

A2013.039, February 13, 2013, HistoryMakers Digital Archive, sess. 1, tape 5, story 5.

74 **today they power 90 percent:** Biography.com editors, "James West," Biography, accessed December 2, 2022, https://www.biography.com/inventor/james -west.

74 **create a new haute cuisine:** Tienlon Ho, "The Noma Way," *California Sunday Magazine*, February 2, 2016, https://story.californiasunday.com/noma-australia -rene-redzepi.

74 **apprenticed in several restaurants:** Ibid.

74 **ingredients native to northern Scandinavia seemed *too* unusual:** Stefan Chomka, "René Redzepi: 'With Noma 2.0, We Dare Again to Fail,'" 50 Best Stories, November 10, 2017, https://www.theworlds50best.com/stories/News /rene-redzepi-noma-dare-to-fail.html.

75 **voted the best restaurant in the world:** Tim Lewis, "Claus Meyer: The Other Man from Noma," *Observer* (blog), *Guardian*, March 20, 2016, sec. Food, https://www .theguardian.com/lifeandstyle/2016/mar/20/claus-meyer-the-other-man-from -noma-copenhagen-nordic-kitchen-recipes.

75 **"explorers of the edible world":** René Redzepi, *René Redzepi Journal* (New York and London: Phaidon, 2013), 44.

75 **led to many a radical new dish:** Ho, "Noma Way."

75 **"farmed, fished, or foraged":** Ibid.

75 **wrote about his restaurant as a kind of laboratory:** Redzepi, *René Redzepi*, 18–19, entry for February 9, 2013.

75 **"one failure after another":** Ibid., 19.

76 **"fail as much as you want":** Chomka, "René Redzepi." See also Pierre Deschamps et al., *Noma: My Perfect Storm* (Documentree Films, 2015).

76 **"learning from every mistake":** Stefano Ferraro, "Stefano Ferraro, Head Pastry-Chef at Noma: Failing Is a Premise for Growth," trans. Slawka G. Scarso, Identità Golose Web Magazine internazionale di cucina, March 1, 2020, https://www .identitagolose.com/sito/en/116/25235/chefs-life-stories/stefano-ferraro-head -pastry-chef-at-noma-failing-is-a-premise-for-growth.html.

76 **"It can't be static":** Redzepi, *René Redzepi*, 25.

76 **creation of a recipe based on live fjord shrimp:** Redzepi, *René Redzepi*, 48–49, Thursday, March 24.

76 **Redzepi and his team experimented:** Ho, "Noma Way."

77 **"again and again and again":** Ibid.

77 **"page after page of red numbers":** Redzepi, *René Redzepi*, 160.

77 **"broader concepts that could nudge us":** Ibid., 26.

77 **experimenting with radical new winter-menu projects:** Alessandra Bulow, "An Interview with René Redzepi," Epicurious, https://www.epicurious.com /archive/chefsexperts/celebrity-chefs/rene-redzepi-interview.

Notes

77 **Credited with increasing Copenhagen's tourism:** Deschamps et al., *Noma.*

77 **three Michelin stars:** "Noma," Michelin Guide, accessed December 1, 2022, https://guide.michelin.com/us/en/capital-region/copenhagen/restaurant/noma.

78 **"everything we have achieved we have done by failing":** Redzepi, *René Redzepi*, 59.

78 **the restaurant would close for good:** Pete Wells, "Noma Spawned a World of Imitators, but the Restaurant Remains an Original," *New York Times*, January 9, 2023, https://www.nytimes.com/2023/01/09/dining/rene-redzepi-closing-noma -pete-wells.html?action=click&module=RelatedLinks&pgtype=Article.

79 **Harvard Business School case study:** See Amy C. Edmondson and Laura R. Feldman, "Phase Zero: Introducing New Services at IDEO (A)," Harvard Business School, Case 605-069, February 2005 (revised March 2013); Amy C. Edmondson and Kathryn S. Roloff, "Phase Zero: Introducing New Services at IDEO (B)," Harvard Business School, Supplement 606-123, June 2006 (revised March 2013).

79 **IDEO, a small innovation consultancy:** For key details about IDEO and their unique approach to design, see Edmondson and Feldman, "Phase Zero."

79 **company traces its history back to 1991:** "Bill Moggridge," IDEO, accessed October 22, 2021, https://www.ideo.com/people/bill-moggridge.

79 **widely used innovations include the computer mouse:** Edmondson and Feldman, "Phase Zero."

79 **"Fail often":** A widely watched ABC *Nightline* segment in 2009 featured an IDEO team designing a radical new supermarket cart in five days. The cart was elegant and functional, but the company's culture was the real star of the show, as was the irresistible charm of David Kelley—not only extolling the need for failure, but cheerfully pointing to a collection of company failures proudly displayed and shared with the television audience. "ABC *Nightline*—IDEO Shopping Cart," December 2, 2009, https://www.youtube.com/watch?v=M66ZU2PCIcM. See also "Why You Should Talk Less and Do More," IDEO Design Thinking, October 30, 2013, https://designthinking.ideo.com/blog/why-you-should-talk-less -and-do-more.

80 **"'we believe you can figure it out'":** Edmondson and Feldman, "Phase Zero," 2.

81 **"involving us earlier in their process":** Ibid., 5.

82 **learn how to usher ideas through corporate systems:** Edmondson and Roloff, "Phase Zero."

84 **failed to establish what's called efficacy:** "Eli Lilly's Alimta Disappoints," Yahoo! Finance, June 4, 2013, http://finance.yahoo.com/news/eli-lillys-alimta -disappoints-183302340.html. See also Steven T. Szabo et al., "Lessons Learned and Potentials for Improvement in CNS Drug Development: ISCTM Section on Designing the Right Series of Experiments," *Innovations in Clinical Neuroscience* 12, no. 3, suppl. A (2015).

84 **$2.5 billion:** Eric Sagonowsky, "Despite Drug Launch Streak, Lilly Posts Rare Sales Decline as Alimta Succumbs to Generics," Fierce Pharma, August 4, 2022, https://www.fiercepharma.com/pharma/lillys-new-launches-shine-alimta -drags-sales.

Chapter 3: To Err Is Human

87 **Citibank employees accidentally transferred $900 million:** Chris Dolmetsch, Jennifer Surane, and Katherine Doherty, "Citi Trial Shows Chain of Gaffes Leading to $900 Million Blunder," Bloomberg, December 9, 2020, https://www .bloomberg.com/news/articles/2020-12-09/citi-official-shocked-over-900 -million-error-as-trial-begins.

88 **a controversial finders-keepers ruling:** Eversheds Sutherland, "The Billion Dollar Bewail: Citibank Cannot Recover $900 Million Inadvertently Wired to Lenders," JD Supra, March 11, 2021, https://www.jdsupra.com/legalnews/the -billion-dollar-bewail-citibank-9578400/.

90 **effective in reducing preventable errors:** Atul Gawande, *The Checklist Manifesto: How to Get Things Right* (New York: Metropolitan Books and Henry Holt, 2010).

90 **crashed into the ice-covered Potomac River:** For an analysis of this accident, see J. Richard Hackman, *Leading Teams: Setting the Stage for Great Performances* (Boston: Harvard Business School Press, 2002).

92 **driver walked away from the accident:** For additional details on this basic failure, see Thomas Tracy, Nicholas Williams, and Clayton Guse, "Brooklyn Building Smashed by MTA Bus at Risk of Collapse, City Officials Say," *New York Daily News*, June 9, 2021, https://www.nydailynews.com/new-york/ny-brooklyn-mta -bus-crash-video-20210609-j5picmqwkfghbipx6w2omdu3dy-story.html.

92 **shopping bags between his feet:** "'Disturbing' Video Emerges in MTA Bus Crash into Brooklyn Building Case" (video), *NBC News 4 New York*, June 9, 2021, at 1:06, https://www.nbcnewyork.com/on-air/as-seen-on/disturbing -video-emerges-in-mta-bus-crash-into-brooklyn-building-case/3097885/.

94 **initially attributed to a simple cause:** Martin Chulov, "A Year on from Beirut Explosion, Scars and Questions Remain," *Guardian*, August 4, 2021, sec. World News, https://www.theguardian.com/world/2021/aug/04/a-year-on-from-beruit -explosion-scars-and-questions-remain.

94 **headline on March 31, 2021, said it all:** Sharon LaFraniere and Noah Weiland, "Factory Mix-Up Ruins Up to 15 Million Vaccine Doses from Johnson & Johnson," *New York Times*, March 31, 2021, sec. U.S., https://www.nytimes .com/2021/03/31/us/politics/johnson-johnson-coronavirus-vaccine.html.

95 **Workers at the plant had accidentally contaminated:** Sharon LaFraniere, Noah Weiland, and Sheryl Gay Stolberg, "The F.D.A. Tells Johnson & Johnson That

About 60 Million Doses Made at a Troubled Plant Cannot Be Used," *New York Times*, June 11, 2021, sec. U.S., https://www.nytimes.com/2021/06/11/us/politics/johnson-covid-vaccine-emergent.html.

95 **wasted doses had climbed:** LaFraniere, Weiland, and Stolberg, "F.D.A. Tells Johnson & Johnson."

96 **error went undetected for days:** LaFraniere and Weiland, "Factory Mix-Up Ruins."

97 **reflected a problematic safety culture:** For further details on the problematic safety culture at the plant, see Chris Hamby, Sharon LaFraniere, and Sheryl Gay Stolberg, "U.S. Bet Big on COVID Vaccine Manufacturer Even as Problems Mounted," *New York Times*, April 6, 2021, sec. U.S., https://www.nytimes.com/2021/04/06/us/covid-vaccines-emergent-biosolutions.html.

97 **"fickle" business:** LaFraniere and Weiland, "Factory Mix-Up Ruins."

97 **a third of adult Americans:** U.S. Centers for Disease Control and Prevention, "Sleep and Sleep Disorders," National Center for Chronic Disease Prevention and Health Promotion, Division of Population Health, September 7, 2022, https://www.cdc.gov/sleep/index.html.

97 **sleep deprivation not only leads to:** For more on the negative impacts of drowsy driving, see U.S. Centers for Disease Control and Prevention, "Drowsy Driving: Asleep at the Wheel," National Center for Chronic Disease Prevention and Health Promotion, Division of Population Health, November 21, 2022, https://www.cdc.gov/sleep/features/drowsy-driving.html.

97 **"probable cause, a contributing factor, or a finding":** Jeffrey H. Marcus and Mark R. Rosekind, "Fatigue in Transportation: NTSB Investigations and Safety Recommendations," *Injury Prevention: Journal of the International Society for Child and Adolescent Injury Prevention* 23, no. 4 (August 2017): 232–38, doi: 10.1136/injuryprev-2015-041791.

97 **sleep-deprived medical interns:** Christopher P. Landrigan et al., "Effect of Reducing Interns' Work Hours on Serious Medical Errors in Intensive Care Units," *New England Journal of Medicine* 351, no. 18 (October 28, 2004): 1838–48, doi: 10.1056/NEJMoa041406.

97 **6 percent increase in fatal car accidents:** Josef Fritz et al., "A Chronobiological Evaluation of the Acute Effects of Daylight Saving Time on Traffic Accident Risk," *Current Biology* 30, no. 4 (February 2020): 729–35.e2, doi: 10.1016/j.cub.2019.12.045.

98 **suspended walkways made of concrete and glass:** For more on this disaster, see R. D. Marshall et al., *Investigation of the Kansas City Hyatt Regency Walkways Collapse*, NIST Publications, Building Science Series 143 (Gaithersburg, MD: National Institute of Standards and Technology, May 31, 1982), https://www.nist.gov/publications/investigation-kansas-city-hyatt-regency-walkways-collapse-nbs-bss-143.

99 **flaw for the walkways was so obvious:** Rick Montgomery, "20 Years Later: Many Are Continuing to Learn from Skywalk Collapse," *Kansas City Star*, July 15, 2001, A1, archived from the original on May 20, 2017, from https://web .archive.org/web/20160108175310/http://skywalk.kansascity.com/articles/20 -years-later-many-are-continuing-learn-skywalk-collapse/.

99 **No one acted to halt construction:** Henry Petroski, *To Engineer Is Human: The Role of Failure in Successful Design*, 1st ed. (New York: Vintage, 1992), 88.

99 **revoked for gross negligence:** Montgomery, "20 Years Later." See also *Duncan v. Missouri Bd. for Architects*, 744 S.W.2d 524, January 26, 1998, https://law.justia .com/cases/missouri/court-of-appeals/1988/52655-0.html.

99 **prior to the walkways' collapse:** Staff, "Hyatt Regency Walkway Collapse," engineering.com, October 24, 2006, https://www.engineering.com/story/hyatt -regency-walkway-collapse.

99 **workers were simply rerouted:** Petroski, *To Engineer Is Human*.

100 **ironically ended up paying:** Kansas City Public Library, "The Week in KC History: Hotel Horror," accessed November 9, 2021, https://kchistory.org/week -kansas-city-history/hotel-horror.

100 **"need to talk about failures":** Montgomery, "20 Years Later."

100 **Champlain Towers South condominium:** "Champlain Towers South Collapse," National Institute of Standards and Technology, June 30, 2021, https://www.nist .gov/disaster-failure-studies/champlain-towers-south-collapse-ncst-investigation.

100 **sock puppet was the mascot:** "Pets.com Latest High-Profile Dot-Com Disaster," CNET, January 2, 2002, https://www.cnet.com/news/pets-com-latest-high-profile -dot-com-disaster/.

101 **IPO raised $82.5 million:** Andrew Beattie, "Why Did Pets.com Crash So Drastically?," Investopedia, October 31, 2021, https://www.investopedia.com/ask/ answers/08/dotcom-pets-dot-com.asp.

101 **selling merchandise for a third *less*:** Kirk Cheyfitz, *Thinking inside the Box: The 12 Timeless Rules for Managing a Successful Business* (New York: Free Press, 2003), 30–32.

101 **forced to liquidate Pets.com:** Beattie, "Why Did Pets.com Crash."

101 **"journey of self-discovery":** Claire Cain Miller, "Chief of Pets.com Is Back, Minus the Sock Puppet," *New York Times*, August 1, 2008, sec. Bits, https:// archive.nytimes.com/bits.blogs.nytimes.com/2008/08/01/chief-of-petscom-is -back-minus-the-sock-puppet/.

101 **"most transformative of my life":** Julie Wainwright and Angela Mohan, *ReBoot: My Five Life-Changing Mistakes and How I Have Moved On* (North Charleston, SC: BookSurge, 2009), 63.

101 **crippled by her very public failure:** Maggie McGrath, Elana Lyn Gross, and Lisette Voytko, "50 over 50: The New Golden Age," *Forbes*, https://www.forbes .com/50over50/2021/.

101 **ignored or hid the glaring early evidence:** John Haltiwanger and Aylin Woodward, "Damning Analysis of Trump's Pandemic Response Suggested 40% of US
COVID-19 Deaths Could Have Been Avoided," *Business Insider*, February 11,
2021, https://www.businessinsider.com/analysis-trump-covid-19-response-40
-percent-us-deaths-avoidable-2021-2.

101 **almost two hundred thousand preventable deaths:** Steffie Woolhandler et al.,
"Public Policy and Health in the Trump Era," *Lancet* 397, no. 10275 (February
20, 2021): 705–53, doi: 10.1016/S0140-6736(20)32545-9. See also Haltiwanger
and Woodward, "Damning Analysis."

101 **hampered by supply-chain challenges:** Gary Gereffi, "What Does the COVID-
19 Pandemic Teach Us about Global Value Chains? The Case of Medical Supplies," *Journal of International Business Policy* 3 (2020): 287–301, doi: 10.1057/
s42214-020-00062-w; Organisation for Economic Co-operation and Development, "The Face Mask Global Value Chain in the COVID-19 Outbreak: Evidence
and Policy Lessons," OECD Policy Responses to Coronavirus (COVID-19), May
4, 2020, https://www.oecd.org/coronavirus/policy-responses/the-face-mask
-global-value-chain-in-the-covid-19-outbreak-evidence-and-policy-lessons
-a4df866d/.

102 **unwillingness to authorize additional production:** Aishvarya Kavi, "Virus
Surge Brings Calls for Trump to Invoke Defense Production Act," *New York
Times*, July 22, 2020, sec. U.S., https://www.nytimes.com/2020/07/22/us/politics
/coronavirus-defense-production-act.html.

103 **assumptions can be made from superficial signals:** Erin Griffith, "What
Red Flags? Elizabeth Holmes Trial Exposes Investors' Carelessness," *New
York Times*, November 4, 2021, sec. Technology, https://www.nytimes.com
/2021/11/04/technology/theranos-elizabeth-holmes-investors-diligence.html.

104 **Research on error management:** Cathy van Dyck et al., "Organizational
Error Management Culture and Its Impact on Performance: A Two-Study
Replication," *Journal of Applied Psychology* 90, no. 6 (2005): 1228–40, doi:
10.1037/0021-9010.90.6.1228; Michael Frese and Nina Keith, "Action Errors,
Error Management, and Learning in Organizations," *Annual Review of Psychology* 66, no. 1 (2015): 661–87; Paul S. Goodman et al., "Organizational Errors:
Directions for Future Research," *Research in Organizational Behavior* 31 (2011):
151–76, doi: 10.1016/j.riob.2011.09.003; Robert L. Helmreich, "On Error Management: Lessons from Aviation," *BMJ* 320, no. 7237 (2000): 781–85.

105 **Mistakes were made:** Carol Tavris and Elliot Aronson, *Mistakes Were Made (but
Not by Me): Why We Justify Foolish Beliefs, Bad Decisions, and Hurtful Acts*, 3rd
ed. (New York: Houghton Mifflin Harcourt, 2020).

105 **view their personality or ability as the cause:** Lee Ross, "The Intuitive Psychologist and His Shortcomings: Distortions in the Attribution Process," *Advances in
Experimental Social Psychology* 10 (1977): 173–220.

106 **Powell's willingness to confront:** Donald Dosman, "Colin Powell's Wisdom," *Texas News Today* (blog), October 19, 2021, https://texasnewstoday.com/colin -powells-wisdom/504875/.

106 **"failures, and setbacks are a normal part":** Dan Schawbel, "A Conversation with Colin Powell: What Startups Need to Know," *Forbes*, May 17, 2012, https://www.forbes.com/sites/danschawbel/2012/05/17/colin-powell-exclusive -advice-for-entrepreneurs/?sh=e72e3600251e.

106 **builds trust and commitment:** Steven M. Norman, Bruce J. Avolio, and Fred Luthans, "The Impact of Positivity and Transparency on Trust in Leaders and Their Perceived Effectiveness," *Leadership Quarterly* 21, no. 3 (2010): 350–64, doi: 10.1016/j.leaqua.2010.03.002.

107 **Paul O'Neill understood this:** For great recounts of Paul O'Neill's successful safety initiative at Alcoa, see Kim B. Clark and Joshua D. Margolis, "Workplace Safety at Alcoa (A)," Harvard Business School, Case 692-042, October 1991 (revised January 2000); Steven J. Spear, "Workplace Safety at Alcoa (B)," Harvard Business School, Case 600-068, December 1999 (revised March 2000); Charles Duhigg, *The Power of Habit: Why We Do What We Do in Life and Business* (New York: Random House Trade Paperback, 2014), chap. 4, 97–126.

107 **"talk to you about worker safety":** Duhigg, *Power of Habit*, 98.

107 **the room fell into a stunned silence:** Ibid.

107 **"he's going to kill the company":** Ibid., 99.

107 **sell the stock immediately:** Ibid.

107 **"metals that are fifteen hundred degrees":** Ibid., 98.

108 **"intend to go for zero injuries":** Ibid.

108 **"a habit of excellence":** Ibid., 99.

108 **help managers build psychologically safe environments:** Quoted from a talk by O'Neill for IHI in an IHI blog: Patricia McGaffigan, "What Paul O'Neill Taught Health Care about Workforce Safety," April 28, 2020, https://www.ihi .org/communities/blogs/what-paul-o-neill-taught-health-care-about-workforce -safety.

109 **"my failure of leadership":** Duhigg, *Power of Habit*, 116.

109 **net income had grown to five times:** Ibid., 100.

109 **could have sold the stock for $5 million:** Ibid.

110 **Toyoda Automatic Loom Works:** "The Story of Sakichi Toyoda," Toyota Industries, accessed November 11, 2021, https://www.toyota-industries.com /company/history/toyoda_sakichi/. See also Nigel Burton, *Toyota MR2: The Complete Story* (Ramsbury, Marlborough, UK: Crowood Press, 2015).

110 **future lay in manufacturing cars:** Satoshi Hino, *Inside the Mind of Toyota: Management Principles for Enduring Growth* (New York: Productivity Press, 2006), 2.

110 **"with a human touch":** Burton, *Toyota MR2*, 10.

110 **power to frontline workers:** James P. Womack, Daniel T. Jones, and Daniel Roos, *The Machine That Changed the World: The Story of Lean Production—Toyota´s Secret Weapon in the Global Car Wars That Is Revolutionizing World Industry* (London: Free Press, 2007).

110 **Pulling the cord immediately sends a signal:** Kazuhiro Mishina, "Toyota Motor Manufacturing, U.S.A., Inc.," Harvard Business School, Case 693-019, September 1992 (revised September 1995).

110 **most (eleven out of twelve) pulls:** Ibid.

111 **pulling an Andon Cord every few seconds:** David Magee, *How Toyota Became #1: Leadership Lessons from the World's Greatest Car Company*, paperback ed. (New York: Portfolio, 2008).

111 **"losing is the way of winning for yourself":** Mary Louise Kelly, Karen Zamora, and Amy Isackson, "Meet America's Newest Chess Master, 10-Year-Old Tanitoluwa Adewumi," *All Things Considered*, NPR, May 11, 2021, https://www.npr.org/2021/05/11/995936257/meet-americas-newest-chess-master-10-year-old-tanitoluwa-adewumi.

112 **"always learn something from mistakes":** "Yani Tseng Stays Positive After 73," *USA Today*, November 1, 2012, sec. Sports, https://www.usatoday.com/story/sports/golf/lpga/2012/11/15/cme-group-titleholders-yani-tseng/1707513/.

113 **punish people for *not* reporting a problem in a timely way:** Tim Grosz, "Success of Proactive Safety Programs Relies on 'Just Culture' Acceptance," Air Mobility Command, February 5, 2014, https://www.amc.af.mil/News/Article-Display/Article/786907/success-of-proactive-safety-programs-relies-on-just-culture-acceptance/.

113 **most effective hospital teams:** Amy C. Edmondson, "Learning from Mistakes Is Easier Said Than Done: Group and Organizational Influences on the Detection and Correction of Human Error," *Journal of Applied Behavioral Science* 32, no. 1 (March 1, 1996): 5–28.

113 **people were not speaking up:** For more-detailed accounts of Mulally's turnaround of Ford, see Bryce G. Hoffman, *American Icon: Alan Mulally and the Fight to Save Ford Motor Company* (New York: Crown Business, 2012); Amy C. Edmondson and Olivia Jung, "The Turnaround at Ford Motor Company," Harvard Business School, Case 621-101, April 2021 (revised March 2022).

114 **"data sets you free":** Hoffman, *American Icon*, 102.

114 **actively managing problems, as a team:** Alan Mulally, "Rescuing Ford," interview by Peter Day, *BBC Global Business*, October 16, 2010, https://www.bbc.co.uk/programmes/p00b5qjq.

114 **To their surprise, Mulally applauded:** Hoffman, *American Icon*, 124.

114 **entire "exchange took twelve seconds":** Alan Mulally, "Alan Mulally of Ford: Leaders Must Serve, with Courage" (video), Stanford Graduate School of Business, February 7, 2011, at 31:25, https://www.youtube.com/watch?v=ZIwz1KlKXP4.

114 **argued that transparency increased performance pressure:** Ibid., at 32:59.

115 **Aviation Safety Reporting System:** Jan U. Hagen, *Confronting Mistakes: Lessons from the Aviation Industry When Dealing with Error* (Houndmills, Basingstoke, Hampshire, UK: Palgrave Macmillan, 2013).

115 **airport names and flight numbers are excluded:** Ibid., 143.

115 **"confidential, voluntary, and non-punitive":** Ibid., 146, Figure 3.10.

115 **human factors involved, such as judgments, decisions, and actions:** Ibid., 145, Figure 3.9b.

115 **sizable database of error reports:** Ibid., 148.

115 **40 percent drop in the pilot errors:** Susan P. Baker et al., "Pilot Error in Air Carrier Mishaps: Longitudinal Trends among 558 Reports, 1983–2002," *Aviation, Space, and Environmental Medicine* 79, no. 1 (January 2008): 2–6, as quoted in Hagen, *Confronting Mistakes*, 143.

115 **8 billion passengers without a fatal crash:** Andy Pasztor, "The Airline Safety Revolution," *Wall Street Journal*, April 16, 2021, sec. Life, https://www.wsj.com /articles/the-airline-safety-revolution-11618585543.

116 **temporal discounting:** For instance, see Kris N. Kirby and R. J. Herrnstein, "Preference Reversals Due to Myopic Discounting of Delayed Reward," *Psychological Science* 6, no. 2 (1995): 83–89. Also note that temporal discounting is sometimes referred to as *present bias*.

116 **drag on the economy from our unwillingness to invest:** Stephen J. Dubner, "In Praise of Maintenance," *Freakonomics*, episode 263, produced by Arwa Gunja, October 19, 2016, at 41:41, https://freakonomics.com/podcast/in-praise-of -maintenance/.

117 **No discussion of codification is complete without:** Gawande, *Checklist Manifesto*.

118 **checklist has become a proven method:** National Academy of Sciences, "The Hospital Checklist: How Social Science Insights Improve Health Care Outcomes," From Research to Reward, https://nap.nationalacademies.org/read/23510/.

118 **saved fifteen hundred lives and $100 million:** "Doctor Saved Michigan $100 Million," *All Things Considered*, NPR, December 9, 2007, https://www.npr.org /templates/story/story.php?storyId=17060374.

118 **"only 20 percent of the way" toward reducing error:** Andy Pasztor, "Can Hospitals Learn about Safety from Airlines?," *Wall Street Journal*, September 2, 2021, https://www.wsj.com/articles/can-hospitals-learn-about-safety-from -airlines-11630598112.

118 **quarter of a million unnecessary deaths of patients:** Ibid.

119 **accidents were attributable to human errors:** Hagen, *Confronting Mistakes*, 7.

119 **crashed into the Florida Everglades:** *Aircraft Accident Report: Eastern Airlines, Inc., L-1011, N310EA, Miami, Florida, December 29, 1972* (Washington, DC: National Transportation Safety Board, June 14, 1973).

120 **(CRM) brought down the accident rate:** For background on the history, principles, and practices of CRM, see Barbara G. Kanki, José M. Anca, and Thomas Raymond Chidester, eds., *Crew Resource Management*, 3rd ed. (London: Academic Press, 2019).

120 **reduced poisoning accidents by 91 percent:** Mark Mancini, "The Surprising Origins of Child-Proof Lids," Mental Floss, February 14, 2014, https://www .mentalfloss.com/article/54410/surprising-origins-child-proof-lids.

120 **"error-proofing" in Japanese:** Shigeo Shingō and Andrew P. Dillon, *A Study of the Toyota Production System from an Industrial Engineering Viewpoint*, rev. ed. (Cambridge, MA: Productivity Press, 1989).

121 **Eminent design researcher Don Norman:** For more on Norman, check out his website, About Don Norman, December 21, 2020, https://jnd.org/about/.

121 **work laid the foundation for the field:** For more on the field of human-centered design, see "What Is Human-Centered Design?," IDEO Design Kit, IDEO.org, accessed November 11, 2021, https://www.designkit.org/human -centered-design.

121 **select Mississippi instead of Minnesota:** Don Norman, "What Went Wrong in Hawaii, Human Error? Nope, Bad Design," *Fast Company*, January 16, 2018, https://www.fastcompany.com/90157153/don-norman-what-went-wrong-in -hawaii-human-error-nope-bad-design.

121 **likely to give familiar tasks less attention:** Pamela Laubheimer, "Preventing User Errors: Avoiding Unconscious Slips," Nielsen Norman Group, August 23, 2015, https://www.nngroup.com/articles/slips/.

121 **can provide contextual error warnings:** Ibid.

122 **fateful day in 1888:** "How a Kitchen Accident Gave Birth to a Beloved Sauce," Goldthread, November 26, 2018, https://www.goldthread2.com/food/how -kitchen-accident-gave-birth-beloved-sauce/article/3000264.

122 **worth more than $17 billion:** Bee Wilson, "The Accidental Chef," *Wall Street Journal*, September 18, 2021, sec. Life, https://www.wsj.com/articles/the -accidental-chef-11631937661.

122 **discovered by accident:** Ibid.

Chapter 4: The Perfect Storm

125 **Captain Pastrengo Rugiati:** Richard Petrow, *The Black Tide: In the Wake of Torrey Canyon*, 1st UK ed. (United Kingdom: Hodder and Stoughton, 1968), 245.

126 **Britain's biggest oil spill:** Adam Vaughan, "*Torrey Canyon* Disaster—the UK's Worst-Ever Oil Spill 50 Years On," *Guardian*, March 18, 2017, sec. Environment, https://www.theguardian.com/environment/2017/mar/18/torrey-canyon-disaster -uk-worst-ever-oil-spill-50tha-anniversary.

Notes

127 **"little things added up to one big disaster":** Petrow, *Black Tide*, 246.

127 **he became as broken as his boat:** Ibid., 158.

128 **terrified man under the bed:** Ibid., 182.

128 **verdict saved them nearly $17 million:** Ibid., 184.

129 **A blame culture:** Amy C. Edmonson, *The Fearless Organization: Creating Psychological Safety in the Workplace for Learning, Innovation, and Growth*, 1st ed. (Hoboken, NJ: John Wiley and Sons, 2019), chap. 3.

130 **"what sounded like a whip":** Wendy Lee and Amy Kaufman, "Search Warrant Reveals Grim Details of 'Rust' Shooting and Halyna Hutchins' Final Minutes," *Los Angeles Times*, October 26, 2021, sec. Company Town, https://www.latimes.com/entertainment-arts/business/story/2021-10-24/alec-baldwin-prop-gun-shooting-halyna-hutchins-search-warrant.

131 **breach of safety protocol:** Wendy Lee and Amy Kaufman, "'Rust' Assistant Director Admits He Didn't Check All Rounds in Gun before Fatal Shooting," *Los Angeles Times*, October 27, 2021, sec. Local, https://www.latimes.com/california/story/2021-10-27/rust-assistant-director-dave-halls-protocol-alec-baldwin-shooting.

131 **unclear how live ammunition:** Julia Jacobs and Graham Bowley, "'Rust' Armorer Sues Supplier of Ammunition and Guns for Film Set," *New York Times*, January 13, 2022, sec. Movies, https://www.nytimes.com/2022/01/12/movies/rust-film-ammunition-supplier-sued.html.

131 **"accidental discharge":** Emily Crane, "'Rust' Set Had Two 'Negligent Discharges' before Fatal Shooting, New Police Report Reveals," *New York Post*, December 5, 2022, https://nypost.com/2022/11/18/rust-set-had-two-negligent-discharges-before-fatal-shooting-cops/.

132 **tragic complex failure that took ninety-eight lives:** Matthew Shaer, "The Towers and the Ticking Clock," *New York Times Magazine*, January 28, 2022, https://www.nytimes.com/interactive/2022/01/28/magazine/miami-condo-collapse.html.

133 **buildings vulnerable from the start:** Ibid.

134 **became hypoxic and drowned:** Kevin Lilley, "Navy Officer, 35, Dies in Off-Duty Diving Mishap," *Navy Times*, June 7, 2018, https://www.navytimes.com/news/your-navy/2018/06/05/navy-officer-35-dies-in-off-duty-diving-mishap/.

134 **hectic training program:** Gareth Lock, *If Only . . .* (documentary) (Human Diver, 2020), at 34:03, https://vimeo.com/414325547.

134 **"I told him to just do it":** Ibid.

134 **"not a blame game for me":** Ibid.

135 **Fed up and frustrated:** Meg James, Amy Kaufman, and Julia Wick, "The Day Alec Baldwin Shot Halyna Hutchins and Joel Souza," *Los Angeles Times*, October 31, 2021, sec. Company Town, https://www.latimes.com/entertainment-arts/business/story/2021-10-31/rust-film-alec-baldwin-shooting-what-happened-that-day.

136 **Too often failure analysis is superficial:** Mark D. Cannon and Amy C. Edmondson, "Failing to Learn and Learning to Fail (Intelligently): How Great Organizations Put Failure to Work to Innovate and Improve," *Long Range Planning* 38, no. 3 (June 1, 2005): 299–319.

136 **"cure was worse than the malady":** Vaughan, "*Torrey Canyon* Disaster."

136 **rolling barrels of detergent off cliff tops:** Raffi Khatchadourian, "Deepwater Horizon's Lasting Damage," *New Yorker*, March 6, 2011, http://www.newyorker.com/magazine/2011/03/14/the-gulf-war.

136 **"thick carpet of black goo":** Vaughan, "*Torrey Canyon* Disaster."

137 **who was in charge and what was entirely legal:** Ved P. Nanda, "The *Torrey Canyon* Disaster: Some Legal Aspects," *Denver Law Review* 44, no. 3 (January 1967): 400–425.

137 **twenty-three of the forty-one thousand-pound bombs:** Vaughan, "*Torrey Canyon* Disaster."

137 **over five hundred miles per hour:** Alan Levin, "Lion Air Jet's Final Plunge May Have Reached 600 Miles per Hour," *Bloomberg*, November 2, 2018, https://www.bloomberg.com/news/articles/2018-11-03/lion-air-jet-s-final-plunge-may-have-reached-600-miles-per-hour.

138 **575 miles per hour:** Tim Hepher, Eric M. Johnson, and Jamie Freed, "How Flawed Software, High Speed, Other Factors Doomed an Ethiopian Airlines 737 MAX," Reuters, April 5, 2019.

138 **FAA grounded the entire 737 MAX fleet:** Bill Chappell and Laurel Wamsley, "FAA Grounds Boeing 737 Max Planes in U.S., Pending Investigation," NPR, March 13, 2019, sec. Business, https://www.npr.org/2019/03/13/702936894/ethiopian-pilot-had-problems-with-boeing-737-max-8-flight-controls-he-wasnt-alon.

139 **significant factor back in 1997:** Sumit Singh, "The Merger of McDonnell Douglas and Boeing—a History," Simple Flying, September 29, 2020, https://simpleflying.com/mcdonnel-douglas-boeing-merger/.

139 **resulted in a company culture shift:** Jerry Useem, "The Long-Forgotten Flight That Sent Boeing off Course," *Atlantic*, November 20, 2019, https://www.theatlantic.com/ideas/archive/2019/11/how-boeing-lost-its-bearings/602188/.

139 **shared engineering sensibility helped engineers:** Ibid.

139 **lack of technical understanding of how aircrafts function:** Natasha Frost, "The 1997 Merger That Paved the Way for the Boeing 737 Max Crisis," Quartz, January 3, 2020, https://www.yahoo.com/video/1997-merger-paved-way-boeing-090042193.html. See also Michael A. Roberto, *Boeing 737 MAX: Company Culture and Product Failure* (Ann Arbor, MI: WDI Publishing, 2020).

139 **significantly more cost-effective aircraft:** Roberto, *Boeing 737 MAX.*

140 **executives decided against expensive and lengthy research:** Ibid.

140 **8 percent more fuel efficient:** Ibid.

140 **shift the engines' location:** Ibid., 6.

Notes

Notes

140 **downplay the 737 MAX's design differences:** Ibid., 7.

140 **chief technical pilot felt pressured:** David Gelles, "'I Honestly Don't Trust Many People at Boeing': A Broken Culture Exposed," *New York Times*, January 10, 2020, sec. Business, https://www.nytimes.com/2020/01/10/business/boeing-737-employees-messages.html.

141 **"put your family on a MAX":** Ibid.

141 **turned down his proposed design upgrades:** Dominic Gates, Steve Miletich, and Lewis Kamb, "Boeing Rejected 737 MAX Safety Upgrades before Fatal Crashes, Whistleblower Says," *Seattle Times*, October 2, 2019, https://www.seattletimes.com/business/boeing-aerospace/boeing-whistleblowers-complaint-says-737-max-safety-upgrades-were-rejected-over-cost/.

141 **"suppressive cultural attitude towards criticism":** Ibid.

141 **fearful of losing their jobs:** Natalie Kitroeff and David Gelles, "Claims of Shoddy Production Draw Scrutiny to a Second Boeing Jet," *New York Times*, April 20, 2019, sec. Business, https://www.nytimes.com/2019/04/20/business/boeing-dreamliner-production-problems.html; Amy C. Edmondson, "Boeing and the Importance of Encouraging Employees to Speak up," *Harvard Business Review*, May 1, 2019, https://hbr.org/2019/05/boeing-and-the-importance-of-encouraging-employees-to-speak-up.

141 **$2.5 billion in fines and compensation:** U.S. Department of Justice, "Boeing Charged with 737 Max Fraud Conspiracy and Agrees to Pay over $2.5 Billion" (press release), Office of Public Affairs, January 7, 2021, https://www.justice.gov/opa/pr/boeing-charged-737-max-fraud-conspiracy-and-agrees-pay-over-25-billion.

142 **credit card numbers of nearly 150 million Americans:** "Equifax Data Breach," Electronic Privacy Information Center, n.d., https://archive.epic.org/privacy/data-breach/equifax/.

142 **breach went undetected for seventy-six days:** *Prepared Testimony of Richard F. Smith before the U.S. House Committee on Energy and Commerce, Subcommittee on Digital Commerce and Consumer Protection* (statement of Richard Smith, CEO, Equifax), October 2, 2017.

142 **James Howells:** "Accidentally threw away a hard drive" is a phrase abbreviating a series of minor domestic events as recounted by D. T. Max. Howells found the hard drive while cleaning out his desk and added it to a garbage bag that held truly disposable items. That evening, a conversation with his wife concluded with the understanding that Howells would dispose of the bag at the town dump. Although by then Howells had realized he should keep the hard drive, he assumed he would have ample time to retrieve it from the bag. The next morning, his wife, without telling him, drove the bag to the dump. Ergo, a very human and seemingly irreversible mistake. For more information, see D. T. Max, "Half a Billion in Bitcoin, Lost in the Dump," *New Yorker*, December 6, 2021, https://

320

www.newyorker.com/magazine/2021/12/13/half-a-billion-in-bitcoin-lost-in
-the-dump.

143 **"far more difficult to predict":** Rita Gunther McGrath, "The World Is More
Complex Than It Used to Be," *Harvard Business Review*, August 31, 2011,
https://hbr.org/2011/08/the-world-really-is-more-compl.

143 **empty shipping containers piled up:** Lazaro Gamio and Peter S. Goodman,
"How the Supply Chain Crisis Unfolded," *New York Times*, December 5,
2021, sec. Business, https://www.nytimes.com/interactive/2021/12/05/business
/economy/supply-chain.html.

144 **wrote the book on complex failure:** Chris Clearfield and András Tilcsik, *Meltdown* (New York: Penguin, 2018), 78.

144 **asking why medical errors persisted:** Amy C. Edmondson, "Learning from
Failure in Health Care: Frequent Opportunities, Pervasive Barriers," *Quality and
Safety in Health Care* 13, suppl. 2 (December 1, 2004): ii3–9.

144 **prevalence of unintended harm in hospitals:** Lucian L. Leape, "Error in
Medicine," *JAMA* 272, no. 23 (December 21, 1994): 1851–57, doi: 10.1001/
jama.1994.03520230061039; Lisa Sprague, "Reducing Medical Error: Can You
Be as Safe in a Hospital as You Are in a Jet?," *National Health Policy Forum* 740
(May 14, 1999): 1–8.

144 **quarter of a million unnecessary patient deaths:** Andy Pasztor, "Can Hospitals Learn about Safety from Airlines?," *Wall Street Journal*, September 2, 2021,
https://www.wsj.com/articles/can-hospitals-learn-about-safety-from-airlines
-11630598112.

144 **nature of complex failure:** Edmondson, "Learning from Failure."

144 **Perrow's groundbreaking book:** Charles Perrow, *Normal Accidents: Living with
High-Risk Technologies* (Princeton, NJ: Princeton University Press, 1999).

145 **institutions have moved into Perrow's danger zone:** Clearfield and Tilcsik,
Meltdown, 57.

146 **tightly coupled and interactively complex:** Perrow, *Normal Accidents*. See also
Andrew Hopkins, "The Limits of Normal Accident Theory," *Safety Science* 32
(1999): 93–102.

147 **Back in 1996, my answers to these questions:** Amy C. Edmondson, "Learning
from Mistakes Is Easier Said Than Done: Group and Organizational Influences
on the Detection and Correction of Human Error," *Journal of Applied Behavioral
Science* 32, no. 1 (March 1, 1996).

148 **seven factors that contributed to the accident:** Amy Edmondson, Michael E.
Roberto, and Anita Tucker, "Children's Hospital and Clinics (A)," Harvard Business School, Case 302-050, November 2001 (revised September 2007), 1–2.

149 **Swiss cheese model:** James Reason, "Human Error: Models and Management,"
BMJ 320, no. 7237 (2000): 768–70.

150 **more behavioral than technical:** Karlene H. Roberts, "New Challenges in Orga-

nizational Research: High Reliability Organizations," *Industrial Crisis Quarterly* 3, no. 2 (June 1, 1989): 111–25; Gene I. Rochlin, "Reliable Organizations: Present Research and Future Directions," *Journal of Contingencies and Crisis Management* 4, no. 2 (June 1996): 55–59, doi: 10.1111/j.1468-5973.1996.tb00077.x.

150 **the culture of HROs:** Karl E. Weick, Kathleen M. Sutcliffe, and David Obstfeld, "Organizing for High Reliability: Processes of Collective Mindfulness," in *Research in Organizational Behavior* 21, eds. R. I. Sutton and B. M. Staw (Amsterdam: Elsevier Science/JAI Press, 1999): 81–123.

151 **more protection for oil tankers:** Bethan Bell and Mario Cacciottolo, "*Torrey Canyon* Oil Spill: The Day the Sea Turned Black," BBC News, March 17, 2017, sec. England, https://www.bbc.com/news/uk-england-39223308.

151 **legal processes for responding:** "The Oil Pollution Act of 1990," U.S. Environmental Protection Agency, Public Law 101-380, 33 U.S. Code §2701, https://www.law.cornell.edu/uscode/text/33/2701.

151 **how France handled the *Torrey Canyon* oil slicks:** Bell and Cacciottolo, "*Torrey Canyon* Oil Spill."

152 **changed how we think about natural resources:** Ibid.

152 **invigorated discussion in the film industry:** Joe Hernandez, "The Fatal Shooting of Halyna Hutchins Is Prompting Calls to Ban Real Guns from Sets," *Morning Edition*, NPR, October 24, 2021, https://www.northcountrypublicradio.org/news/npr/1048830998/the-fatal-shooting-of-halyna-hutchins-is-prompting-calls-to-ban-real-guns-from-sets.

152 **safety culture to prevent drownings:** Lock, *If Only . . .*

153 **doomed the mission:** *Columbia* shuttle story taken from Michael Roberto, Richard M. J. Bohmer, and Amy C. Edmondson, "Facing Ambiguous Threats," *Harvard Business Review* 84, no. 11 (November 2006): 106–13.

153 **worried that a chunk of insulating foam:** Rodney Rocha, "Accidental Case Study of Organizational Silence & Communication Breakdown: Shuttle *Columbia*, Mission STS-107" (presentation), HQ-E-DAA-TN22458, September 2011, https://ntrs.nasa.gov/citations/20150009327.

153 **confirmation bias:** For an early study demonstrating confirmation bias, see Clifford R. Mynatt, Michael E. Doherty, and Ryan D. Tweney, "Confirmation Bias in a Simulated Research Environment: An Experimental Study of Scientific Inference," *Quarterly Journal of Experimental Psychology* 29, no. 1 (February 1977): 85–95, doi: 10.1080/00335557743000053.

154 **blind eye to the risk of mortgage-backed securities:** Federal Deposit Insurance Corporation (FDIC), *Crisis and Response: An FDIC History, 2008–2013* (Washington, DC: FDIC, 2017).

154 ***Columbia* Accident Investigation Board:** Columbia *Accident Investigation Board Report*, vol. 1 (Washington, DC: National Aeronautics and Space Administration, August 2003).

156 **would have provided experience with malfunctions:** Roberto, *Boeing 737 MAX*.

157 **reduced the frequency of heart attacks:** "Rapid Response Teams: The Case for Early Intervention," Improvement Stories, https://www.ihi.org/resources/Pages /ImprovementStories/RapidResponseTeamsTheCaseforEarlyIntervention.aspx.

157 **award-winning undergraduate honors thesis:** Jason Park, *Making Rapid Response Real: Change Management and Organizational Learning in Patient Care* (Lanham, MD: University Press of America, 2010).

158 **reported an early warning signal:** Majid Sabahi et al., "Efficacy of a Rapid Response Team on Reducing the Incidence and Mortality of Unexpected Cardiac Arrests," *Trauma Monthly* 17, no. 2 (2012): 270–74, doi: 10.5812/traumamon .4170.

159 **following RRT implementation:** Ibid.

159 **false alarms are celebrated:** Michael A. Roberto, *Know What You Don't Know: How Great Leaders Prevent Problems Before They Happen* (Upper Saddle River, NJ: Pearson Prentice Hall, 2009); Park, *Making Rapid Response Real*.

159 **detecting smoke rather than fighting fire:** Roberto, *Know What You Don't Know*, 5–6.

Chapter 5: We Have Met the Enemy

168 **reap vast returns:** Bridgewater, a hedge fund, faced little restrictions on its investment decisions. Hedge funds are financial services organizations that use sophisticated investment techniques to buy and sell financial assets for those willing to take on greater risk in pursuit of higher returns. Unlike retail banks or mutual funds, hedge funds face little government regulation, and their investors are typically wealthy people and institutions. For additional information see "Hedge Funds," U.S. Securities and Exchange Commission, https://www .investor.gov/introduction-investing/investing-basics/investment-products/pri vate-investment-funds/hedge-funds.

168 **one of the longest periods of growth:** David John Marotta, "Longest Economic Expansion in United States History," *Forbes*, January 21, 2020, https://www .forbes.com/sites/davidmarotta/2020/01/21/longest-economic-expansion-in -united-states-history/.

168 **"like a blow to my head with a baseball bat":** Ray Dalio, "Billionaire Ray Dalio on His Big Bet That Failed: 'I Went Broke and Had to Borrow $4,000 from My Dad,'" CNBC, December 4, 2019, https://www.cnbc.com/2019/12/04/billionaire -ray-dalio-was-once-broke-and-borrowed-money-from-his-dad-to-pay-family -bills.html.

168 **"failure was one of the best things that ever happened":** Ibid.

169 **"especially so publicly wrong—was incredibly humbling":** Ibid.

171 **cognition, group dynamics, and institutional systems:** Daniel Goleman, *Vital Lies, Simple Truths: The Psychology of Self-Deception* (New York: Simon & Schuster, 1985).

171 **reaffirming your existing interpretation of certain events:** Rich Ling, "Confirmation Bias in the Era of Mobile News Consumption: The Social and Psychological Dimensions," *Digital Journalism* 8, no. 5 (2020): 596–604.

172 **score high in narcissism:** Yiran Liu et al., "Narcissism and Learning from Entrepreneurial Failure," *Journal of Business Venturing* 34, no. 3 (May 1, 2019): 496–521, doi: 10.1016/j.jbusvent.2019.01.003.

172 **"Narcissism levels have been rising":** Tomas Chamorro-Premuzic, "Why We Keep Hiring Narcissistic CEOs," *Harvard Business Review*, November 29, 2016, https://hbr.org/2016/11/why-we-keep-hiring-narcissistic-ceos; Jean M. Twenge et al., "Egos Inflating over Time: A Cross-Temporal Meta-Analysis of the Narcissistic Personality Inventory," *Journal of Personality* 76, no. 4 (July 2008): 875–902, discussion at 903–28, doi: 10.1111/j.1467-6494.2008.00507.x.

172 **low road and the high road:** Joseph LeDoux, *The Emotional Brain* (New York: Simon & Schuster Paperbacks, 1996).

172 **popularized this distinction:** Daniel Kahneman, *Thinking, Fast and Slow* (New York: Farrar, Straus and Giroux, 2011).

174 **rejected by a group as a survival-based prepared fear:** Jennifer J. Kish-Gephart et al., "Silenced by Fear: The Nature, Sources, and Consequences of Fear at Work," *Research in Organizational Behavior* 29 (December 31, 2009): 163–93.

175 **rather than promoting learning, actually *undermines* it:** Lauren Eskreis-Winkler and Ayelet Fishbach, "Not Learning from Failure—the Greatest Failure of All," *Psychological Science* 30, no. 12 (December 1, 2019): 1733–44.

176 **failure is "ego threatening":** Ibid., 1733.

176 **less likely to share information about their failures:** Lauren Eskreis-Winkler and Ayelet Fishbach, "Hidden Failures," *Organizational Behavior and Human Decision Processes* 157 (2020): 57–67.

176 **The surgeons learned more from their own successes:** K. C. Diwas, Bradley R. Staats, and Francesca Gino, "Learning from My Success and from Others' Failure: Evidence from Minimally Invasive Cardiac Surgery," Harvard Business School, Working Paper 12-065, July 19, 2012, https://hbswk.hbs.edu/item/learning-from-my-success-and-from-others-failure-evidence-from-minimally-invasive-cardiac-surgery.

177 **growing body of research:** For a few examples, see Catherine H. Tinsley, Robin L. Dillon, and Matthew A. Cronin, "How Near-Miss Events Amplify or Attenuate Risky Decision Making," *Management Science* 58, no. 9 (September 2012): 1596–1613; Palak Kundu et al., "Missing the Near Miss: Recognizing Valuable Learning Opportunities in Radiation Oncology," *Practical Radiation Oncology* 11, no. 2 (2021): e256–62; Olivia S. Jung et al., "Resilience vs. Vulnerability:

Psychological Safety and Reporting of Near Misses with Varying Proximity to Harm in Radiation Oncology," *Joint Commission Journal on Quality and Patient Safety* 47, no. 1 (January 2021): 15–22.

178 **"warm wash of shame":** Brené Brown, "Listening to Shame," TED2012, at 14:47, https://www.ted.com/talks/brene_brown_listening_to_shame?language=sc.

178 **"intensely painful feeling or experience":** Brené Brown, "Shame Resilience Theory: A Grounded Theory Study on Women and Shame," *Families in Society* 87, no. 1 (2006): 43–52, doi: 10.1606/1044-3894.3483.

178 **"preeminent cause of emotional distress":** Robert Karen, "Shame," *Atlantic Monthly*, February 1992, 40–70; Paul Trout, "Education & Academics," *National Forum* 80, no. 4 (Fall 2000): 3–7.

178 **"aggression, bullying, suicide, eating disorders":** Brown, "Listening to Shame," at 14:13.

179 **feelings about using Instagram:** "Instagram Worsens Body Image Issues and Erodes Mental Health," *Weekend Edition Sunday*, September 26, 2021, https://www.npr.org/2021/09/26/1040756541/instagram-worsens-body-image-issues-and-erodes-mental-health.

179 **concluded that social media usage is harmful:** Nicole Wetsman, "Facebook's Whistleblower Report Confirms What Researchers Have Known for Years," Verge, October 6, 2021, https://www.theverge.com/2021/10/6/22712927/facebook-instagram-teen-mental-health-research.

180 **"worse for one in three teen girls":** Georgia Wells, Jeff Horwitz, and Deepa Seetharaman, "Facebook Knows Instagram Is Toxic for Teen Girls, Company Documents Show," *Wall Street Journal*, September 14, 2021.

180 **"overwhelming feelings of inadequacy":** Nadia Khamsi, "Opinion: Social Media and the Feeling of Inadequacy," *Ryersonian.Ca* (blog), September 25, 2017, https://ryersonian.ca/opinion-social-media-and-the-feeling-of-inadequacy/.

180 **the amount of time you spend on social media:** Melissa G. Hunt et al., "No More FOMO: Limiting Social Media Decreases Loneliness and Depression," *Journal of Social and Clinical Psychology* 37, no. 10 (December 2018): 751–68, doi: 10.1521/jscp.2018.37.10.751.

180 **"ironic that reducing your use of social media":** Alice G. Walton, "New Studies Show Just How Bad Social Media Is for Mental Health," *Forbes*, November 16, 2018, https://www.forbes.com/sites/alicegwalton/2018/11/16/new-research-shows-just-how-bad-social-media-can-be-for-mental-health/.

180 **helped people behave in ways that contributed:** For a review of social comparison theory, see this excellent review: Abraham P. Buunk and Frederick X. Gibbons, "Social Comparison: The End of a Theory and the Emergence of a Field," *Organizational Behavior and Human Decision Processes* 102, no. 1 (January 2007): 3–21.

181 **"life is cooler or better":** Walton, "New Studies Show."

181 **"most decorated Olympian":** Jeré Longman, "Simone Biles Rejects a Long Tradition of Stoicism in Sports," *New York Times*, July 28, 2021, sec. Sports, https://www.nytimes.com/2021/07/28/sports/olympics/simone-biles-mental-health.html.

181 **"most decorated gymnast":** Camonghne Felix, "Simone Biles Chose Herself," Cut, September 27, 2021, https://www.thecut.com/article/simone-biles-olympics-2021.html.

181 **"basically life-or-death":** Ibid.

182 **support her teammates' success:** Ibid., where it states, "'I'm sorry, I love you guys, but you're going to be just fine,' Biles reassured her teammates, hugging them one by one."

182 **"You're imperfect, and you're wired for struggle":** Brené Brown, *The Power of Vulnerability* (TEDxHouston, Houston, TX, 2010), https://www.ted.com/talks/brene_brown_the_power_of_vulnerability/, 17:00.

182 **learn to challenge our automatic thinking:** Adam Grant, *Think Again: The Power of Knowing What You Don't Know* (New York: Viking, 2021).

183 **elucidated the power of reframing:** Viktor E. Frankl, *Man's Search for Meaning* (Boston: Beacon Press, 2006).

184 **contrasts a *fixed mindset* with a *growth mindset*:** Carol Dweck, "Developing a Growth Mindset with Carol Dweck" (video), Stanford Alumni, October 9, 2014, at 9:37, https://www.youtube.com/watch?v=hiiEeMN7vbQ. See also Carol Dweck, "The Power of Believing That You Can Improve," TEDxNorrkoping, December 17, 2014, at 10:11, https://www.ted.com/talks/carol_dweck_the_power_of_believing_that_you_can_improve?language=en.

185 **"game changer":** Zoom interview with Satya Nadella, SIP (Short Intensive Program): Putting Purpose to Work 5033, Harvard Business School, December 14, 2021.

186 **Model 2 was rare but could be learned:** I wrote at more length about the work of Chris Argyris in Amy C. Edmondson, "Three Faces of Eden: The Persistence of Competing Theories and Multiple Diagnoses in Organizational Intervention Research," *Human Relations* 49, no. 5 (1996): 571–95. I also recommend Argyris's book *Reasoning, Learning and Action* (San Francisco: Jossey-Bass, 1982), which first introduced me to his brilliant insights about interpersonal behavior.

186 **"it didn't always feel that way":** Jonathan Cohen (@JonathanCohenMD), "One of My Favorite Parts of GRs: Sharing #PsychologicalSafety Lessons," Twitter, January 9, 2022, 11:07 a.m., https://twitter.com/JonathanCohenMD/status/1480209559159513091.

187 **he had reframed his thinking about failure:** For more information about Larry Wilson, see Larry Wilson and Hersch Wilson, *Play to Win: Choosing Growth over Fear in Work and Life* (Austin, TX: Bard Press, 1998).

188 **rational behavior therapy (RBT):** Maxie C. Maultsby Jr., *Rational Behavior Therapy* (Seaton Foundation, 1990).

188 **pioneered cognitive behavioral therapy:** Albert Ellis and Debbie Joffe Ellis, *All Out! An Autobiography* (Amherst, NY: Prometheus Books, 2010).

188 **How we *think* about events is what matters:** Mariusz Wirga, Michael DeBernardi, and Aleksandra Wirga, "Our Memories of Maxie C. Maultsby Jr., 1932–2016," *Journal of Rational-Emotive & Cognitive Behavior Therapy* 37 (2019): 316–24, doi: 10.1007/s10942-018-0309-3.

189 **inspired to study psychiatry after hearing stories:** Ibid.

189 **biggest obstacle he ever faced:** Ibid., 319, drawing from Charles H. Epps, Davis G. Johnson, and Audrey L. Vaughan, *African American Medical Pioneers* (Betz Publishing, 1994).

189 **"short-term efficiency and long-term effectiveness":** Wirga, DeBernardi, and Wirga, "Our Memories," 319, drawing from Maxie C. Maultsby Jr., "Rational Behavior Therapy," in *Behavior Modification in Black Populations*, eds. Samuel S. Turner and Russell T. Jones (New York: Plenum Press, 1982), 151–70.

189 **his legacy included:** Wirga, DeBernardi, and Wirga, "Our Memories."

190 **begun to expect he'd do well in whatever he tried:** Maxie Clarence Maultsby Jr., *Help Yourself to Happiness: Through Rational Self-Counseling* (New York: Institute for Rational Living, 1975), 22–23.

191 ***playing to win*? Or *playing not to lose*?:** Wilson and Wilson, *Play to Win*.

193 **insights I gained from studying with Chris:** For an example of his work, see Chris Argyris, *Knowledge for Action: A Guide to Overcoming Barriers to Organizational Change* (San Francisco: Jossey-Bass, 1993).

194 **Cognitive Habits for Responding:** Wilson and Wilson, *Play to Win*.

195 **"*know* I'm right?'":** Ray Dalio, *Principles: Life and Work* (New York: Simon & Schuster, 2017), 36.

195 **"seek out the smartest people who disagreed with me":** Ibid.

195 **"don't care if the right answer comes from me":** Ibid.

195 **"lies our growth and our freedom":** Franz J. Vesely, "Alleged Quote," https://www.viktorfrankl.org/quote_stimulus.html.

Chapter 6: Contexts and Consequences

199 **"we can adjust the sails!":** Dolly Parton (@DollyParton), "We Cannot Direct the Wind, but We Can Adjust the Sails!," Twitter, September 25, 2014, 12:59 p.m., https://twitter.com/dollyparton/status/515183726918389761.

199 **the Electric Maze:** Boyd Watkins, "Guest Gamer: An Interview with Boyd Watkins," interview by Sivasailam "Thiagi" Thiagarajan and Raja Thiagarajan, Thiagi

Gameletter, 2009, https://thiagi.net/archive/www/pfp/IE4H/september2009.html#GuestGamer.

202 **Participants in the learning condition outperformed:** Fiona Lee et al., "The Mixed Effects of Inconsistency on Experimentation in Organizations," *Organization Science* 15, no. 3 (May–June 2004): 310–26, doi: 10.1287/orsc.1040.0076.

204 **companies encompass a range of contexts:** Amy C. Edmondson, *Teaming: How Organizations Learn, Innovate, and Compete in the Knowledge Economy* (San Francisco: Jossey-Bass, 2012), chap. 1.

205 **In the chaos it was easy to assume:** "'I'm Not Wrong': Taxi Driver Says He's Not Responsible for Sleeping Boy Left Alone in Cab," WBZ-CBS Boston, March 3, 2022, https://boston.cbslocal.com/2022/03/03/child-left-alone-in-taxi-weston-dorchester-massachusetts-state-police-logan-airport/.

209 **"no one can see you":** Jeff Nilsson, "'It Doesn't Have to Be Perfect': Honoring the Julia Child Centennial," *Saturday Evening Post*, August 11, 2012, https://www.saturdayeveningpost.com/2012/08/julia-child/.

212 **naïve realism gives you an erroneous sense:** Lee Ross and Andrew Ward, "Naïve Realism: Implications for Social Conflict and Misunderstanding," in *Values and Knowledge*, ed. Terrance Brown, Edward S. Reed, and Elliot Turiel (Mahwah, NJ: Lawrence Erlbaum Associates, January 1996), 103–35.

214 **how Coca-Cola got caught up in this situation:** Bill Garrett, "Coke's Water Bomb," BBC News Online, June 1, 2004, sec. BBC Money Programme, http://news.bbc.co.uk/2/hi/business/3809539.stm.

214 **a "PR catastrophe":** Michael McCarthy, "Pure? Coke's Attempt to Sell Tap Water Backfires in Cancer Scare," *Independent*, March 20, 2004, sec. Environment, https://web.archive.org/web/20080522154932/http:/www.independent.co.uk/environment/pure-cokes-attempt-to-sell-tap-water-backfires-in-cancer-scare-567004.html.

214 **watched by 20 million people:** Tom Scott, "Why You Can't Buy Dasani Water in Britain" (video), March 9, 2020, at 9:58, https://www.youtube.com/watch?v=wD79NZroV88.

214 **"some consumers may be put off":** "Water World Braced for Dasani," *Grocer*, September 5, 2003.

215 **forced to recall half a million bottles of Dasani:** "Coke Recalls Controversial Water," BBC News, March 19, 2004, http://news.bbc.co.uk/2/hi/business/3550063.stm.

215 **and the company wrote off:** Scott, "Why You Can't Buy Dasani."

215 **"don't think the Dasani disaster was inevitable":** Ibid.

215 **over a billion dollars of funding:** Alex Wayne, "Obamacare Website Costs Exceed $2 Billion, Study Finds," Bloomberg, September 24, 2014, https://www.bloomberg.com/news/articles/2014-09-24/obamacare-website-costs-exceed-2-billion-study-finds.

215 **"unintuitive, clunky to navigate":** Leonard A. Schlesinger and Paras D. Bhayani, "HealthCare.gov: The Crash and the Fix (A)," Harvard Business School, Case 315-129, June 9, 2015 (revised November 1, 2016).

216 **how to design the technology to connect millions:** Brian Kenny, "The Crash and the Fix of HealthCare.gov," *Cold Call* (podcast), n.d., https://hbr.org/podcast /2016/11/the-crash-and-the-fix-of-healthcare-gov.

217 **"well-documented disaster":** Robert Safian, "President Obama: The Fast Company Interview," *Fast Company*, June 15, 2015, https://www.fastcompany .com/3046757/president-barack-obama-on-what-we-the-people-means-in-the -21st-century.

217 **"ignored problems until it was too late":** Amy Goldstein, "HHS Failed to Heed Many Warnings That HealthCare.gov Was in Trouble," *Washington Post*, February 23, 2016, sec. Health & Science, https://www.washingtonpost.com/national /health-science/hhs-failed-to-heed-many-warnings-that-healthcaregov-was-in -trouble/2016/02/22/dd344e7c-d67e-11e5-9823-02b905009f99_story.html.

217 **psychologically safe, no-blame culture:** Leonard A. Schlesinger and Paras D. Bhayani, "HealthCare.gov: The Crash and the Fix (B)," Harvard Business School, June 9, 2015, 4.

218 **"meetings are for solving problems":** Steven Brill, *America's Bitter Pill: Money, Politics, Backroom Deals, and the Fight to Fix Our Broken Healthcare System* (New York: Random House, 2015), 362.

218 **admitted that his coding mistake:** Ibid., 2. See also Brill, *America's Bitter Pill*, 361–62.

220 **90 percent of newly developed drugs fail:** Asher Mullard, "Parsing Clinical Success Rates," *Nature Reviews Drug Discovery* 15, no. 447 (2016).

Chapter 7: Appreciating Systems

227 **"bad system will beat a good person every time":** W. Edwards Deming, Dr. Deming's Four Day Seminar, Phoenix, AZ, February 1993, https://deming.org /a-bad-system-will-beat-a-good-person-every-time/.

227 **3M's central research laboratory:** Richard Sandomir, "Spencer Silver, an Inventor of Post-it Notes, Is Dead at 80," *New York Times*, May 13, 2021, sec. Business, https://www.nytimes.com/2021/05/13/business/spencer-silver-dead.html.

227 **doomed to sit on the lab shelf as a curiosity:** Claudia Flavell-While, "Spencer Silver and Arthur Fry: In Search of an Application," *Chemical Engineer*, March 9, 2018.

228 **difference lies in the geometric relationships:** Amy C. Edmondson, *A Fuller Explanation: The Synergetic Geometry of R. Buckminster Fuller*, Design Science Collection (Boston: Birkhäuser, 1987), chap. 2.

229 **gave rise to a handful of innovative materials:** E. A. Katz, "Chapter 13: Fullerene Thin Films as Photovoltaic Material," in *Nanostructured Materials for Solar Energy Conversion*, ed. Tetsuo Soga (Amsterdam: Elsevier, 2006), 363.

231 **will not do justice to entire fields:** A few of the works that influenced me are David Kantor and Lehr William, *Inside the Family* (HarperCollins, 1976); Jay W. Forrester, "Industrial Dynamics—after the First Decade," *Management Science* 14, no. 7 (1968): 398–415; Peter M. Senge, *The Fifth Discipline: The Art and Practice of the Learning Organization* (New York: Currency, 1990); W. Richard Scott and Gerald F. Davis, *Organizations and Organizing: Rational, Natural and Open Systems Perspectives* (Abingdon-on-Thames, Oxfordshire, UK: Routledge, 2015); Elinor Ostrom, "A General Framework for Analyzing Sustainability of Social-Ecological Systems," *Science* 325, no. 5939 (2009): 419–22.

231 **classroom exercise called the Beer Game:** Peter Dizikes, "The Secrets of the System," *MIT News*, May 3, 2012, https://news.mit.edu/2012/manufacturing-beer-game-0503.

233 **the bullwhip effect:** Hau L. Lee, V. Padmanabhan, and Seungjin Whang, "The Bullwhip Effect in Supply Chains," *MIT Sloan Management Review*, Spring 1997, 11.

233 **described the exercise in his seminal 1990 book:** Senge, *Fifth Discipline*.

236 **the "fix that fails":** Ibid.

238 **fifty-seven container ships were idled:** Michael Waters, "Supply Chain Container Ships Have a Size Problem," *Wired*, December 12, 2021, https://www.wired.com/story/supply-chain-shipping-logistics/.

238 **giant ship stuck in the Suez Canal:** Nadeen Ebrahim, "*Ever Given* Container Ship Leaves Suez Canal 106 Days after Getting Stuck," Reuters, July 7, 2021, https://www.reuters.com/world/ever-given-container-ship-set-leave-suez-canal-2021-07-07/.

238 **"creating a backlog that directly explains why":** Waters, "Supply Chain Container Ships."

239 **"extensive ocean-dredging projects":** Ibid.

239 **nurses confronted "process failures" surprisingly often:** Anita L. Tucker and Amy C. Edmondson, "Why Hospitals Don't Learn from Failures: Organizational and Psychological Dynamics That Inhibit System Change," *California Management Review* 45, no. 2 (Winter 2003): 55–72, doi: 10.2307/41166165.

241 **a balancing loop:** Senge, *Fifth Discipline*.

243 **an apparent equilibrium between two activities is *illusory*:** Tucker and Edmondson, "Why Hospitals Don't Learn."

244 **burgeoning green shipping movement:** U.S. Department of State, "Green Shipping Corridors Framework" (fact sheet), April 12, 2022, Office of the Spokesperson, https://www.state.gov/green-shipping-corridors-framework/.

245 **"which in turn drives absenteeism and turnover":** Zeynep Ton, "The Case for Good Jobs," *Harvard Business Review*, November 30, 2017, https://hbr .org/2017/11/the-case-for-good-jobs.

247 **3M's innovation system: the Technical Forum:** Paul Rosenthal, *Art Fry's Invention Has a Way of Sticking Around* (podcast), Smithsonian Lemelson Center, June 13 2008, https://invention.si.edu/podcast-art-frys-invention-has-way -sticking-around.

247 **coating a bulletin board with the adhesive:** Flavell-While, "Spencer Silver and Arthur Fry."

247 **the moniker Mr. Persistent:** Sandomir, "Spencer Silver."

247 **spend 15 percent of their paid time pursuing crazy ideas:** Rosenthal, *Art Fry's Invention.*

248 **pieces would often flutter out:** Jonah Lehrer, *Imagine: How Creativity Works*, 1st ed. (New York: Houghton Mifflin, 2012).

248 **would solve the problem:** Rosenthal, *Art Fry's Invention.*

248 **colleagues were not sold on the idea:** Ibid.

248 **"wasn't an accident":** Ibid.

248 **"eureka, head-flapping moment":** Sarah Duguid, "First Person: 'We Invented the Post-it Note,'" *Financial Times*, December 3, 2010.

249 **convinced to launch an intensive marketing campaign:** "Arthur L. Fry: How Has He Transformed the Scene?," Minnesota Science & Technology Hall of Fame, accessed June 18, 2022, https://www.msthalloffame.org/arthur_l_fry.htm.

250 **"creates *a community of scientists*":** Steven Spear and H. Kent Bowen, "Decoding the DNA of the Toyota Production System," *Harvard Business Review*, September 1, 1999, 3, https://hbr.org/1999/09/decoding-the-dna-of-the-toyota -production-system.

251 **the story told by James Wiseman:** Charles Fishman, "No Satisfaction at Toyota," *Fast Company*, December 1, 2006, https://www.fastcompany.com/58345/no -satisfaction-toyota.

251 **"please talk to us about your problems":** Ibid.

251 **"a lightning bolt" moment:** Ibid.

253 **the pursuit of "100 percent patient safety":** Amy Edmondson, "The Role of Psychological Safety: Maximizing Employee Input and Commitment," *Leader & Leader* 2019, no. 92 (Spring 2019): 13–19.

253 **the influential report *To Do No Harm*:** Julianne M. Morath and Joanne E. Turnbull, *To Do No Harm: Ensuring Patient Safety in Health Care Organizations*, with a foreword by Lucian L. Leape (San Francisco: Jossey-Bass, May 2005).

253 **helping create the Lucian Leape Institute:** "Julianne M. Morath," MedStar Health: Advisory Board Bios, accessed June 17, 2022, https://www.medstarhealth .org/innovation-and-research/institute-for-quality-and-safety/about-us/advisory -board/julianne-m-morath.

254 **"Accuse, Blame, Criticize":** Amy Edmondson, Michael E. Roberto, and Anita Tucker, "Children's Hospital and Clinics (A)," Harvard Business School, Case 302-050, November 2001 (revised September 2007), 7.

254 **come together to create a surprisingly effective system:** Ibid.

254 **ninety-eight thousand preventable deaths:** Ibid.

254 **"a complex error-prone system":** Edmondson, "Role of Psychological Safety," 14.

255 **"Was everything as safe as you would have liked":** Amy C. Edmondson, *The Fearless Organization: Creating Psychological Safety in the Workplace for Learning, Innovation, and Growth*, 1st ed. (Hoboken, NJ: John Wiley and Sons, 2019), 170.

255 **"health-care situation where something did not go well":** Edmondson, Roberto, and Tucker, "Children's Hospital and Clinics (A)," 4.

255 **Patient Safety Steering Committee:** Ibid.

256 **Words to Work By:** Ibid.

257 **Safety Action Teams and Good Catch Logs:** Ibid.

Chapter 8: Thriving as a Fallible Human Being

259 **expected to retreat to a quiet life of motherhood:** This story draws from Tilar J. Mazzeo's excellent biography *The Widow Clicquot: The Story of a Champagne Empire and the Woman Who Ruled It* (New York: HarperCollins, 2008).

261 **"we must invent the things of tomorrow":** Ibid., 181.

263 **she intuited the concept of intelligent failure:** Natasha Geiling, "The Widow Who Created the Champagne Industry," *Smithsonian Magazine*, November 5, 2013, https://www.smithsonianmag.com/arts-culture/the-widow-who-created-the-champagne-industry-180947570/.

265 **"the license it gives some to fail without fear":** Adam Bradley, "The Privilege of Mediocrity," *New York Times*, September 30, 2021, https://www.nytimes.com/2021/09/30/t-magazine/mediocrity-people-of-color.html.

265 **"get to the point where Joe Schmo Black guy is just safe":** Ibid.

265 **being mistaken for a janitor while employed as a scientist:** "James West: Digital Archive," HistoryMakers, accessed October 23, 2021, https://www.thehistorymakers.org/biography/james-west.

265 **"a culture in science and academia":** Veronika Cheplygina, "How I Fail S02E08—Jen Heemstra (PhD'05, Chemistry)," *Dr Veronika CH* (blog), January 8, 2021, https://veronikach.com/how-i-fail/how-i-fail-s02e08-jen-heemstra-phd05-chemistry/.

265 **"responsibility to share our failures is proportional":** Ibid.

266 **"ended up seismically shifting my worldview and priorities":** Ibid.

266 **focusing on your emotions:** Noelle Nelson, Selin A. Malkoc, and Baba Shiv,

Notes

"Emotions Know Best: The Advantage of Emotional versus Cognitive Responses to Failure," *Journal of Behavioral Decision Making* 31, no. 1 (January 2018): 40–51, doi: 10.1002/bdm.2042.

266 **experience with the right kind of wrong:** Jennifer M. Heemstra et al., "Throwing Away the Cookbook: Implementing Course-Based Undergraduate Research Experiences (CUREs) in Chemistry," in *ACS Symposium Series* 1248, ed. Rory Waterman and Andrew Feig (Washington, DC: American Chemical Society, 2017), 33–63, doi: 10.1021/bk-2017-1248.ch003.

267 **In his seminal book:** Judith Halberstam, *The Queer Art of Failure* (Durham, NC: Duke University Press, 2011).

267 **lead toward a "mindless conformity":** Ibid., 51.

267 **"free space of reinvention":** Ibid., 60.

267 **competition reality-television show:** David Canfield, "There Has Never Been a Show Like *RuPaul's Drag Race*," *Vanity Fair*, August 27, 2021, https://www.vanityfair.com/hollywood/2021/08/awards-insider-rupauls-drag-race-emmy-impact.

268 **1.3 million viewers via simulcast:** Dino-Ray Ramos, "'RuPaul's Drag Race' Season 13 Premiere Slays as Most-Watched Episode in Franchise's History," *Deadline* (blog), January 4, 2021, https://deadline.com/2021/01/rupauls-drag-race-season-13-premiere-vh1-ratings-most-watched-episode-1234664587/; Brad Adgate, "Ratings: The 2020–21 NBA Season in Review and a Look Ahead," *Forbes*, July 21, 2021, https://www.forbes.com/sites/bradadgate/2021/07/21/the-2020-21-nba-season-in-review-and-a-look-ahead/.

268 **"I am not myself upset about it":** S. Jocelyn Bell Burnell, "PETIT FOUR," *Annals of the New York Academy of Sciences* 302, no. 1 (Eighth Texas Symposium on Relativistic Astrophysics, December 1977): 685–89, doi: 10.1111/j.1749-6632.1977.tb37085.x.

269 **collected regrets from more than sixteen thousand people:** Daniel H. Pink, *The Power of Regret: How Looking Backward Moves Us Forward* (New York: Riverhead Books, 2022).

269 **did *not* regret having taken a chance and failing:** Ibid.

270 **excessively high standards:** Thomas Curran and Andrew P. Hill, "Perfectionism Is Increasing over Time: A Meta-Analysis of Birth Cohort Differences from 1989 to 2016," *Psychological Bulletin* 145, no. 4 (April 2019): 410–29, doi: 10.1037/bul0000138.

270 **"sensitive and vulnerable to those setbacks and failures":** Adam Grant, "Breaking Up with Perfectionism," interview with Thomas Curran and Eric Best, *WorkLife with Adam Grant* (TED podcast), May 3, 2022, https://www.ted.com/podcasts/worklife/breaking-up-with-perfectionism-transcript.

270 **enjoy a healthier relationship to our work or hobbies:** Ibid.

270 **few things you want to improve:** Nelson, Malkoc, and Shiv, "Emotions Know Best."

271 **"people I respect most are those who fail well":** Ray Dalio (@RayDalio), "Everyone Fails. Anyone You See Succeeding Is Only Succeeding at the Things You're Paying Attention To," Twitter, October 20, 2022, 10:06 a.m., https://twitter .com/RayDalio/status/1583097312163004417.

275 **the risk of failure:** Kayt Sukel, *The Art of Risk: The New Science of Courage, Caution, and Change* (Washington, DC: National Geographic Society, 2016).

275 **Manufacturers and patent lawyers laughed:** Sara Blakely, "How Spanx Got Started," *Inc.*, https://www.inc.com/sara-blakely/how-sara-blakley-started -spanx.html.

276 **what they'd failed at that day:** Kathleen Elkins, "The Surprising Dinner Table Question That Got Billionaire Sara Blakely to Where She Is Today," Business Insider, April 3, 2015, https://www.businessinsider.com/the-blakely-family-dinner -table-question-2015-3.

276 **calls grit:** Angela Duckworth, *Grit: The Power of Passion and Perseverance* (New York: Scribner, 2016).

276 **youngest self-made billionaire:** Rachel Makinson, "How Spanx Founder Sara Blakely Created a Billion-Dollar Brand," *CEO Today* (blog), October 28, 2021, https://www.ceotodaymagazine.com/2021/10/how-spanx-founder-sara-blakely -created-a-billion-dollar-brand/.

276 **give half of her wealth to charity:** "About," *Spanx by Sara Blakely Foundation* (blog), accessed June 27, 2022, https://www.spanxfoundation.com/about/.

276 **effort over time is crucial for success:** Angela L. Duckworth et al., "Grit: Perseverance and Passion for Long-Term Goals," *Journal of Personality and Social Psychology* 92, no. 6 (2007): 1087–101, doi: 10.1037/0022-3514.92.6.1087.

277 **"failed my way through years":** Rob Knopper, "About," https://www.robknopper .com/about-3.

278 **record of obstacles encountered and solutions:** Rob Knopper, "What My Practice Journal Looks Like," *Auditionhacker* (blog), June 25, 2016, https://www .robknopper.com/blog/2016/6/25/what-my-practice-journal-looks-like.

278 **"Bad performances give you":** Rob Knopper, "What to Do When You Have a Disastrous Snare Drum Performance," *Percussionhacker* (blog), March 4, 2018, https://www.robknopper.com/blog/2018/3/2/pg0qmqdy07akmm6cmh8q8i1y sus4s1.

280 **recent research on forgiveness:** Charlotte V. O. Witvliet et al., "Apology and Restitution: The Psychophysiology of Forgiveness after Accountable Relational Repair Responses," *Frontiers in Psychology* 11 (March 13, 2020): 284, doi: 10.3389/fpsyg.2020.00284.

280 **Good apologies, alas, are not the norm:** Karina Schumann, "The Psychology of Offering an Apology: Understanding the Barriers to Apologizing and How to

Overcome Them," *Current Directions in Psychological Science* 27, no. 2 (2018): 74–78, doi: 10.1177/0963721417741709.

280 **a threat to your self-image:** Ibid.

281 **the belief that an apology won't help:** Ibid.

281 **set of attributes of an effective apology:** Christine Carter, "The Three Parts of an Effective Apology," Greater Good, November 12, 2015, https://greatergood .berkeley.edu/article/item/the_three_parts_of_an_effective_apology.

282 **value proposition was to be customers' "third place":** Matthew Dollinger, "Starbucks, 'the Third Place,' and Creating the Ultimate Customer Experience," *Fast Company*, June 11, 2008, https://www.fastcompany.com/887990/starbucks -third-place-and-creating-ultimate-customer-experience.

283 **call the police on you:** Christine Hauser, "Starbucks Employee Who Called Police on Black Men No Longer Works There, Company Says," *New York Times*, April 16, 2018, sec. U.S., https://www.nytimes.com/2018/04/16/us/starbucks -philadelphia-arrest.html.

283 *possibly* **ascertain whether data had been compromised:** Cale Guthrie Weissman, "Equifax Wants You to Enter Your Social Security Number Here to Find Out If It Was Hacked," *Fast Company*, September 7, 2017, https://www .fastcompany.com/40464504/equifax-wants-you-to-enter-your-social-security -number-here-to-find-out-if-it-was-hacked.

283 **she apologized *in a tweet*:** Will Oremus, "Marissa Mayer Personally Apologizes for Yahoo Mail Debacle," Slate, December 16, 2013. See also Marissa Mayer (@marisssamayer), "An Important Update for Our Users," Twitter, December 11, 2013, 2:31 p.m., https://twitter.com/marissamayer/status/410854397292593153.

283 **"am committed to earning your confidence back":** Jennifer Bendery, "Kathleen Sebelius Takes Blame for Obamacare Glitches While Being Grilled by Marsha Blackburn," HuffPost, October 30, 2013, https://www.huffpost.com/entry /kathleen-sebelius-marsha-blackburn_n_4177223.

283 **Obama acknowledged his own contribution to the failure:** Chuck Todd, "Exclusive: Obama Personally Apologizes for Americans Losing Health Coverage," NBC News, November 7, 2013, https://www.nbcnews.com/news/us-news /exclusive-obama-personally-apologizes-americans-losing-health-coverage -flna8c11555216.

284 **"your trust in us is our absolute priority":** Tiffany Hsu, "Neiman Marcus Says Social Security Numbers, Birth Dates Not Stolen," *Los Angeles Times*, January 16, 2014, https://www.latimes.com/business/la-xpm-2014-jan-16-la-fi-mo-neiman -marcus-breach-20140116-story.html.

284 **made a public apology in his podcast:** Megan McCluskey, "Dan Harmon Gives 'Full Account' of Sexually Harassing Community Writer Megan Ganz," *Time*, January 11, 2018, https://time.com/5100019/dan-harmon-megan-ganz-sexual -harassment-apology/.

285 **"deliberately chosen to work on hard problems"**: Astro Teller, "Tips for Unleashing Radical Creativity," *X, the moonshot factory* (blog), February 12, 2020, https://blog.x.company/tips-for-unleashing-radical-creativity-f4ba55602e17.

286 **"how are we going to kill our project"**: Astro Teller, "The Unexpected Benefit of Celebrating Failure," TED Talk, https://www.ted.com/talks/astro_teller_the_unexpected_benefit_of_celebrating_failure.

286 **teams pivoted to a new:** "Waymo: Transforming Mobility with Self-Driving Cars," accessed June 16, 2022, https://x.company/projects/waymo/.

286 **"35 different ideas before they found the one"**: Teller, "Tips for Unleashing."

286 **what psychologists call malicious envy:** Alison Wood Brooks et al., "Mitigating Malicious Envy: Why Successful Individuals Should Reveal Their Failures," *Journal of Experimental Psychology: General* 148, no. 4 (April 2019): 667–87, doi: 10.1037/xge0000538.

287 **"CV of Failures"**: Melanie Stefan, "A CV of Failures," *Nature* 468 (November 2010): 467, doi: 10.1038/nj7322-467a.

288 **"more attention than my entire body of academic work"**: Johannes Haushofer, "Johannes Haushofer Personal Page," accessed June 18, 2022, https://haushofer.ne.su.se/.

288 **also talk about what they've learned:** Jeffrey R. Young, "Encouraging Teachers to Share Their Mistakes on Stitcher," *EdSurge* (podcast), October 19, 2021, https://listen.stitcher.com/yvap/?af_dp=stitcher://episode/87639474&af_web_dp=https://www.stitcher.com/episode/87639474.

288 **This "wake-up call"**: Jon Harper, "Pandemic Lesson #2: I Pushed My Teachers Too Hard; in Fact, I Pushed Some over the Edge," *My BAD* (podcast), accessed June 27, 2022, https://podcasts.apple.com/us/podcast/pandemic-lesson-2-i-pushed-my-teachers-too-hard-in/id1113176485?i=1000508349340.

288 **life-changing evening honestly sharing their biggest failures:** "Failure Institute: About Us," Failure Institute, accessed June 18, 2022, https://www.thefailureinstitute.com/about-us/.

289 **a Heroic Failure Award:** Gwen Moran, "Fostering Greater Creativity by Celebrating Failure," *Fast Company*, April 4, 2014, https://www.fastcompany.com/3028594/a-real-life-mad-man-on-fighting-fear-for-greater-creativity.

290 **kitty litter product, freshly "soiled"**: Sue Shellenbarger, "Better Ideas through Failure," *Wall Street Journal*, September 27, 2011, sec. Careers, https://online.wsj.com/article/SB10001424052970204010604576594671572584158.html.

290 **Dare to Try Award:** Ramakrishnan Mukundan, Sabeel Nandy, and Ravi Arora, "'Dare to Try' Culture Change at Tata Chemicals," *HQ Asia* 3 (2012): 38–41.

290 **Lean Forward, Fail Smart:** "Building a Better Workplace," Partnership for Public Service, https://ourpublicservice.org/about/impact/building-a-better-workplace/.

Index

Page numbers in *italics* refer to illustrations. Page numbers beginning with 299 refer to notes.

A

ABC *Nightline*, 309
accountability, 150, 178, 279–80
  blame vs., 129
  mutual, 114
Adewumi, Tanitoluwa, 111–12
adhesives, 227–28
Aesop, 158
Affordable Care Act (ACA), 215–18
Ager, David, 157
Airbus, 139–40
Air Florida Flight 90, 90–91, 118, 222
Air Force, U.S., 113, 189
Alcoa, 107–9, 162
Alcott, Louisa May, 7
Alexander I, Czar of Russia, 262
Alimta, 84
Alphabet (company), 62, 285–86
Amazon.com, 101
ambiguous threats, 152, 153, 154, 156
  amplifying, 157–58, 162
  vigilance vs. amplification of, 158–59

amygdala, 33, 37, 84, 173, 188
analysis, of failures:
  self-serving, *67*
  skipping, *67*
  superficial, 66, *67*, 98
Anderson, Patty, 23–24
Andon Cords, 110–11, 157, 158–60,
    249–50, 252
angle grinders, 212–13
anonymity, in reporting errors, 115
anxiety, 31
apologies, 280–85
Apple, 79, 231
apple cider, 69
Argyris, Chris, 185–86, 193, 195–96
Armagh Planetarium, 55
assembly lines, 32–34, *35*, 40
assumptions, faulty, 88, 102–3, 121
  judgment errors vs., 102
AstraZeneca, 95
Atal, Bishnu, 61
athletes, 30, 111–12

Index

Attrill, Martin, 152
autosave function, 121
aversion, 25–32, *41*
aviation industry, 8–9, 90–91, 115, 118,
    119–20, 137–41, 278
Aviation Safety Reporting System
    (ASRS), 115, 156
Avogo avocado tool, 58, 60
Awbery, Sarah, 58

B
balancing loops, *241*
Baldwin, Alec, 130–31, 132
balloon clamps, 46–47
banking failures, 87–88
baseball teams, 245–46
Beer Game, 231–35, 241, 249–50, 257
Bell Burnell, Jocelyn, 54–56, 60, 73,
    268
Bell Labs, 61, 72–74, 81, 265
belonging, psychological safety vs.,
    268–69
Berman, Ben, 162, 223–25, 285
Best, Eric, 270–71
Bezos, Jeff, 101
Biles, Simone, 181–82
bitcoin, 142–43, 320
"black boxes" on airplanes, 119
Blakely, Sara, 275–77
blame, 41–42, *41*, 50, 84, 127–29, 170,
    218, 254
    accountability vs., 129, 279–80
    dodging, 27–29
    fundamental attribution errors and,
        105, 279
    preventing failures and, 134–35
blameless reporting, 111, 112–17, 120,
    129, 255–56
blind dates, 11, 42, 56–57, 61, 64–65
Bloomberg, 87–88
body image issues, 179–80

Boeing 737 MAX, 137–41, 156, 161, 162
Boeing aircraft company, 137–41, 154,
    161
Boer, Giny, 287
Bohmer, Richard, 154
Bohne, Louis, 260, 262
Bonanza Creek Ranch, 130–31, 132
bottled water, 214–15
boundaries redrawing, 241–44, *242*, 258
Bowen, Kent, 250
"Boy Who Cried Wolf, The" (Aesop),
    158
Bradley, Adam, 265
bragging, 251–52, 287
Breault, Henri, 120
Breeden, Jake, 273–74
bridge (card game), 190–91, 271, 272
Bridgewater Associates, 167–69, 323
Brighton College, 58–59
British Petroleum, 136
Brotherhood of Sleeping Car Porters,
    70–71
Brown, Annie, 45
Brown, Brené, 178, 182
Brown, Joseph, 45
Brown, Tim, 80
Buckminsterfullerene (buckyballs),
    229
Bugge, Ashley, 134–35
Bugge, Brian, 134–35, 152
building collapses, 98–100, 132–33,
    135–36, 153
Bulli, El, 74
bullwhip effect, 233
burnout, 15, *242*, 243
bus crashes, 92–93

C
Cadillac, 289
Cambridge University, 55
Campori, Morano, 60

Index

C&A, 287

cannulas, 44–45

cars, 115–16

catch and correct, 159–61

cause and effect, 237

Centers for Disease Control and
    Prevention (CDC), U.S., 97

certainty, 40, 204

challenge, *41*, 42

Chamorro-Premuzic, Tomas, 172

champagne, 259–64, 292

Champlain Towers South
    condominium, 100, 132–33,
    135–36, 153

Channel Pilot, The (maritime manual),
    126–27, 128

checking out, *39*

Checklist Manifesto, The (Gawande), 90,
    117–18

checklists, 90–91, 117–18

chemotherapy drugs, 84

Cheplygina, Veronika, 266

chess, 111–12

Child, Julia, 208–9

child-proof caps, 120

children, 5, 28, 58–59, 68, 94, 113, 117,
    128–29, 158, 184, 230, 237–38, 240,
    245–46, 252, 271, 275–76, 278

Children's Hospital and Clinics
    (Minneapolis), 253–57, 285

Cho, Fujio, 251–52

Churchill, Winston, 5

Citibank, 87–88

Clearfield, Chris, 143–44, 145

Clicquot, Barbe-Nicole Ponsardin,
    259–64, 276, 292

Clicquot, François, 260

Clicquot, Philippe, 261

climate change, 171, 174, 272

close calls, 177, 222, 278

Coca-Cola, 214–15

code blues, 157–59

codification, 117–18, 121

cognitive behavior therapy, 188

Cohen, Jonathan, 186, 195

Columbia Accident Investigation Board
    (CAIB), 154

Columbia space shuttle, 152–55, 156,
    161, 162, 290

Community (TV show), 284

computer mouse, 79

concentration camps, 183

confidence, 32, 206

    see also overconfidence

confirmation bias, 153–54, 169, 171–72,
    174

confusion, 25, 32–36, *41*, 47–48

consequentiality, three dimensions of,
    210

contact tracing, 143

container ships, 143, 238–39, 244

contexts, 32–33, 199–208, *211*, 212–24

    calling attention to, 285–86

    certainty and uncertainty in, 40,
        203–5, 260–61

    consistent, 33–34, *35*, 204–7, *211*,
        219, 222, *223*

    misconstruing, 201

    navigating, *211*

    novel, 33–34, *35*, 204–6, 207–8, *211*,
        215–18, 220–21, 222, *223*

    preparation and, 223–26

    relationship to failures, 218–23,
        223

    variable, 33–34, *35*, 204–7, *211*,
        214–15, 217, 219–20, 222, *223*

    what is known, 202–3

    what's at stake, 202–3

contextual awareness, 203, 222

cooking, 74–78, 117

cortex, 188

counterfactual thinking, 30–31

coupling, 229
  in hospitals, 147–49
  in Perrow's model, 145–47, *146*
COVID-19 pandemic, 33, 34–35, 94–97, 155
  failures during, 101–2, 131, 143, 222, 233, 235, 238–39
crew resource management (CRM), 9, 119–20
cross-circulation, 44–45
Crown Center Redevelopment Corporation, 99–100
Crystal Pepsi, 59–60
curiosity, 60–61, 72, 84, 169, 183, 185–86
Curl, Robert, 229
Curran, Thomas, 270

D
Dalio, Ray, 167–69, 171–72, 195, 271
Dare to Try Award, 290
Dasani water, 214–15
data breaches, 142
dating websites, 59, 64–66
daylight savings time, 97
Dayton, Douglas, 78–83
Defense Department, U.S., 153
defensiveness, 182, 186, 256, 281
Deming, W. Edwards, 227
Dennis, Clarence, 23–25, 26, 43, 45
dentistry, 115–16
depression, 31, 181, 270
Detert, James, 174
Dickerson, Mickey, 217–18
dignity, employees treated with, 108
Dimmock, Aaron, 160–61
discernment, 292–93
diversity, equity, and inclusion, 265–69, 282–83
diving, 270–71
DNA, 49–52

doctor-patient relationships, 282
drag performance, 267–68
Dried Kitchen, 77
driving, alcohol and, 113, 156
Dubner, Stephen, 116
Duckworth, Angela, 276, 291
due diligence, 103
Duhigg, Charles, 107, 109
Duncan, Arne, 184
Dweck, Carol, 68, 184, 251, 281

E
E*Trade, 289
Eastern Air Lines Flight 401, 119
Edison, Thomas A., 49, 53–54
effort, relationship to success, 36
Eisenberger, Naomi, 37
Eisenmann, Thomas, 59
electret microphones, 72–74, 265
Electric Maze, 199–202, 209, 211
Eli Lilly, 62, 79, 84, 289
Ellis, Albert, 188
Emergent Biosolutions, 95, 97
emotions, learning from, 266
environmental movement, 151–52
Equifax, 142, 283
equity, 265–69, 282–83
errors:
  actual vs. detected, 15*n*
  anonymity in reporting, 115
  aversion to, 104–5
  befriending, 104–6
  and building trust, 106
  catching, 109–11
  defined, 17, 52, 88–89
  design and, 121
  fundamental attribution errors, 105, 279
  judgment, 102
  knowledge and, 201, 202–3
  learning from, 89, 111–12

owning, 106–7
poka-yoke and, 120–21
psychological safety and reporting of,
    12–16, 38, 106, 107–9
punishment of, 91
repercussions of, 89
unintended nature of, 91
Eskreis-Winkler, Lauren, 175–76, 177
Ethiopian Airlines Flight 302, 138
evaluation, systems of, systems of
    learning vs., 113
evolution, 37
excuses, 281, 284–85
exercider, 69
experimentation, *41*, 70–83, 201,
    209–10, *211*

F
Facebook, 179–80
"fail fast, fail often," 32, 59, 79, 80, 103–4
failure bonuses, 62
Failure Fridays, 287
Failure Institute, 288–89
failure landscape, *223*
failure parties, 62, 84, 289
failures:
    analysis of, 29, 64–70, *67*, 98
    of author, 1–3, 9–10, 12–14
    blameworthy, 41–43, *41*, 50, 84,
        127–29
    causes of, *41*
    collecting data from, 65–66
    covering up of, *39*
    CV of, 287–88
    defined, 17
    destigmatizing, 40
    emotional aversion to, 18, 25–32, 34,
        38, 48, 80, 84, 170–75, 176, 178,
        191, *194*, 200, 201, 279
    flexible thinking and, 74
    as fuel, 30

good, defined, 16
healthy cultures of, *291*
high standards and, 39–40, *39*
humor and, 52
learning from, 18, 40, 64–70, *67*, 89,
    175–78, 195–96
new, 43
normalizing, 50
off-diagonal, 221–22, *223*
power and, 28
praiseworthy, 41–42, *41*, 50
preventable, 6, 15, 19, 38, 83–84, 88,
    91, 97, 101, 104, 138, 174, 202, 205,
    212–18, 235, 254, 258, 278, 279
privilege and, 265–69
prohibitions of, 34–36
reframing of, 30–32, *41*, 48, 65, 162,
    177, 179, 182–86
relationship of contexts to, 218–23,
    223
relief at those of others, 28–29
reputation and, 61–62
rewarding, 289–91
sharing lessons of, 40, 176, 286–89
social stigma of, 25, 40
time and resources consumed by, 61
types of, distinguishing, 25, 40, *41*
typology of, 6–7, 33
failures, basic, 34, 35, *35*, 87–123, *89*,
    219, *223*
checklists and, 90–91, 117–18
codification and, 117–18, 121
complex failures vs., 94, 100, 129–30
errors and, 91–92
failure-proofing, 120–21
faulty assumptions and, 88, 102–3,
    121
inattention and, 88, 93, 94–98,
    120–21
intelligent failures vs., 66, 70, 88,
    93–94, 104

Index

failures, basic (*cont.*)
  known territory and, 93–94
  leading to success, 122
  learning from, 89
  as most preventable, 104
  neglect and, 88, 93, 98–100
  overconfidence and, 88, 93, 100–103,
    121, 131
  predictable contexts and, 219
  preventing, 88, 89–91, 104–23, 278
  prevention systems for, 112–21
  preventive maintenance for, 115–17
  psychological safety and, 40, *41*
  recognizing, 92–94
  single causes of, 94
failures, complex, 35, *35*, 89, 118,
    125–63, 205, 219–20, *223*
  basic failures vs., 94, 100, 129–30
  blame and prevention of, 134–35
  catching and correcting, 159–61
  coupling and, 145–49, *146*
  early warnings of, 152–55
  external factors and, 133–35
  false alarms and, 156–59
  familiar settings and, 130–32, 138
  intelligent failures vs., 130
  interactive complexity and, 145–49,
    146, 229
  learning from, 151–52
  multicausal nature of, 132–33, 138,
    229–30
  overconfidence and, 131
  practicing for, 162–63
  preventing and reducing, 29, 138–39,
    150–63, 278
  recovery windows and, 155–56
  rising number of, 141–44
  slow unfolding of, 137–42
  Swiss cheese model and, 149–50
  systems and, 144–50
  warning signs of, 135–36

failures, intelligent, 11–12, 35, *35*,
    53–67, *89*, 220–21, 222, *223*, 248,
    263
  action and, 67–70
  basic failures vs., 10, 66, 70, 88, 93–94
  as basis for iterative action, 66, 67–70,
    80
  complex failures vs., 129
  in educational settings, 58–59
  errors vs., 12
  four key attributes of, 53–64, *64*, 168
  growth mindset and, 68
  hypothesis-driven preparation and,
    49–53, 59–61
  innovation and, 11, 75–76
  intelligent failure strategy, 67–70
  learning from, 29, 64–70, *64*, *67*
  new/unknown territory and, 53–57,
    64, 130, 168, 200–201
  nonrepeatable nature of, 40, 62
  opportunity driven, 57–59, *64*, 168
  original thinking and, 56
  pilot tests and, 62–64
  play and, 58–59
  psychological safety and, 40, *41*
  scientists and, 49–53
  small size of, 53, 61–64, *64*, 168
  sunk costs and, 62
  as unpreventable, 83–84
fallibility, of humans, 6, 16, 18, 20, 32,
    104, 106, 112, 149, 264–76, 279,
    280, 287, 292
false alarms, 156–59
families, psychological safety in, 40, 113,
    156
Fast Company, 251
fatigue, 41–42, 97–98
  in pilots, 8–9, 225
fears, 25, *41*, 52, 173, 182
  interpersonal, 27, 37–41
  learning inhibited by, 37

342

prepared, 174–75
psychological safety and, 38, 46–48
Federal Aviation Administration (FAA),
    115, 137–38
Ferraro, Stefano, 76
Field, Mark, 114
Fifth Discipline, The (Senge), 233
fight-or-flight response, 33, 37
film sets, accidents on, 130–31, 132,
    135, 152, 156, 162, 230
financial industry, 154
Finkelstein, Sydney, 28
Fishbach, Ayelet, 175–76, 177
fixed mindset, 184–85
"fix that fails," 236–38, 244
flexible thinking, 74
flight simulators, 8–9, 140–41
folic acid, 84
Forbes, 64–65, 101, 180, 276
Ford Edge, 114
Ford Motor Company, 113–14
forgiveness, 280
Forrester, James, 25
Forrester, Jay, 231, 233
Fourneaux, Alexandre Jérôme, 261
Foushee, H. Clayton, 8–9, 222
framing, *see* reframing
framing statement, 224
Frankl, Victor E., 167, 183, 195
Freakonomics (podcast), 116
Frebel, Thomas, 77
Frost, Natasha, 139
Fry, Arthur, 246–49
Fuckup Nights, 288–89
Fuller, Buckminster, 2, 229
fundamental attribution errors, 105, 279

G

Ganz, Megan, 284–85
gardeners, 60
Gattaca (film), 50–51, 304

Gawande, Atul, 90, 117–18
GE, 69
Gibbon, John, 45
Gillum, Jack, 98–100
Gino, Francesca, 176–77
Glaeser, Edward, 116
Glidden, Gregory, 44–45
Glidden, Lyman, 44–45
glyoxal, 51
Goleman, Daniel, 170–71
Good Catch Logs, 256–57
Google, 62, 217, 247, 290
Grant, Adam, 182, 270–71
Great Britain, 137
Gretzky, Wayne, 30
Grey Advertising, 289–90
grit, 276, 291
Grocer (magazine), 214
growth mindset, 68, 184–85, 251
guilt, shame vs., 178–79
Gutierrez-Reed, Hannah, 131

H

Hackman, Richard J., 9, 12, 14
Halberstam, Jack, 267
Halls, David, 131
Harmon, Dan, 284–85
Harmontown (podcast), 284
Harper, Jon, 288
Harvard Business School, 28–29, 78–79,
    231
Harvard University, 1–3, 157, 191, 250,
    287
Harvey, Sam, 58
Haushofer, Johannes, 287–88
Havens Steel Company, 99–100
Hawkins, Stephen J., 136
headphones, 72–74
Healthcare.gov, 215–18, 283
heart failures, 157–59, 278
heart-lung machine, 43–45

heart surgery, 23–25, 43–48, 176–77
hedgefunds, 323
Heemstra, Jennifer, 49–52, 57, 81, 222, 265–66
Heroic Failure Award, 289–90
heteronormative culture, 267–69
Hewish, Antony, 55, 268
high reliability organizations (HROs), 150
highway accidents, 97
hobbies, 272–73
Hoge, James, 69
Holmes, Elizabeth, 103
hospitals:
    errors in, 7–10, 113, 118, 144–45, 147, 239–43, 253–57
    loose coupling in, 147–49
    rapid response teams (RRTs) in, 157–59
    systems thinking in, 253–57
Howells, James, 142–43, 320
humility, 19–20, 168, 169
Hunt, Melissa, 180–81
Hutchins, Halyna, 130–31, 132, 152, 156
Hyatt Regency Hotel, Kansas City, Mo., 98–100
hypotheses, intelligent failure and, 49–53

I

IBM, 45
IDEO, 78–83, 207, 247, 250, 287, 309
impostor syndrome, 186
inability, 41, 42
inattention, 41, 42, 88, 93, 94–98, 120–21
inclusion, 265–69, 282–83
information technology (IT), 142–43
innovation:
    corporate systems and, 80–83, 290
    intelligent failures and, 11, 75–76
    psychological safety and, 16, 38

innovation strategy services, 81–83
Instagram, 179–81
insulin injectors, 79
insurance companies, 105
interactive complexity, 229
    in hospitals, 147–49
    in Perrow's model, 145–47, 147
interaural time delays, 72–74
interdependence, 36, 143
Isles of Scilly, 126
iterative action, 66, 67–70, 80

J

Jennings, John, 265
jidoka, 110
Johnson & Johnson, 94–97
Jones, Jacqueline, 44
Journal of Social and Clinical Psychology, 180
Judge, Sheryl, 24–25
judgment errors, faulty assumptions vs., 102
Justice Department, U.S., 141
just-in-time (JIT) production, 249–50

K

Kahneman, Daniel, 27, 172–73
Katz, Karen, 283–84
Kelley, David, 79–80, 309
Kennedy, Robert F., 23, 26
Kickstarter, 58
King, Billie Jean, 259
Kitslaar, Benjamin, 288
Knight, John Peake, 68–69
Knopper, Rob, 277–78
knowing, learning vs., 169, 182–83, 193, 196
Know What You Don't Know (Roberto), 159
Knutson, Steve, 51–53, 60
Kroto, Harold, 229

L

laboratories, 11, 34, *35*, 49–54, 222
Lancet, 101
Langley Research Center, 71
leadership:
  nonhierarchical, 46–48
  psychological safety and, 46–48
Lean Forward, Fail Smart Award, 290
Leape, Lucian, 7–9, 13, 14, 282
learning, knowing vs., 169, 182–83, 193, 196
"Learning from Mistakes Is Easier Said Than Done" (Edmondson), 3
Lee, Fiona, 201–2
Lee Kum Kee, 122
Lee Kum Sheung, 122
Lewis, F. John, 44
LGBTQIA people, 267–68
Lieberman, Matthew, 37
light bulbs, incandescent, 53
Lillehei, Clarence Walton "Walt," 24–25, 43–45
linear predictive coding, 61
Lion Air Flight 610, 137, 141
London Design Museum, Design Ventura competition of, 58
looms, steam-powered, 107–9
loss aversion, 27, 172–73
low-stakes situations, 208–9
Lucian Leape Institute, 253–54
luck, 19, 36, 133, 215, 253

M

malicious envy, 286–87
Man's Search for Meaning (Frankl), 183
manufacturing plants, 146–47, *146*
Maultsby, Maxie, 186, 187–89, 190–91, 192, 195–96, 264
Mayer, Marissa, 283
McDonnell Douglas, 139
McGrath, Rita, 143

median sternotomy, 46, 47
medical errors, 3, 7–10, 113, 144–45, 147
medical interns, 97
Medstar Health, 118
Meltdown (Clearfield and Tilcsik), 143–44, 145
Menlo Park, N.J., Edison's laboratory in, 53
mental models, 236–37
Metropolitan Opera Orchestra, 277–78
Meyer, Claus, 75
Miami Beach, 132–33
microphones, electret, 72–74, 265
Microsoft, 185
Miller, G. Wayne, 43
minorities, failure and, 265
mischief, misconduct, 41, 92
mistakes, *see* errors
Model 1 and 2 theories-in-use, 185–86
Moggridge, Bill, 79
molecular gastronomy, 74
Molinsky, Andy, 14
Moltke, Helmuth von, 36–37
Morath, Julianne, 253–57, 285
Morgan, Garrett, 69
morphine, 147–49
mortgage-backed securities, 154
Mulally, Alan, 113–14
Mullard Radio Astronomy Observatory, 55–56
My BAD (podcast), 288
Myhren, Tor, 289–90

N

NAACP, 71
Nadella, Satya, 185
naïve realism, 212
Napoléon I, Emperor of the French, 261
narcissism, 172

NASA, 8–9, 71, 115, 223–24, 290
  Space Shuttle program of, 29, 152–55, 156
NASA Industrial Workshop, 119
National Center for Human Factors in Healthcare, 118
National Institutes of Health (NIH), 8
National Patient Safety Foundation, Lucian Leape Institute of, 253
National Transportation Safety Board, 97, 223–24
Nature, 287–88
Navy, U.S., 160
NBC News, 283
negativity bias, 27
neglect, 88, 93, 98–100
Neiman Marcus, 283–84
Nelson, Noelle, 266
New York Times, 94, 265
Niebuhr, Reinhold, 292–93
Nobel Prize, 268
Noma, 76–78
non-learning theories in use, 195
normal accidents, 145
Normal Accidents (Perrow), 144, 145
Norman, Don, 121
nuclear power plants, 145–46, *146,* 150
nurses, 239–43, 253–57

O

Obama, Barack, 184, 216–18, 283
Obstfeld, David, 150
Oil Pollution Act, 151–52
oil spills, 125–28, 130, 131, 136–37, 145, 151–52
Olympic medals, 30–31
O'Neill, Paul, 107–9, 162
Only Fools and Horses (TV show), 214–15
operating rooms, 23–25, *35,* 43–48, 176–77

organizational behavior, 1, 2, 7, 15, 100, 174–75
outcome, process vs., 68
outsiders, 61
overconfidence, 88, 93, 100–103, 121, 131
overdoses, accidental, 147–49
oyster sauce, 122

P

packing lists, 117
pain, social and physical, 37
Palm N Turn caps, 120
Park, Jason, 157
Parton, Dolly, 199
Pasztor, Andy, 115
Patel, Shiven, 60
pausing, to disrupt automatic emotional responses, 189–94, *194,* 237
Paz Linares, Matias, 60
Pepsi, Crystal, 59–60
perfectionism, 31, 225, 270–71
Perrow, Charles, 125, 144–47, *146,* 254
  coupling/interaction model of, *146*
persistence, 275–77
Pets.com, 100–101
Phelps, Michael, 181
Pignatti, Pietro, 60
pill bottles, 120
pilot tests, full-scale launches vs., 62–64
Pink, Daniel, 269
pipettes, 52
pivoting, 273–74
plane crashes, 90–91, 118, 119–20, 137–41, 156, 162, 222
Platt Brothers, 110
playing to win, 192, 262, 271, 285
Pogo (comic strip), 197
polymers, 73–74
positive psychology, 31–32
Post-it notes, 227–28, 246–49
Powell, Colin, 106

Power of Habit, The (Duhigg), 107
practicing, for failures, 162–63
preventability, uncertainty and, *89*
problem-solving:
   first-order, 239–44, *241, 242*
   psychological safety and, 38, 244
   second-order, 240, *242*, 243–44, 256
process, outcome vs., 68
process failures, 239–41, *242*, 243
Pronovost, Peter, 118
psychological safety, 15–16, 161, 184,
   185, 256
   avoiding complex failures with, 29,
   38, *41*, 139, 141, 156
   belonging vs., 268–69
   diversity, equity, and inclusion and,
   268–69
   error reporting and, 12–16, 38, 106,
   107–9, 113–14, 129, 217–18
   in families, 40, 113, 156
   fear and, 38, *41*, 46–48
   importance to failing well, 15–16
   innovation and, 38, 46–48, 75–76,
   79–80
   in operating rooms, 46–48
   problem-solving and, 38, 244, 251–52
   standards and, 38–40, *39*
   teamwork and, 38–39, 80
pulsars, 54–56, 268
pupitres bottle racks, 263

Q
Queer Art of Failure, The (Halberstam),
   267
questions, freedom to ask, 40

R
radios, 71–72
railroads, *146*
rapid response teams (RRTs), 157–59,
   278

rational behavior therapy (RBT), 186,
   187–89
Ratwani, Raj, 118
Reason, James, 149
recognition, for employees, 108
recovery windows, 155–56
Redzepi, René, 74–78
reflection, 277–78
reframing, 30–32, *41*, 48, 65, 162, 177,
   179, 182–86
regrets, 269
rejection, fear of, 27, 37–38, 40, 48
research and development departments,
   33–34, 53, 204
resiliency, 31, 50, 73, 150, 183, 219,
   263
resources, for employees, 108
respect, employees treated with, 108
restaurant industry, 74–78, 117
Revlon, 87–88
Rick and Morty (TV show), 284
Rickard, Seth, 60
risks:
   interpersonal, 15, 37–41, 174
   mitigation of, *39*, 72, 81, 83
risk-taking, 15, 37, 72, 173, 174, 184
RNA, 51–53
Roberto, Mike, 154, 157, 159, 257
Roberts, Karlene, 150
Rocha, Rodney, 153, 154, 161
Rome, ancient, 116–17
Roosevelt, Theodore, 87
Ross, Lee, 105, 212
Royal Navy, 137
Rugiati, Anna, 128
Rugiati, Pastrengo, 125–27, 128, 130,
   131, 145
rumination, 31
Ru-Paul's Drag Race (TV show),
   267–68
Rust (film), 130–31, 135, 156, 162, 230

S

sabotage, 41, *41*, 42, 92
Safety Action Teams, 256–57
safety practices, 107–9, 146
    violation of, 41–42
sailboats, 95–96, 104–5
science, technology, engineering, and
    mathematics (STEM), 58–59, 266
scientists:
    communities of, 250–51
    intelligent failure and, 49–53
Scott, Tom, 215
scuba diving, 134–35, 152
Sebelius, Kathleen, 283
segregation, 189
self-awareness, 32, 197
self-criticism, 31
self-driving cars, 286
self-esteem, 29, 172, 177, 179–80, 182,
    191, 280
self-flagellation, 31
self-image, 105, 280–81
self-management, 18
self-protection, 171, 173, 183, 186, 281,
    285
Seligman, Martin, 31–32, 83–84
Senge, Peter, 233, 236, 240–41
Serenity Prayer, 292–93
Sessler, Gerhard, 73–74
Seven Stones Reef, 126, 136
sexual misconduct, 284–85
shame, 31, 32, 84, 104–5, 178–82, 209,
    279
    guilt vs., 178–79
shipping containers, 143, 238–39, 244
shrimp, 76
Silicon Valley companies, 11, 32, 79,
    217, 247
Silver, Spencer, 227–28, 246–47
Simmons mattress manufacturer, 78–79,
    80–83

simple-fix dynamic, 240–41, *241*
Sitkin, Sim, 11
situational awareness, 197, 212–18,
    225–26, 260–61
skiing, 67–68
sleep deprivation, *see* fatigue
Smalley, Richard, 229
Smith, Richard, 142
social media, 38, 143, 169, 179–81, 182
social rejection, 37
software designers, 121
Sony, 74
Souza, Joel, 130–31
Space Shuttle program, 29, 152–55, 156
Spanx, 275–77
Spear, Steven, 250
Staats, Bradley, 176–77
stakes:
    high, 210–11, *211*
    low, 208–9, *211*
standards:
    failure and, 39–40, *39*
    psychological safety and, 38–40, *39*,
        129
    unrealistic, 31
Stanford University, 159
Starbucks, 282–83
Stark, Chris, 69–70
status quo, *39*
Stefan, Melanie, 287–88
STEM (science, technology,
    engineering, and mathematics),
    58–59, 266
stock market, 167–69, 171–72, 195
Stop—Challenge—Choose technique,
    191–93, *194*, 203
stress, 40
strokes, 192–93
success, relationship to failure, 36
sunk cost fallacy, 62, 172
SUNY Downstate Medical Center, 26

Super Bowl, ads for, 289

supply chains, 101, 143, 222, 231–35, 238–39

surgical operating rooms, 23–25, *35*, 43–48, 176–77

Sutcliff, Kathie, 150

Swiss cheese model, 149–50, 254

system awareness, 197, 228, 230–31

system dynamics, 236

systems, 227–58
    designed for innovation, 246–49, 290
    designing, 245–54
    redrawing boundaries of, 241–44, *242*, 258
    synergy in, 228–31, 256–57

systems thinking, 98, 235, 236–44
    in families, 245–46, 252, 258
    specialization and, 229, 258

T

Taittinger, Pierre, 261

Takeda, 273–74

Tata Group, 290

taxi cabs, 205

teachers, 60

teamwork, 8–11
    psychological safety and, 38–39, 80

teens, 38, 156, 179–80, 290–91

telephone calls, 61

telescopes, 55–56

Teller, Astro, 62, 285–86, 290

temporal discounting, 116–17, 121, 236

tenure, 265–67

Texas News Today, 106

thalamus, 188

Theranos, 103

Think Again (Grant), 182

Thinking, Fast and Slow (Kahneman), 172–73

Thompson, W. Leigh, 62

threats, ambiguous, *see* ambiguous threats

3M, 227–28, 246–49, 250

Three Mile Island nuclear power plant, 145–46

thumbs-up/thumbs-down interaction, 79

Tilcsik, András, 143–44, 145

TiVo, 79

To Do No Harm (Morath), 253

Torrey Canyon, SS, 125–27, 133, 136–37, 151–52

Toyoda, Kiichiro, 110

Toyoda, Sakichi, 109–10, 249

Toyoda Automatic Loom Works, 110

Toyota Motor Company, 110–11, 120–21, 157, 159, 249–52

Toyota Production Systems (TPS), 249–52

traffic lights, 68–69

training, 93, 140–41, 154

Trash Cooking, 77

trial and error, as misnomer, 12, 84

Triangulate (dating site), 59

truck drivers, 97–98

Truman, Harry, 28

trust, errors and, 106

Tseng, Yani, 112

Tucker, Anita, 239, 257

twisties, 181–82

Twitter, 121

U

uncertainty, *41*, 42, 203–5, 218, 260–61
    preventability and, *89*

undo function, 121

universities, *146*, 147

University Hospital (Minnesota), 23

Index

V

vaccines, 94–97
ventricular septal defect (VSD), 44–45
Veuve Clicquot, 259–64
vigilance, 150, 159–60, 219
    amplifying ambiguous threats vs.,
        158–59
    titrating, 209–11
violations, defined, 17
Vital Lies, Simple Truths (Goleman),
        170–71
vulnerability, 106–7, 178, 269

W

Wainwright, Julie, 101, 181–82
Wambach, Abby, 30
Waters, Michael, 238–39
Watkins, Boyd, 199
Watson, Thomas, 45
Webb, Amy, 64–66
Weick, Karl, 150
West, James, 49, 70–74, 81, 265
West, Matilda, 71

West, Samuel, 70–71
whiteness, 265
Wilson, Larry, 187–88, 191–92, 196,
        220, 272
    see also Stop—Challenge—Choose
        technique
wine, 259–64
Winstanley, Felix, 60
Wired, 238
Wiseman, James, 251–52
women, failure and, 52, 265–66
work-arounds, *see* problem-solving,
        first-order
Worklife (podcast), 270–71

X

X laboratories, 62, 285–86, 290

Y

Yahoo!, 283

Z

Zolten, Amanda, 289–90

About the Author

AMY EDMONDSON is the Novartis Professor of Leadership and Management at the Harvard Business School, where she studies people and organizations seeking to make a positive difference in the world through the work they do. She has pioneered the concept of psychological safety for over twenty years and was recognized in 2021 as number one on the Thinkers50 global ranking of management thinkers. She also received that organization's Breakthrough Idea Award in 2019 and Talent Award in 2017. In 2019 she was first on *HR Magazine*'s list of the 20 Most Influential International Thinkers in Human Resources.

Amy's research has been published in *Harvard Business Review* and *California Management Review*, as well as in academic journals such as *Administrative Science Quarterly* and the *Academy of Management Journal*. Her most recent prior book, *The Fearless Organization* (Wiley & Sons, 2018), explains psychological safety—what it is, why it matters, and how to build it—and has been translated into fifteen languages. In addition to publishing several books and numerous articles in top academic outlets, Edmondson has written for, or her work has been covered by, media such as the *Wall Street Journal*, the *New York Times*, the *Washington Post, Financial Times, Psychology Today, Fast Company*, and *strategy + business*. Her TED Talk on teaming has been viewed more than 3 million times.

Before her academic career, Amy was director of research at Pecos River Learning Centers, where she worked with CEO Larry Wilson to design and implement change programs in large companies. In this role she discovered a passion for understanding how leaders can build organizations as places where people can learn, grow, and contribute to making a better world. In the early 1980s, she was chief engineer for the legendary architect and inventor Buckminster Fuller, who, not incidentally, was a strong advocate of learning from failure. Edmondson received her PhD in organizational behavior, AM in psychology, and AB in engineering and design from Harvard University.

She lives in Cambridge, Massachusetts, with her husband, George Daley, a physician/scientist intimately familiar with the science of failing well, and relishes all visits from their twentysomething sons.